BY SIMONE BECK, LOUISETTE BERTHOLLE, AND JULIA CHILD

Mastering the Art of French Cooking, Volume One

(1961)

———————————

BY SIMONE BECK AND JULIA CHILD

Mastering the Art of French Cooking, Volume Two

(1970)

———————————

These are Borzoi Books published in New York by Alfred A. Knopf

Simca's Cuisine

SIMCA'S CUISINE

Simone Beck

IN COLLABORATION WITH

Patricia Simon

ILLUSTRATIONS BY JOHN WALLNER

*many based on sketches done
in France by Michel Beck*

Alfred A. Knopf / New York / 1972

THIS IS A BORZOI BOOK
PUBLISHED BY ALFRED A. KNOPF, INC.

Library of Congress Cataloging in Publication Data
Beck, Simone. Simca's cuisine.
1. Cookery, French. I. Simon, Patricia. II. Title.
TX719.B389   641.5'944   72–2234
ISBN 0–394–47449–X

Manufactured in the United States of America
FIRST EDITION

To Judith Jones, editor *extraordinaire*

Acknowledgments

No book is the work of one person; this is especially true of a cookbook. We wish particularly to acknowledge our indebtedness to the following people whose assistance was invaluable in helping to bring this book from conception to realization.

Simone Beck wishes to express her appreciation as follows:

I wish to thank, first my beloved husband, Jean Fischbacher, who helped me daily. Next, Julia Child, my partner and friendly sister for twenty-three years: also her husband, Paul. The experienced counsel of these two friends is represented in this book.

James A. Beard, generous friend and great American cook, and his collaborator, John Ferrone, were invaluable and expert aids.

To these must be added other friends in America: Mrs. Malvina Kinard of Westport, Connecticut; Dr. Selma Hyman and Mrs. Mildred Tuhy of Portland, Oregon, who made it possible for me to talk to my first American audiences; Mrs. Lucille Tyree of Grosse Pointe, Michigan; Mrs. Grace Gadsby of Allentown, Pennsylvania, Mrs. Bernard Cutler of Washington, D.C.; and Mrs. Florence Bolton Love of Orlean, Virginia, all of whom were faithful and generous with their time and advice.

I add to them with pleasure my compatriots and fellow members of the "Cercle des Gourmettes": the president of the club, Mme. L. Poussard; our vice-president, Mme. Jean Régnier; Mme. Marcheix Thoumyre; Mme. Louisette (Bertholle) de Nalèche; and Mme. Robert Glaëzner, whose enthusiasm and knowledge have been immensely helpful over the years.

Two others of my countrymen must be included: Messieurs Pierre Androuët of Paris and Jean Ferreyrolles of Monte Carlo. One specializes in cheese, the other in Cognac; each is an expert in his field, each is a friend, and each was willing to share his expertise with me.

I am particularly grateful to Nancy Nicholas, not only for her skillful help in testing some of the recipes, but also for her valuable editorial assistance.

Patricia Simon wishes to express her appreciation to Claire S. Felix, Nancy J. Cunniff, and Jeanne M. Simon, of Philadelphia, and Henrietta G. Susser, of Leonia, New Jersey, for their assistance in testing recipes; and to Lois Straub, of Philadelphia, for her work in typing the manuscript.

Contents

More Formal Occasions

Special Occasions

Les Autres Plats de Choix

Pot Pourri

Foreword

*T*his is a book for those, no longer quite beginners, who adore to cook and partake of *la véritable cuisine à la française*—the true French cuisine.

To be sure, I had no thought of writing such a book on the occasion of my last visit to the United States. That trip, in the fall of 1970, was for the publication of Volume II of *Mastering the Art of French Cooking,* the book on which I had collaborated for so many years with my colleague and dear friend, Julia Child. And we had vowed, Julia and I, to terminate our collaboration there—she to pursue her television program and other work, and I to devote myself to my private life. At the age of sixty-six, and after twenty-two years in the professional practice of the cuisine, I wanted a rest!

But during the tour of cooking demonstrations that I gave that year —in New York City, at the school of my friend James Beard; in Connecticut at the invitation of my friend Malvina Kinard; in Portland, Oregon; and at the homes of friends in Washington, D.C., and Virginia —it seemed that a great many people were urging me to do one more book, a book all my own. I ended by taking the course of least resistance (and undoubtedly giving in most of all to my own real desire) in undertaking to write this little book—which would, finally and in truth, be my last.

I wanted to collect some menus of the kind that I serve to my family and friends in France, chosen especially as being suitable for Americans. Through these menus I hope to convey—although so much has changed and is changing every day—how many of us still live and dine in France in a style that still differs in many respects from that of any other country in the world.

I wanted also to publish certain recipes—some very old, but most of them new—which would not be strictly classical (because all of that has been done and done), but would reflect the individual cuisines of the three provinces that have formed the basis of my own cuisine.

First, the province of Normandy, where I was born and where I lived for more than eighteen years in the home of my parents—the beautiful province of orchards and pasture land, whose apples, butter, and cream are the finest in France. And many of the *normand* recipes in this book go back fifty years or more to the black notebooks of my mother and of my grandmother Beck before her.

Second, the province of Alsace, whose many interesting dishes I have come to know and appreciate through my husband, Jean Fischbacher, whose family came from there. (And some of these recipes have come directly from his mother and his grandmother and his aunt.)

And, finally, Provence. This ravishing southern province became my own twelve years ago when my husband and I acquired a house and land there. And it is in Provence that I have made what I feel have been the most interesting culinary experiments. Provence, full of sunlight, brings forth vegetables and herbs with magnificent perfumes and flavors that allow of combinations so various as to be inexhaustible. One can change the same recipe twenty times over, replacing one seasoning with another, and the dish will be completely different. The Provençal flavor remains for me the most exciting with which to experiment and create.

The cuisine of these three provinces forms the basis for a great many of the recipes in this book; but not for all. There are recipes based on the cooking of other French provinces, or on that of her former colonies, or (and perhaps mostly) on a whim that I had one day a few months ago, or two years ago—or forty years ago!

Then there are some little "secrets," or *trucs*.

In the practice of the cuisine, especially after so many years in the profession, one always finds something new; each time one makes the same recipe, one learns something new. And if you are passionate about cuisine, as I am, and want to arrive at good, even perfect, results, it is useful to know little processes that improve your results, or eliminate tedious or needless work—little secrets, shortcuts, and tricks. In French (in the vernacular), such things are called *trucs*. It is with the realization that some little *trucs* I have discovered or developed along my way could be as useful to my future readers as they have been to me and my private students that I want to share them in this book.

There are one or two observations that I might make about the menus and dishes. The menus, of course, are not always for every day of the week. Some of them are perhaps too rich for that, some too expensive, and some take time. I have not included here, for example, the simple roast meats, or plain fish or egg dishes, that I serve very frequently to my family and friends in France, because recipes for them have been given in many other books, including our *Mastering*. The menus here are for times —with one's immediate family, with one's close friends, and of course on formal occasions—when one wants to be a little bit special, a little festive. A great many of the dishes, however, are easily realizable for any ordinary day of the week.

I have been very much impressed by the wonderful generation of American cooks who have emerged since the last war. I know that in most cases they have no servants, or servants only on occasion, and I know how important it is for them to have recipes that will not require too much attention at the last moment.

Therefore, a very special aspect of this book is that almost all of the dishes can be made in advance. A great many can be made one, and sometimes two, days ahead, and reheated or completed just before serving. All of the soups can be reheated—they will only be better. All of the stews and dishes in sauce as well. All of the vegetables, all of the quiches, all of the gratins, and almost all of the desserts can be made in advance. A few special dishes cannot be—some soufflés, a sabayon, a gigot. . . . But I hope that I will find the forgiveness of my readers by offering results that will make these dishes worthy of the last-minute attention or little extra trouble that they may require.

This same concern for practicality has led me not to complicate the work of my readers by imposing on them dishes whose ingredients they would have difficulty in finding. As I have had the opportunity to cook in the United States, I know that it will be possible to realize these recipes.

Finally, some very brief words of advice, which can never be repeated too often. *Always* read through to the end of the recipe before beginning to cook, even before shopping. Always assemble the utensils and ingredients needed before starting. Special French equipment is occasionally recommended here, but in all cases I have indicated acceptable substitutes. And as an ardent advocate of the art of improvisation, I would hope that my readers will sometimes be more clever than I in finding substitutes should they need to. The idea of improvisation and substitution applies to the menus as well. They are intended simply as *ideas* and *suggestions*—in no way meant to be rigid or dogmatic. When the reader wants to make a complete menu, suggestions for its organization, and notes about what can be prepared ahead of time, will be found in a paragraph of *Conseils,* or Advice, which precedes the recipes for that menu. However, I realize that one does not always use a book like this to prepare an entire menu; I am sure that often my readers will simply want to locate a single recipe—or find inspiration for a new vegetable dish or a bouchée to serve at a cocktail party. The index is therefore organized so that one can locate the recipes there not only alphabetically by title but also under categorical headings.

Another small word of advice. If you have decided to execute *un menu de gala*—a very special dinner or a very special dish—I suggest that you try it in advance for your family. Then you won't be taken unaware by an unexpected problem, and you will be able to resolve it easily, without getting yourself excited. Because on that day the dish or menu will be only for you and your family. When you make it again for your "party," all problems will have been anticipated and it will seem easy to execute. Then you will be able to enjoy your friends and your drink before dinner without any apprehensions at all.

I have all my life loved to share good cooking with my good friends who love life, who love to eat, to drink wine, to converse together. One feels so close to people with whom one shares a wonderful meal and a wonderful wine. Eating something well conceived and well made is one of life's very great pleasures. I want to share the happiness that I have had with you, my readers, and I know that you in turn will share it with others—and they with others still. And then the circle will be complete. . . .

Simone Beck

INFORMAL OCCASIONS

———◆———

En famille et entre nous

Ten Dinners for Family and Close Friends

1. Un menu des quatre saisons

A MENU FOR ALL SEASONS

Porc braisé au whiskey (chaud ou froid)
Pork braised with bourbon;
prunes steeped in bouillon (hot or cold)

Pain de laitues/Timbales of lettuce
puréed with shallots and cream
or Brocoli sautés/Sautéed broccoli

Salade de saison/Green salad vinaigrette

Crème au chocolat meringuée/Frozen
chocolate mousse made with meringue

Vin rouge de Bourgogne: Beaune

*I*t will not always, I am afraid, be possible for me to remember the origins of each dish in this book; after almost five decades of experimenting with the cuisine, the sources of some recipes are simply lost in the mists of the past! Some have been recorded in the notebooks of my family and the family of my husband, some in the notebooks of my own teenage years of experimenting (at that time mostly with cakes, for as a girl I had a very special fondness for sweets). After that, the sources diffuse: from restaurants, from friends, from my studies at the Cordon Bleu, from culinary journals and other publications, from various societies to which I belong; from chefs, from cooks, from strangers, from students long forgotten—and then hundreds that I have created over the years. Even today, when I am in the mood, I sometimes originate or adapt several in the course of a week. It seems that one can never stop.

So that I cannot recall exactly how and when I acquired this recipe for pork braised with bourbon whiskey. It is true that the Touraine has a dish of pork with prunes, but that is done quite differently. I think that this particular dish resulted from my casting about for an interesting way to serve pork cold—for I find cold pork delicious but often unattractive. This recipe, which I like even better cold, has an unexpectedly delicate taste; the flavors of the Dijon mustard, brown sugar, and bourbon blend during the braising so that the residue is subtle; the prunes give an interesting contrast, and each pale piece of pork, studded with tongue or ham, is ringed with a dark brown border, beautiful against the pale green of the lettuce timbales and the dark green of watercress.

The next day you will have a delicious cold leftover—or you could concoct a new dish, substituting the pork for the beef in the *chou en farce Tante Caroline* on page 52 or the ham in the *charlotte de jambon* on page 67. You could also use it in the eggplant timbale on page 28.

The lettuce timbales can be made either in individual timbale molds —a presentation I find very charming—or in one larger mold. If for some reason you want to omit the timbales, a salad might very well substitute if the dish is served cold. With hot pork, broccoli would be excellent.

This *crème au chocolat meringuée* is a favorite of my husband Jean —and for me that remains the supreme compliment, for he is so fond of chocolate desserts that he has one literally every day of his life. I am therefore hard-pressed to devise a never-ending and interesting supply and this may explain the fact, which can hardly escape notice, that there is an abundance of chocolate desserts in this small book: two chocolate cakes, two chocolate mousses, a chocolate cream, a chocolate soufflé, and chocolate truffles, as well as three desserts with chocolate sauce!

The *crème au chocolat meringuée* is a combination of chocolate, egg yolks, and meringue, and is very easily accomplished; it becomes richer and more festive still if one stirs into it some crushed nougatine— a brittle, related to praline, made with nuts and a caramel syrup, hardened, and then crushed. The word comes from *nougat,* which in turn derives from the Latin word *nux* for nut. Thousands and thousands of pounds of nougat are made each year in Montélimard, Provence, from the almond trees that grow there.

In France we use a type of chocolate that is of a consistency and composition such that it can be stirred over direct heat without burning. American unsweetened and semisweet chocolate is different; it has a high quantity of cocoa butter and will burn over direct heat. The best substitute for French chocolate is German's sweet chocolate.

Conseils: The pork can be partially cooked in advance and reheated, covered with foil, in a low oven. If it is to be served cold, it can be made a day or two ahead of time. The lettuce timbales can be fully cooked and reheated in a bain-marie—7 to 8 minutes for the small timbales and 15 minutes for a large one. The dessert is preferably made a day or more in advance; but if the circumstances require, you could make it as little as an hour ahead; it will still be good, but it won't have the springy consistency that it will achieve after a long chilling.

Porc braisé au whiskey (chaud ou froid)

PORK BRAISED WITH BOURBON; PRUNES STEEPED
IN BOUILLON (HOT OR COLD)

For 6:

3 pounds pork loin, *in one piece, boned and tied*

18 prunes

1½ to 2 cups, or more, beef bouillon

¼ pound pickled tongue, or prosciutto, or smoked ham, *cut in thick slices*

½ cup Dijon mustard

⅔ cup dark brown sugar

2 tablespoons peanut or vegetable oil

⅔ cup bourbon whiskey

Salt

Black pepper, *freshly ground*

Bouquet garni of thyme, sage, and parsley

½ teaspoon arrowroot or cornstarch (*optional*)

Preheat the oven to 375°.

Dry the meat. Put the prunes to steep in about 1 cup tepid bouillon to cover.

Cut the tongue, prosciutto, or ham into strips to fit a larding needle and lard the meat along its length. (If you have no larding needle, poke the ham or tongue into the meat with a thin sharp knife.) Paint the meat with the mustard; then roll it in the brown sugar.

Heat the oil in a heavy ovenproof cooking pot and brown the meat in it, turning it when one side is colored so that it browns evenly (10 to 15 minutes). The sugar will caramelize; watch carefully to see that it does not burn.

Pour half the whiskey over the meat and set it aflame. When the flame goes out, pour in ½ cup of the remaining bouillon, cover the pot, and set into the preheated oven to cook for 1¾ hours.

Halfway through the cooking, turn the meat, season with salt and pepper, add the bouquet garni, and lower the heat to 350°.

About 10 minutes before the end of the cooking time add the prunes and their liquid.

If the pork is to be served hot, remove the meat to a warm platter, strain the cooking liquid, and remove the fat (*technique, p. 320*). Return the liquid to the pot, set over heat, and bring the sauce to the boil, adding the remaining whiskey and stirring to dislodge the sediments. (The sauce can be thickened by bringing it to a boil with the arrowroot or cornstarch mixed with a little cold stock or water.) Taste, and correct the seasoning.

If the pork is to be served cold, add ½ cup of bouillon to the cooking liquid, bring the sauce to a boil, stirring to dislodge the sediment, and set aside to cool. Taste the sauce and correct the seasoning.

To serve

A bunch of watercress

To serve in the French manner, slice half of the pork and present it on the serving dish with the unsliced pork. If serving hot with lettuce timbales, coat them with some of the sauce and serve the rest in a sauceboat. If the pork is cold, the sauce will have jelled. In that case, remove the hardened fat, chop the jellied sauce, and spoon around the sliced meat. Hot or cold, decorate the dish with the prunes and watercress.

Pain de laitues

TIMBALES OF LETTUCE PURÉED WITH
SHALLOTS AND CREAM

For 6 to 8:

6 to 8 tight heads of lettuce
Salt
4 tablespoons shallots or scallions, *minced*
4 tablespoons butter
1¾ cups very stale bread crumbs, *homemade from good bread*

1 cup cold milk
4 eggs
½ cup Parmesan or ¾ cup imported Swiss cheese, *grated*
⅓ cup heavy cream
Black pepper, *freshly ground*
Nutmeg, *freshly grated*

Recommended equipment: 8 individual ½-cup baking dishes, or a 1-quart charlotte mold or deep baking dish.

Trim the lettuce and separate the leaves. Put them into a large quantity of boiling water and add a handful of salt when the water returns to the boil. Boil rapidly, uncovered, for 8 to 10 minutes to blanch the lettuce—the base of the leaves should still be hard and the leaves limp. Drain and refresh under cold running water; then squeeze by handfuls to press out all the surplus moisture. Chop roughly and set aside.

Sauté the minced shallots or scallions in the butter until they are soft but not colored. Add the chopped lettuce leaves and cook gently for about 10 to 15 minutes until the remaining moisture in the leaves has evaporated.

Soak the bread crumbs in the milk and mash them with a fork until all of the milk is absorbed. Beat the eggs with a fork and combine them with the bread crumbs, lettuce, grated cheese, and cream. Blend thoroughly, and season highly with salt, pepper, and nutmeg.

To assemble, cook, and serve

Butter and bread crumbs to coat
    the molds or mold

Preheat the oven to 375°.

Butter the molds or mold, line the bottom with buttered waxed paper (buttered side up), and sprinkle with bread crumbs. Fill the molds or mold with the lettuce mixture, then place in a shallow pan and pour water into the pan to come about a third of the way up the sides of the molds or mold. Bring the water to a simmer on top of the stove, then set the pan in the oven to cook for 30 to 35 minutes for the large mold, or about 15 minutes for the small ones—until the mixture is firm and has drawn away from the sides.

Unmold, peel off the paper, coat the timbales with a spoonful or two of the sauce from the pork (preceding recipe), and serve.

If the timbales are being served without the pork they can be decorated with finely minced parsley.

---•●•---

Brocoli sautés

SAUTÉED BROCCOLI

For 8:

3 pounds fresh broccoli
Salt
6½ tablespoons butter
Black pepper, *freshly ground*

1 egg, *hard boiled, or about*
1½ tablespoons parsley,
finely chopped

Separate the broccoli into stems and flowerets, and cut the stems into large pieces. Peel each piece of stem very carefully. In a salad basket or a colander wash the broccoli under cold running water, being gentle with the broccoli tops. Plunge the stems into a large quantity of boiling water, adding salt as soon as the water returns to the boil. Boil the stems uncovered for 2 minutes; then add the flowerets and boil 3 minutes longer, until a knife pierces a stalk easily. Refresh the broccoli under cold running water, drain, and set aside. *The broccoli can be prepared a few hours in advance to this point.*

Melt the butter in a large pan. Add the broccoli, and shake the pan to coat the pieces with butter. Season with salt and pepper, still tossing the pan, until the broccoli is heated through.

Serve sprinkled with sieved hard-boiled egg or very finely chopped parsley.

———◄•►———

Crème au chocolat meringuée

FROZEN CHOCOLATE MOUSSE MADE WITH MERINGUE

This can be served after only 1 or 2 hours in the freezer, but it is at its best when made several hours or a day in advance.

For 6:

1½ tablespoons powdered instant coffee	½ cup granulated sugar
	7 egg whites
7 ounces German's sweet choco- late, *broken into small pieces*	Pinch of salt
	½ teaspoon vanilla extract
4 egg yolks	5 tablespoons confectioners' sugar

Put the coffee and 1½ tablespoons of boiling water in the top of a double boiler or a saucepan set in simmering water. Stir to dissolve the coffee, add the chocolate, and continue to stir over heat until the chocolate is melted and smooth. Set aside.

Beat the egg yolks with the granulated sugar until they are a pale creamy yellow. Put the pan of chocolate back over the water, add the egg yolk and sugar mixture, and stir until the mixture barely reaches a boil. Remove from the heat.

Beat the egg whites with the pinch of salt until they are white and frothy; add the vanilla extract and the confectioners' sugar, and continue to beat until the meringue is firm and very white.

Lightly fold the meringue into the tepid chocolate mixture (rewarm it if it is cold). Put into the freezer to set.

Optional: Stir the following crushed nougatine into the dessert before freezing it, and serve with a pitcher of heavy cream.

Nougatine

½ cup walnuts or other nuts   ½ cup granulated sugar

Preheat the oven to 300°.

Put the walnuts into the oven to warm but not brown. Oil a metal baking sheet. Put 3 tablespoons of water with the sugar into an enameled saucepan and boil to form a light caramel syrup. Immediately add the warmed walnuts, stir over heat for a few seconds to distribute the nuts through the syrup, and pour the nougatine onto the oiled baking sheet, spreading it out into a layer. Set aside to cool and harden. Then chop it into rough pieces.

2. *Un menu Normandie-Provence*

FLAVORS NORMANDE AND PROVENÇALE

Les amuse-gueule/Small cocktail delicacies

Filets de poisson à la provençale,
sauce bouillabaisse
Fillets of fish in bouillabaisse sauce

Riz au blanc/Buttered rice with herbs

Vin blanc: Côtes de Provence

Salade de saison/Green salad vinaigrette

Fromage: Pont-l'Évêque

Vin rouge de Bordeaux

Omelettes normandes/Apple-cream omelets,
flamed with Calvados or rum

*T*he fillets of fish in *sauce bouillabaisse*—an adaptation of the classic fish and shellfish dish from Marseilles, and the *omelette normande*—a dessert omelet filled with sautéed apples and cream—are two dishes representing the two provinces that have most influenced my cuisine. The herbs and tomatoes permeate the sauce for the fish with the strong flavors of Provence; the apples, cream, and Calvados bring to the omelet the mellowness of Normandy.

The tomato sauce should be made with the finest, ripest tomatoes. But if you are making this dish with tomatoes that are underripe, there is a quite startling *truc* that will rid them of their excess acidity: simply stir ½ teaspoon of instant coffee, dissolved in ½ cup of the sauce, into the finished sauce! Try first half the amount of coffee; then add the rest if necessary.

This would become a completely *normand* menu if you were to substitute for the fish in bouillabaisse the *filets de poisson à la normande* to be found on page 268. Both of these are dishes that I devised in response to requests from my students for recipes that can be quickly made with fish fillets.

Conseils: The bouillabaisse base can be made as far in advance as you wish, the filling for the omelet can be prepared several hours ahead of time. The fish and the rice require only a quarter hour's cooking. The omelets, of course, must be made between the entree and the dessert, but this is quickly done.

Les amuse-gueule

Small cocktail delicacies; see pages 227–39 for suggestions.

Filets de poisson à la provençale, Sauce bouillabaisse

FISH FILLETS IN BOUILLABAISSE SAUCE

For 6:

Fish fillets and fish fumet

3 pounds fillets of halibut, red snapper, flounder, cod, or any firm-fleshed fish

Bones, skin, and trimmings from the fish if obtainable; otherwise, 2½ cups chicken bouillon

Trim the fish fillets and remove any skin. If you have the fish bones and trimmings, use them to prepare 2½ cups of fish fumet (*p. 298*). Otherwise, use chicken bouillon.

Bouillabaisse sauce

2½ tablespoons olive oil
1 cup onions, *minced*
½ cup leeks, *diced*
4 pounds well-ripened tomatoes, *roughly chopped*
3 large cloves garlic, *unpeeled*
2 cups dry white wine
2½ cups fish fumet or chicken bouillon (*above*)

2 chili peppers, *ground,* or Tabasco to taste
1 tablespoon fennel or dill seeds
A large bouquet garni of thyme, savory, basil, oregano, and a 1-inch piece of dried orange peel (*technique, p. 324*)
Pinch of saffron
Salt
Black pepper, *freshly ground*

Warm the olive oil in a large, heavy skillet. Add the onions and leeks and cook gently, stirring occasionally with a wooden spoon, until the vegetables are tender but not browned (about 15 minutes). Add the chopped tomatoes and the unpeeled garlic, cover the skillet, and simmer for about 10 minutes longer while the tomatoes render more of their juice. Then uncover and boil rapidly for about 2 minutes until the tomatoes have softened.

Purée the vegetable mixture in a food mill. Then return to the skillet, stir in the wine, and bring to the simmer. Add the fish fumet or chicken bouillon, the chili peppers or Tabasco to taste, the dill or fennel seeds, the bouquet garni, the saffron, salt, and pepper. Simmer for 35 to 40 minutes to reduce the sauce and enhance its flavor.

Remove the bouquet garni, taste, and correct the seasoning.

To assemble, bake, and serve

Salt
Black pepper, *freshly ground*
About 1½ tablespoons parsley, *minced*

6 slices lemon, *fluted*
2 tablespoons flour or 1 teaspoon cornstarch (*optional*)

Preheat the oven to 375°.

Season the fish fillets lightly with salt and pepper. Pour half of the bouillabaisse sauce into a shallow baking dish. Arrange the fish fillets in the dish and cover them with the remaining sauce. Bring to the simmer on top of the stove, cover with a piece of buttered waxed paper (buttered side down), and bake in the preheated oven for 8 to 12 minutes, depending on the thickness of the fillets.

Remove the waxed paper and serve the fish in the baking dish, decorated with minced parsley and fluted slices of lemon.

If a thicker sauce is desired, stir in either 2 tablespoons flour dissolved in 2 tablespoons stock or water or 1 teaspoon cornstarch dissolved in 2 tablespoons stock or water.

Riz au blanc

Buttered Rice with Herbs. See page 309.

———— ●◆● ————

Omelettes normandes

TWO DESSERT OMELETS, FILLED WITH
SAUTÉED APPLES AND CREAM, AND FLAMED
WITH CALVADOS OR DARK RUM

For 6:

To cook the apples

1¼ pounds tart apples, *to make
  about 3 cups when pared,
  cored, and sliced*
Juice of 1 lemon
6 tablespoons unsalted butter

¾ cup sugar
6 tablespoons fine Calvados or
  dark rum
⅓ cup heavy cream

Peel and core the apples, sprinkling them each immediately with lemon juice to keep them white. Cut them into slices about ¼ inch thick, measure out about 3 cups, and set aside.

In a large, heavy omelet pan or skillet, heat half the butter until it is brown and foaming. Add only as many apples as will fit in one layer, and sauté them over high heat for 7 to 10 minutes, stirring occasionally to keep them from burning. Remove the cooked apples, add more butter, and repeat until all the apples are cooked.

Return all the apples to the pan, sprinkle them with the sugar, and stir for a couple of minutes until the sugar caramelizes. Then pour in half of the Calvados or rum, set aflame, and shake the pan until the flame goes out. Remove the pan from the heat, wait for the bubbling to subside, and stir in the cream. Put the apple mixture into a bowl. Clean the pan. *The recipe can be made about 2 hours in advance to this point.*

To make the omelets

8 medium-sized eggs
Pinch of salt

4 tablespoons sugar
6 tablespoons butter

Ten minutes before serving, warm a large oval serving platter.

Separate 3 of the eggs. Beat the 3 egg whites with a pinch of salt until firm; add 2 tablespoons of the sugar, and continue to beat until stiff. Beat the whole eggs, the remaining sugar, and the egg yolks lightly with a fork. Fold the beaten eggs into the stiffly beaten whites (*technique, p. 321*).

Separate the omelet mixture into two batches, to make two omelets. Set the omelet pan over high heat, and melt half the butter until it is nut brown and foaming. When the foam subsides, pour in one batch of the eggs. Let the eggs cook just long enough to set the exterior—less than half a minute. (Resist the temptation to let them cook longer.) Remove the pan from the heat, and put half the apples in the center of the omelet. Then fold the omelet: First slide it down to the edge of the pan, grasping the handle of the pan from underneath. In one motion invert the pan over the middle of the serving dish, so that the bottom of the omelet will be on top. Make the other omelet exactly the same way and put it on the serving dish.

Sprinkle each omelet with 2 tablespoons of sugar. Heat the Calvados or rum and pour it over the omelets. Bring them to the table and set them aflame. As the Calvados or rum runs to the bottom of the dish, spoon it over the omelets to caramelize them.

3. *Un dîner à la campagne*

A COUNTRY DINNER

Melon suivant saison glacé au Porto
Chilled melon with port, in season

Épaule d'agneau de Mortagne
Lamb and vegetables in velouté sauce

Pommes de terre vapeur, persillées
Steamed potatoes with herbs

Salade de saison/Green salad vinaigrette

La tarte pour Jim
Apple-almond tart for Jim

Vin blanc sec de Bordeaux: Graves

*I*n August, at our home in Provence, we frequently have dinner out of doors, and I have often served this menu on such occasions. We eat on a table overlooking the valley; in the near and far distance the gently rolling hills—the foothills of the Alps—stretch away. As the evening darkens in the distance the lights come on in Grasse, the medieval French town where the roses that grow over the hillsides in May and June are turned into the essence of perfume by the perfume factories there.

But this dinner might be served for another kind of "country" occasion: If, for example, you have a weekend residence outside of the city, and you would like something ready for guests the night you arrive, this is the kind of dinner that lends itself well to advance preparation; all but the potatoes can be made in advance and carried with you to be reheated after your arrival.

The rule in France is not to serve a cold dish to begin a dinner. Especially in the winter, the only cold dishes that are served are smoked salmon, or oysters, or, for a very chic dinner, caviar; but melon is such a simple and appropriate beginning for the summertime, when fresh melons are in season, that I make this exception. The melon that I most frequently use is cantaloupe, especially good when sliced in half, scooped out, and filled with port wine. If you cannot obtain good melons, you could substitute the tomato tart on page 234—a hearty tart of tomatoes, herbs, and cheese.

The *épaule d'agneau,* shoulder of lamb, is an adaptation of a delicate stew called a blanquette—classically made with veal, small onions, and mushrooms, cooked in stock or water, and then finished with a liaison of egg yolks, cream, and a little lemon juice.

The *pommes de terre vapeur*—steamed potatoes—is also a classic recipe, often called *pommes à l'anglaise.* The potatoes are peeled and carved into attractive oval shapes and steamed, which gives them a delicate texture. They can be cooked, wrapped in cheesecloth, either in a steamer or in a colander lined with cheesecloth and suspended over boiling water. The important thing is that the potatoes do not touch the water. I have found that these potatoes assume a subtle versatility if different herbs are added to the water that steams them. Here I have recommended parsley and chervil in addition to the classic bouquet garni of bay leaf, thyme, parsley, and celery. But if I am serving the potatoes with fish, I add instead some fennel; for a leg of lamb, mint; with boiled beef, tarragon or basil; with a beef stew, thyme—all, of course, in addition to the classic bouquet garni.

In Provence in the summertime I use only fresh herbs; their aroma and flavor is one of the things that gives Provençal cooking its incomparable flavor and pungency. In Paris in the winter, of course, I use dried herbs. The proportions of fresh to dried are difficult to assess; it depends so much on the particular herb and the age of the herb if dried, but one should always use a smaller amount of dried herbs. I have indicated exact proportions in many instances, but I hope that my readers will also feel free to use their own judgment.

The apple tart is a very special one that I created for my dear friend James Beard during his most recent visit to us in Provence. It consists of grated raw apples, almonds, sugar, egg yolks, and cinnamon, which bake together with the pastry shell and are spread with melted butter for the final cooking. This tart will keep for several days.

Conseils: The melon should be cut into halves, filled with port, and chilled. The potatoes will be made just before serving. The lamb can be reheated and the sauce completed at the same time. The tart, as indicated, can be made several days in advance.

———— •◦• ————

Épaule d'agneau de Mortagne

LAMB, ONIONS, CARROTS, AND MUSHROOMS
IN VELOUTÉ SAUCE

For about 6:

4 pounds boned lamb shoulder,
*cut into pieces about 2½
inches square and 1 inch
thick, without fat or gristle*
4 cups light bouillon, beef stock,
or water
Bones from the lamb, if available
1 large onion, *peeled and stuck
with 2 cloves*
1 large carrot, *quartered*

2 cloves garlic, *peeled*
1 cup dry white wine
Bouquet garni of parsley, thyme,
½ bay leaf, celery stalk
¼ pound small white mushrooms
(or larger ones, *quartered*),
cleaned
Salt
Black pepper, *freshly ground*

If necessary, trim the meat, removing any little pieces of fat or gristle, and cut it into pieces, as above.

Bring the bouillon, stock, or water to a boil in a heavy skillet, add the lamb bones, the onion (stuck with cloves), the quartered carrot, and the peeled garlic, and boil for 5 minutes.

Skim the cooking liquid. Add the white wine and boil briefly. Then add the lamb, the bouquet garni, and more liquid if necessary to cover the lamb. Reduce to a simmer, cover, and let simmer slowly for about 20 minutes.

Add the mushrooms, salt lightly, and simmer for 25 to 35 minutes longer until the meat is tender. Then season with pepper and turn into a colander set over a large bowl. Discard the bones, the bouquet garni, and the cloves. Return the meat and vegetables to the skillet and keep them warm while making the sauce. (There should be about 3½ cups of cooking liquid. If not, add some stock or bouillon.)

Sauce velouté

Cooking liquid from the lamb
3 tablespoons butter
4 tablespoons flour

Salt
Black pepper, *freshly ground*

Let the cooking liquid cool briefly and remove the fat (*technique, p. 320*). Put about ¼ cup of the liquid aside for later use. Melt the butter in an enameled saucepan. Stir in the flour, and cook, stirring, for a few seconds. Off the heat, pour in the lamb cooking liquid, and beat vigorously with a wire whip until smooth. Return to the heat, bring the sauce to a boil, still stirring, and simmer for 5 or 6 minutes, stirring occasionally. Remove from the heat, season with salt and pepper, and pour over the meat. *The recipe can be made a day in advance to this point.*

To serve

3 egg yolks
¼ cup reserved lamb cooking liquid
1 teaspoon cornstarch, dissolved in 2 tablespoons cold bouillon or water

Salt
Black pepper, *freshly ground*
Juice of ½ lemon
About 1½ tablespoons parsley, *chopped*

Reheat the lamb slowly in the sauce for 20 minutes.

Beat the egg yolks into the reserved cooking liquid. Stir in the dissolved cornstarch, and then 1 cup of the velouté sauce. Pour the mixture back into the remaining sauce, and bring it to just under a boil, stirring constantly; the sauce should coat a spoon nicely. Correct the seasoning, adding lemon juice to taste.

Stir the lamb in the sauce. Then put all into a shallow preheated serving dish and surround it with the mushrooms. Sprinkle with chopped parsley, and serve at once.

------◣•◆------

Pommes de terre vapeur, persillées

STEAMED POTATOES WITH HERBS

For about 6:

18 medium-sized potatoes, prefer- ably new potatoes
Salt

A bouquet garni of ½ bay leaf, a sprig of thyme, 2 stalks pars- ley, and 1 stalk celery, plus about 1 tablespoon mixed parsley and chervil

Wash and peel the potatoes. Pare them into uniform balls or olive shapes about 1¼ inches in diameter or length.

Bring about 2 cups of water to a boil in a large saucepan. Add a tablespoon of salt and the bouquet garni.

Drape a piece of cheesecloth over a colander. Put the potatoes on the cheesecloth, sprinkle them lightly with salt, and fold the cheesecloth over them. Set the colander in the saucepan so that it is suspended over, but not in, the water. Steam the potatoes for 20 to 30 minutes, testing them after 20 minutes with a sharp knife. (If the potatoes are not new potatoes, they will require a longer cooking time.)

When the potatoes are tender, but not overcooked, put them into a warmed serving dish, sprinkle them with salt and some more minced parsley and chervil; serve at once.

La tarte pour Jim

APPLE-ALMOND TART FOR JIM

Recommended equipment: a large tart mold or flan ring, 10 inches in diameter and 1 inch deep.

Tart shell

1 recipe *pâte sablée* (*p. 314*)   6 tablespoons apricot jam

Make the pastry and chill it well in the refrigerator.

Roll out the pastry to a thickness of ⅛ inch and line the mold (*technique, p. 324*). Paint with a thick coating of apricot jam and refrigerate to firm the pastry again.

Filling

4 egg yolks
½ cup sugar
Pinch of salt
½ cup almonds, *pulverized* (*technique, p. 317*)
⅓ cup raisins
½ lemon

About 2 large cooking apples like Rome Beauties or 3 medium-sized tart apples to make 1½ cups, *loosely packed grated*
½ teaspoon cinnamon
4 tablespoons butter, *melted*

Preheat the oven to 350°.

Beat the egg yolks and slowly add the sugar and salt, beating continuously until the sugar is absorbed and the eggs are thick and lemon-colored. Add the pulverized almonds and the raisins. Peel the apples, rub them with the cut lemon, and then grate the apples to measure 1½ loosely packed cups. Stir the grated apples into the egg mixture and add the cinnamon. Fill the pastry shell and bake in the preheated oven for 20 minutes. Then remove the tart from the oven, raise the heat to 375°, prick the top in several places, and pour the melted butter over so that it seeps down inside the filling. Return the tart to the oven, and bake at 350° for 20 minutes more. Unmold onto a rack, and serve tepid.

4. Un dîner
"à la bonne franquette"
A DINNER PLAIN AND HEARTY

Les *croque-madame*/Hot open cheese sandwiches

Timbale d'aubergines du charcutier
Molded casserole of meat and eggplant

Salade de cresson et laitue
Watercress and lettuce salad with walnuts

Crème glacée au caramel/Frozen caramel mousse

Vin rouge de Beaujolais, ou vin rouge de Provence

A la bonne franquette indicates a way of dining and entertaining in a very plain and informal way. Perhaps the word is related to the English word "frankness"—direct, without pretension, without ceremony. You wouldn't dream of putting your wonderful lace cloth on the table. I have often served this menu on such occasions, and no one will ever suspect that in the timbale you have made something very good out of leftovers.

To begin, some *croque-madame*—little warm open cheese sandwiches flavored with Cognac, kirsch, or rum. This word, *croque,* also bears some explanation: it means something crunchy and hard when you bite into it. The recipe is a light adaptation of the classic *croque-monsieur*—a fried sandwich made with toasted, buttered bread, ham, and cheese. The dish makes a nice little beginning which you can have while the eggplant timbale is finishing or being reheated, if you have made it in advance.

I have served this timbale for many years; I believe my original inspiration was the Turkish dish moussaka. Made from leftovers of meat mixed with chopped eggplant, cooked in olive oil, and bound with a tomato sauce, it is baked in a mold lined with slices of fried eggplant; it unmolds very easily and is accompanied by a tomato sauce.

When I was a child, one thing I especially loved was toffee. It seemed that we were forever making toffee—sometimes out of doors on a tiny little stove. For me, ever since, there is nothing more wonderful than the smell of warm caramel. This *crème glacée au caramel* is a simple mousse, almost an ice cream, with a delicate taste of caramel, and it is very quickly made with whipped cream, egg yolks, sugar, and vanilla. A light garnish of whipped cream and crystallized violets or fresh fruit rolled in sugar completes it.

Conseils: The *croque-madame* should be made right before dinner, but can wait for twenty minutes while you have an apéritif or whiskey. Everything else can be made in advance. The dessert, like all frozen desserts, will only be better if made the day before. The timbale can be prepared in advance, but in that case do not cook it completely; as dinnertime approaches, put it in a bain-marie and bring the water slowly to the simmer on top of the stove. Keep it simmering for about 15 minutes. At the same time, slowly reheat the tomato sauce.

Les croque-madame

HOT OPEN CHEESE SANDWICHES WITH
COGNAC, KIRSCH, OR RUM

The bread used in this recipe should be sliced the day before and set out to stale.

For 6 as an appetizer or 24 cocktail bouchées:

¼ cup cold milk
2 tablespoons flour
½ teaspoon baking powder
4 eggs
½ pound imported Swiss cheese, *grated*
2 tablespoons Cognac, kirsch, or rum
½ teaspoon paprika

Salt
Cayenne pepper or Tabasco
6 slices good white sandwich bread, *stale, with crusts cut off, in rectangular slices 4 by 3 inches, about ⅓ inch thick*
Butter for baking sheet
6 tablespoons butter, *melted*

Put the cold milk in a mixing bowl, add the flour and the baking powder, and stir thoroughly to blend. Add the eggs, the grated cheese, and the Cognac, kirsch, or rum, and season with paprika, salt, and a dash of cayenne or Tabasco. Mix thoroughly. *The recipe can be made one or two hours in advance to this point, and the mixture left in the coolest part of the kitchen.*

Preheat the broiler.

Put the slices of bread on a buttered baking sheet, spread each piece evenly with a ⅓-inch layer of the mixture, and pour over each a tablespoon of melted butter. Run under the preheated broiler for 3 or 4 minutes until the top of each sandwich is evenly golden brown.

When the sandwiches have cooled to tepid, cut them into two rectangles. (For cocktails, slice into quarters.) These can be served immediately or kept warm for about 20 minutes in aluminum foil. They should be served tepid.

———— •◦• ————

Timbale d'aubergines du charcutier

MOLDED CASSEROLE OF EGGPLANT WITH
LEFTOVER MEAT OR CHICKEN

For 6:

3 pounds eggplant (if available, tiny ones 6 inches long and 1½ inches in diameter)

Salt

3 medium-sized yellow onions, *to make 1½ cups, chopped*

About ¼ cup olive, peanut, or vegetable oil

3 large cloves garlic, *peeled*

Black pepper, *freshly ground*

1¼ cups *purée de tomate provençale,* or canned tomatoes, *drained, puréed, and refreshed with herbs* (*p. 299*)

6 eggs

1¼ to 1½ cups leftover chicken, pork, or veal, or boiled ham (or combination), *cut into ⅓-inch dice*

Tabasco

Recommended equipment: A 2-quart charlotte mold, soufflé dish, or casserole.

To cook the eggplant and line the mold

Cut part of the eggplant, unpeeled, into enough slices approximately ⅓ inch thick to line the bottom and sides of the mold. Test them by placing them in the mold in overlapping rows. Then cut 5 or 6 more slices to allow for shrinking of the eggplant when fried.

Spread the eggplant slices on a board, sprinkle them with salt, and leave them to disgorge their liquid for about 15 minutes, turning them once. Rinse, drain, and dry on absorbent paper, and set aside.

Peel the remaining eggplant and cut into ½-inch dice. Sauté the chopped onions in 3 tablespoons of oil for about 10 minutes until tender. Add the diced eggplant, a handful at a time, and cook for 10 minutes, stirring occasionally, until it is well colored. Add the peeled garlic and cook 10 minutes longer until the eggplant is tender. Drain the eggplant in a colander to remove excess oil, pressing lightly with a fork. Season liberally with salt and pepper and set aside.

If necessary, add a little more oil to the pan, and warm the oil. Add a layer of the sliced eggplant and fry on each side for one or two minutes until just tender. Drain on paper towels. Repeat with the succeeding batch or batches.

Line the mold with the sliced eggplant, overlapping the pieces so that there will be no gaps.

To assemble and bake   *Preheat the oven to 375°.*

Put the tomato purée into a mixing bowl, and beat in the eggs. Add the meat and the diced eggplant and blend well. Correct the seasoning, adding drops of Tabasco to taste. Put the mixture into the lined mold, filling it to the top.

Put the mold into a shallow pan and pour about 1½ inches of water into the pan. Bring the water to a simmer on top of the stove; then cover the mold, and set the pan into the oven for 30 or 40 minutes until the timbale has drawn away from the sides of the mold, and the slices of eggplant are tender. While the timbale is baking, prepare the sauce.

Tomato sauce

2 tablespoons butter
2 tablespoons flour
⅔ cup chicken bouillon or water
1¼ cups tomato purée

½ cup heavy cream (*optional*)
Salt
Black pepper, *freshly ground*

Melt the butter in an enameled saucepan. Stir in the flour, and cook, stirring, for a few seconds. Remove from the heat, and pour in the bouillon or water, stirring until smooth; then stir in the tomato purée, return to the heat, and continue to stir while the sauce simmers and blends. Fold in the heavy cream if you wish. Season with salt and pepper. Keep warm over low heat while unmolding the timbale.

To serve

basil or parsley, *chopped*

Unmold the timbale onto a warm serving dish. Coat the top with 3 or 4 tablespoons of the sauce and sprinkle with chopped basil or parsley. Serve the remaining sauce in a sauceboat.

Crème glacée au caramel

FROZEN CARAMEL MOUSSE

This dessert is best when made a day ahead of time. It must be made at least 2½ hours in advance.

For 6:

4 egg yolks
⅔ cup sugar

1½ cups heavy cream
½ teaspoon vanilla extract

Beat the egg yolks until they are a pale creamy yellow.

In a small saucepan set over moderate heat, boil the sugar with 2 tablespoons of water to form a golden-brown caramel syrup. At the same time bring half a cup of water to the boil.

Remove the caramel from the heat and, being careful of spattering, immediately pour in the boiling water. Stir, and return to the boil to dissolve the caramel, scraping the bottom of the pan to collect it all.

Beat the hot caramel, a little at a time, into the egg yolks, whipping hard until the mixture is creamy. Then set over a bowl of ice cubes and continue to whip while the mixture thickens and cools. Set aside.

Now whip the cream with the vanilla over the ice cubes. Reserve a quarter of the whipped cream for decoration, and fold the remainder into the cool caramel. Scrape the mousse into an ice cube tray and freeze for at least 2 hours or until set.

To serve

Crystallized flowers, or raspber-
    ries or small strawberries
    rolled in sugar

Spoon the mousse into chilled dessert dishes and decorate each serving with some of the reserved whipped cream and a sugared raspberry or strawberry or a crystallized flower.

5. Le menu des tourangeaux

A SPRING DINNER FROM TOURAINE

Soupe tourangelle aux asperges
Purée of asparagus soup with tarragon

*Paupiettes de veau ou de porc à la tourangelle,
farçie à l'oignon et au fromage*
Rolls of veal or pork with onions and cheese

Riz au blanc/Rice

Salade verte, vinaigrette à l'huile de noix
Green salad with walnut-oil dressing

Fraises avec crème fraîche ou sauce sabayon
Fresh strawberries with thick cream
or sabayon sauce

Vin rouge de Chinon, ou de Bourgueil

*T*his is a menu for spring, when the fresh asparagus and little strawberries are coming into season. In the face of springtime abundance, one can afford to use asparagus in ways other than au naturel. Here it is used to make this simple asparagus soup, which I have named for the Touraine because in the Touraine grow the most beautiful asparagus in France. The salad will be more typically Tourangelle if the dressing is made with walnut oil, which is used in all the provinces where the walnut trees grow. (In the fall we would add fresh walnuts and apples to the salad.) I understand that walnut oil is now available in the United States in "health food" stores.

I believe that this unusual way of preparing rolls of pork or veal came from my mother. The mustard, onions, and cheese give a marked and unusual flavor; the sauce is finished with cream.

The strawberries would be served in France with *crème fraîche*— the thick fresh cream, slightly sour, that is found throughout France. But an even more festive dessert can be made by placing on each serving a few spoonfuls of sabayon—a sauce of warm, foamy egg yolks and Sauternes.

Conseils: The soup, like all soups, is excellent reheated—slowly. To make the *paupiettes* in advance, stop the cooking 15 minutes early. After that, they can be refrigerated for as long as 2 days. Finish cooking them for 20 to 30 minutes under buttered waxed paper or a piece of foil in a heavy-bottomed ovenproof skillet with a lid, in a 375° oven. While the *paupiettes* are reheating, make the sauce. The sabayon must be made at the last minute—but it is worth waiting for.

Soupe tourangelle aux asperges

PURÉE OF ASPARAGUS SOUP WITH TARRAGON

For 6:

2 pounds fresh asparagus
Salt
2 cups milk or unsweetened evaporated milk
3 large, full branches of tarragon (or about 1 teaspoon dried tarragon)

1 cup full-bodied white wine (preferably of Touraine)
Black pepper, *freshly ground*
6 tablespoons butter
6 tablespoons flour
6 cups chicken bouillon
2 tablespoons fresh tarragon (or 1 teaspoon dried tarragon)

Peel the asparagus to remove the scales and put aside a few of the finest tips to decorate the soup. Cut the tenderest part of the asparagus into quarters and then into thin sticks to facilitate the cooking. Boil in a large quantity of salted water for 12 to 15 minutes until tender. Drain thoroughly and pass through a food mill to make a purée. (If you have no food mill, use a sieve.) Then return to the saucepan with the milk, set over moderate heat, and simmer, stirring until smooth.

If using fresh tarragon, roughly chop the leaves. Put the tarragon into a saucepan with the white wine, add some freshly ground black pepper, bring to a simmer, and simmer for 20 minutes. The liquid should reduce by evaporation to about a tablespoon. Set aside.

In an enameled saucepan set over moderate heat, melt 4 tablespoons of butter. Stir in the flour, and cook, stirring, for a few seconds. Add the chicken bouillon, simmer several minutes, add the asparagus purée.

Pour a cup of the soup into the saucepan containing the reduced wine and tarragon. Stir over heat; then pour through a sieve back into the soup. Bring to a boil, taste, and correct the seasoning.

Blend 2 tablespoons fresh or 1 teaspoon dried tarragon into the remaining butter and stir into the soup. If the reserved asparagus tips are large, cut them into halves or quarters lengthwise and garnish each serving with two or three pieces.

———— •◦• ————

Paupiettes de veau ou de porc à la tourangelle (farçie à l'oignon et au fromage)

SMALL ROLLS OF VEAL OR PORK, STUFFED WITH
ONIONS AND CHEESE, IN CREAM SAUCE

For 6:

About ⅓ cup vegetable or peanut oil

About 5 medium-sized yellow onions (*to make 2 cups, chopped*)

6 veal or pork scallops, about 3 x 5 inches, *to be rolled*

Salt

Black pepper, *freshly ground*

6 tablespoons Dijon mustard

1 tablespoon fresh oregano, *minced* (or 1 teaspoon dried)

6 very thin slices imported Swiss cheese

4 tablespoons butter

Bouquet garni of thyme, ½ bay leaf, oregano

Warm 2 or 3 tablespoons of the oil in a heavy-bottomed ovenproof skillet with a lid. Add the chopped onions, and cook them very gently, stirring occasionally, until they are tender and lightly colored (about 15 minutes). Remove them with a slotted spoon, set them aside, and season with salt and pepper. (Do not clean the pan.)

Flatten the veal or pork scallops between pieces of waxed paper with a heavy bottle, the side of a cleaver, or a rolling pin, to make them as thin as possible. Sprinkle them with salt and pepper. Brush each scallop with mustard and sprinkle lightly with oregano. Reserving 1 cup of onions for later, spread each scallop with a thin layer of onions and cover with a slice of cheese. Roll up the scallops into *paupiettes* and secure them with toothpicks or tie them with string. (It is easier to brown them if you use string.)

Preheat the oven to 350°.

Put the *paupiettes* into the pan in which the onions were cooked, adding more oil if necessary, and brown them on all sides over moderate heat (about 15 minutes).

Remove the meat to a plate and clean the skillet. Melt the butter in the skillet, and add the meat, the remaining onions, and the bouquet garni. Cover with a piece of waxed paper, put the lid on the skillet, and set it in the preheated oven. Cook 35 to 40 minutes for veal; about 45 minutes to 1 hour for pork, according to the tenderness of the meat. The meat will be done when it is easily pierced with a sharp knife.

Put the *paupiettes* on a warmed serving dish, discarding the string or toothpicks. Spread the onions around the meat and keep the platter warm while making the sauce.

Sauce

2 tablespoons flour

¼ to ⅓ cup heavy cream

Juice of 1 medium-sized lemon, *strained*

1 cup beef bouillon, fresh or canned

Salt

Black pepper, *freshly ground*

1½ tablespoons parsley, *chopped*

Put the flour in a small saucepan and gradually stir in the cream to make a smooth paste. Stir in the strained juice of the lemon and set aside.

Pour the bouillon into the skillet in which the meat was cooked, and set over heat. Let boil half a minute, scraping the bottom to deglaze. Pour 4 or 5 tablespoons of the bouillon into the flour mixture and mix well; then pour back into the skillet and simmer, stirring constantly while the sauce thickens. Taste, and correct the seasoning.

Cover the *paupiettes* with the sauce and serve them sprinkled with chopped parsley.

Variation: Try replacing the Swiss cheese with goat cheese. In this case, omit the Dijon mustard, which will kill the flavor of goat cheese.

Riz au blanc

Rice. See page 309.

Fraises à la crème fraîche ou sauce sabayon

Serve the strawberries either with *crème fraîche* (*p. 320*) or with a sabayon (half the recipe on p. 290 will be sufficient).

6. *Un dîner en hiver après une marche en forêt*

AFTER A WINTER WALK IN THE WOODS

Les amuse-gueule/Small cocktail delicacies

Estouffade aux trois viandes
Stew of beef, lamb, and pork with cognac,
wine, and vegetables

Les nouilles cuites à point/Buttered noodles

Vin rouge: Côtes de Provence ou Beaujolais

Salade de saison/Green salad vinaigrette

Soufflé à la banane pour Paul, sauce abricot
Banana soufflé with apricot-rum sauce

Vin blanc de Bordeaux: Sauternes

*A*fter a beautiful day's walk brightened with sunshine, there is great comfort in this robust Provençal stew, and nothing could leave more of a glow on a cold day than this banana soufflé with warm apricot sauce.

On Sundays after the hunting season ends in January, my husband and I often go with some close friends, perhaps three other couples, for walks in the forests around Paris; southwest to the Fontainebleau, or to Rambouillet, St. Germain, Marly, or Senlis. We walk for two or three hours; then we eat a picnic lunch and return to our cars by another route. There are places, especially in the Fontainebleau, where you can sit down, out of the wind, out of the snow, under a tree, and have a drink and a picnic, and often we picnic on sandwiches that each of us has made and brought with us. There is a certain spirit of competition among us to outdo one another; each is always jealous of what the other has brought, and there are frequent exchanges. You might be interested in the sandwiches that I remember from a recent walk: Strasbourg sausage on *pain de mie,* our fine-textured bread, garnished with mustard butter; *canapés basques,* puréed sardines on toast with lemon and butter (these can be found on page 238); sandwiches of Chester cheese on well-buttered bread with crushed nuts; roast beef sandwiches on bread spread with mustard butter . . .

After our walk, we almost always dine at one of our homes. *Après* walk, *après* skating, *après* ski—this is a wonderful dinner for such an occasion.

The *estouffade,* with three kinds of meat stewed slowly in wine with onions, olives, herbs, and cognac, is a dish of Marseilles. Typical of the Provençal cuisine that it expresses is the use of a piece of dried orange peel, which adds a special zest to stews, sauces, and to almost all dishes made with tomatoes. It is so easy to dry it and have it on hand that I am never without it. To make this dinner more Provençal still, you could begin it with a Pastis—an apéritif based on anise, which every true *marseillais* drinks before his meal; it is yellow in color, and when you add cold water, it becomes cloudy. It has a very fresh taste, but beware— drink it only if you like the taste of licorice!

I created this banana soufflé especially for Paul Child, the husband of Julia, because he is as fond of bananas as my husband is of chocolate. Just as my husband has a chocolate dessert every night, Paul Child has a banana for breakfast; curiously, by contrast, my husband will have nothing to do with bananas.

Like all of the soufflés in the book, this one can wait for almost an hour before being baked. This is because the soufflé base is folded into the egg whites while it is still warm; the whites, lightly poached by the warmth, keep their firmness and the air stays in. The folding technique used here and throughout this book should also be noted; it is one that I developed with my very dear and much-mourned friend, the late Michael Field. The base, lightened with a large spoonful or two of the beaten egg whites, is folded into the egg whites rather than, as is the usual practice, the other way around. This causes the heavier base to be layered between the lighter whites so that they are evenly blended and well distributed. I find that one achieves very satisfactory results with this technique and have recommended it throughout this book.

Conseils: The stew is best when made in advance and reheated. (In reheating any stew, I always add two or three tablespoons of water, which helps to dilute the coagulated juices. If the stew has been underseasoned, bouillon may be used instead.) The noodles are to be cooked just before serving. The soufflé, as noted above, can wait for an hour before being baked.

Les amuse-gueule

For cocktail bouchées to have before dinner with an apéritif or whiskey, or at the table with wine, as you prefer, *croustades savoyarde,* cheese tartlets (*p. 230*), or *demi-lunes aux crustacés,* small pastries filled with shrimp and crabmeat (*p. 235*), would be delicious. Both can be prepared in advance and quickly be heated.

———◆•◆———

Estouffade aux trois viandes

BEEF, LAMB, AND PORK, MARINATED IN COGNAC
AND WINE, STEWED WITH VEGETABLES

For 6:

To marinate the meat

1 pound beef: pot roast, chuck, or
    bottom round
1 pound neck or shoulder of lamb,
    boned

1 pound pork: shoulder, blade end,
    or picnic shoulder
¼ cup Cognac
2 cups dry white wine
2 tablespoons olive oil

Cut the beef, lamb, and pork into pieces about 2½ inches square and 1 inch thick. Put them into a bowl with the Cognac, white wine, and olive oil, and marinate overnight in the coolest part of the kitchen, turning two or three times. (Six hours, if time is short, would be acceptable.)

To stew the meat

¼ pound green olives, *pitted*
¼ pound chunk of bacon or salt
    pork, *cut into 1-inch cubes*
5 tablespoons olive oil
2 or 3 medium onions, *to yield 1*
    heaping cupful, sliced
Pinch of saffron (*optional*)

2 cloves
Bouquet garni of thyme, ½ bay
    leaf, parsley stalks, and the
    dried peel, bought or home-
    made (*p. 324*), of 1 orange
About 2 cups beef bouillon
Salt

Black pepper, *freshly ground*   2 tablespoons parsley, *minced*
2 tablespoons tomato paste

Recommended equipment: A shallow cast-iron or earthenware casserole, about 4-quart capacity, with a lid.

Drain the meat, reserving the marinade. Dry each piece of meat thoroughly and leave between layers of paper towels. Blanch the olives for 10 minutes in simmering water; then refresh under cold running water. Put the bacon into cold water, bring to the boil, and blanch for 4 or 5 minutes. Rinse and dry.

Preheat the oven to 375°.

Heat the olive oil in the casserole. Add the sliced onions and the saffron, and sauté slowly, turning from time to time, until the onions are lightly browned. Remove them with a slotted spoon and set them aside. Sauté the bacon in the same oil until it is nicely browned; remove and put it to drain on paper towels. Next, brown the beef on all sides; remove it, replace it with the pork, then replace the pork with the lamb. When all is nicely browned, return all the meats except the lamb to the casserole. Add the onions, the bacon, the cloves, the reserved marinade, and the bouquet garni. Pour in enough bouillon to come just ⅓ inch below the ingredients. Season with salt and pepper, being careful not to add too much salt.

Set the casserole over heat and bring the liquid to a boil. Lay a piece of waxed paper over the meat and cover the casserole. Cook in the preheated oven for about 1 hour, then add the lamb, the tomato paste, the parsley, and the olives, cover again, and continue cooking for another hour, or until the meat is tender. Warm a serving platter.

To finish the sauce and serve

1 teaspoon arrowroot or corn-   Parsley, *chopped*
    starch, *dissolved in* 2 table-
    spoons cold bouillon (*op-*
    tional)

Remove the meat from the casserole and keep it warm on the serving platter. Strain the cooking juices, discarding the bouquet garni and the cloves, and put the onions, bacon, and olives on top of the meat. Skim the fat from the cooking juices (*technique, p. 320*). If the sauce does not seem thick enough, stir in the arrowroot or cornstarch dissolved in the cold bouillon, and stir over heat until nicely smooth.

Taste again, correct the seasoning, pour the hot sauce over the meat, and serve sprinkled with parsley.

Les nouilles cuites à point

BUTTERED NOODLES

For 6:

1 pound broad noodles	Black pepper, *freshly ground*
Salt	Nutmeg, *freshly grated*
5 tablespoons butter	

Bring at least 3 quarts of water to the boil. Add salt. Add the noodles and stir them well. As soon as the water returns to the boil, lower the heat. The noodles will be finished as soon as they roll themselves easily around a fork. They must not be overcooked.

Immediately pour the noodles into a colander and refresh them under tepid running water. Do not try to drain them thoroughly: the seasoning will blend with them more easily if they retain a little moisture. Reheat them with butter, and season with salt, freshly ground pepper, and a little grated nutmeg to taste.

Serve at once.

Soufflé à la banane pour Paul

PAUL'S BANANA SOUFFLÉ,
SERVED WITH APRICOT-RUM SAUCE

For 6:

2 tablespoons butter and 3 tablespoons sugar to coat the soufflé mold	4 fine ripe bananas Juice of 1 lemon

Bouillie base

⅓ cup flour	6 egg whites
1 cup cold milk	½ cup granulated sugar
4 egg yolks	⅓ cup almonds, *pulverized*
2 tablespoons dark rum	(*technique, p. 317*)
Salt	

Recommended equipment: A 3-quart soufflé or charlotte mold.

Heavily butter the soufflé mold and sprinkle the bottom and sides with granulated sugar.

Slice the bananas, sprinkle them with lemon juice, and purée them in a food mill or briefly in a blender at low speed. There should be 1⅓ cups of purée. Set aside.

Make the bouillie base: Put the flour into a heavy-bottomed enameled saucepan. With a wire whisk, stir in the cold milk in small quantities to make a smooth paste. Then beat in all the remaining milk and blend well. Set over moderate heat and stir constantly until the mixture has thickened into a *bouillie;* remove from the heat and stir vigorously until smooth.

Drop the 4 egg yolks into the *bouillie;* stir until smooth, then beat in the rum, a pinch of salt, and banana purée.

Beat the 6 egg whites with a pinch of salt until they are stiff but not dry. Sprinkle in the ½ cup of sugar mixed with the pulverized almonds, and beat again for a few seconds until the mixture is homogenous.

If the *bouillie* base is no longer warm, reheat it to tepid. Blend a large spoonful of the beaten egg whites into the warm *bouillie* to lighten it. Fold all back into the remaining egg whites (*technique, p. 321*). Then fill the soufflé mold. *The soufflé can be kept for an hour or more before being cooked.*

To bake and serve   Preheat the oven to 375°.

Bake the soufflé in the preheated oven for 25 to 35 minutes. If you like the center moist, remove it after 25 minutes; the sides will be solid like a cake and the center will remain a little liquid. If you like to serve a well-cooked soufflé, leave it in the oven for 35 minutes.

Apricot-rum sauce

1 cup apricot preserves   3 tablespoons dark rum

Melt the apricot preserves with 1 tablespoon of water and half of the rum, stirring over low heat until it comes to the boil. Strain, return to the saucepan, and set briefly over low heat, adding the remaining rum. Serve the sauce in a sauceboat.

7. *Un menu rapide mais delicieux*

A QUICK AND DELICIOUS MEAL

Demi-poussin grillé à la limousine
Chicken, squabs, or Cornish hens grilled with
Madeira and cream

Pommes de terre rissolées Jeanette
Potatoes sautéed with unpeeled garlic

*Salade de romaine et de cresson avec
fromage de Roquefort*/Romaine and watercress
salad vinaigrette with Roquefort cheese

Fruits de saison/Fresh fruit

Vin rouge de Bordeaux

*T*he *demi-poussin grillé* is a simple and informal method of cooking chickens, squabs, or Cornish hens easily and quickly. I use very tiny chickens—the *demi-poussin*—but I know they are rarely found in the United States, and the dish is equally delicious when made with larger chickens, Cornish hens, or squabs. Either Madeira or Malaga wine—both sweet brown wines—can be used for the sauce; Malaga wine will give a slightly more delicate flavor. At the end of the cooking, after deglazing with cream, you can thicken the sauce, if you like, with arrowroot or cornstarch. But my own preference is not to thicken simple sauces of this kind; you may arrive at a more attractive consistency, but I think you disturb some of the flavor. I prefer the juices just as they are, with their own natural flavor.

The potatoes are the idea of our dear Jeanette, a native Provençale who looks after our property in Provence when we are in Paris. She has a great love for animals, an extraordinary flair for arranging flowers, great charm and humor—and she is also a fine earthy cook. I have learned from her many things about the true cooking of Provence.

Although these potatoes are made with five or six cloves of garlic, they do not really have a very pronounced garlic flavor; the garlic is removed when they are served. The garlic cloves that grow in Provence are usually larger than those normally found in the United States, and for that reason I have specified "large" cloves in all recipes. But if you are especially fond of garlic, you might even want to add an extra clove or two. It is very important that the potatoes be thoroughly dried before they are sautéed, and you must add them to the skillet a handful at a time to allow the oil to return each time to the proper temperature for browning them well.

Conseils: This "express" dinner is not designed to be made in advance. Everything is easily cooked shortly before serving.

Demi-poussin grillé à la limousine

CHICKENS, SQUABS, OR CORNISH
HENS GRILLED WITH MADEIRA AND CREAM

For 6:

6 tablespoons chicken stock
3 young chickens, 1½ to 2 pounds each, if obtainable; otherwise 3 squabs or Cornish hens, or 2 or 3 larger chickens
Salt

Black pepper, *freshly ground*
3½ tablespoons butter, *softened*
3 tablespoons olive or peanut oil
⅔ cup Madeira wine
½ cup heavy cream
1 teaspoon arrowroot or cornstarch (*optional*)

Remove the broiler pan and put the chicken stock into it.

Preheat the broiler.

Cut the small chickens, squabs, or Cornish hens into halves, or larger chickens into quarters. Season with salt and pepper, brush with butter, sprinkle with oil, and place in the broiler pan.

Broil the birds about 6 inches from the heat for 25 to 30 minutes, turning and basting them every 10 minutes. They will be done when the juice runs yellow. Remove them to a warm serving dish, cover with foil, and keep in the turned-off oven while finishing the sauce.

Deglaze the pan with the Madeira, scraping the bottom with a fork to gather all the sediment. Set the pan over heat, warm the liquid slightly, and then stir in the cream by spoonfuls. Let simmer for about 3 minutes, taste, and season with salt and pepper. If you wish to thicken the sauce, stir in the arrowroot or cornstarch diluted in 1 or 2 tablespoons cold water.

Coat the birds with some of the sauce, serving the remaining sauce in a sauceboat.

Pommes de terre rissolées Jeanette

POTATOES SAUTÉED WITH UNPEELED GARLIC

For 6:

2½ pounds boiling potatoes
3 tablespoons lard and 1 table-
    spoon peanut oil (or ¼ cup
    olive oil)

5 or 6 large cloves garlic, *unpeeled*
Salt
About 1 tablespoon each parsley
    and chives, *minced*

Peel the potatoes, cut them into rough pieces about 1 inch square, and put them aside on absorbent paper.

Heat the lard and oil in a large heavy skillet. Add the unpeeled garlic and fry over medium heat for about 2 minutes. Dry the potatoes again, if necessary, and put them into the skillet in one layer. Then sauté them until they are golden, shaking the skillet every few minutes to toss them.

Sprinkle the potatoes with about ¼ teaspoon of salt, lower the heat, and cover the skillet. Continue to cook them for 10 or 15 minutes longer until they are tender and easily pierced with a sharp pointed knife.

Remove the potatoes with a slotted spoon and drain them thoroughly. Discard the garlic. Taste, and add more salt if necessary. Serve in a hot dish, sprinkled with minced parsley and chives.

8. *Un dîner alsacien*

AN ALSATIAN SUPPER

Bouillon de poule, comme en Alsace
Alsatian chicken bouillon

Chou en farce Tante Caroline/Casserole of
cabbage, ground meat, and apples, with cream

Vin blanc sec de Riquewihr

Salade de saison/Green salad vinaigrette

Fromage de Münster

Sorbet à la framboise/Raspberry sherbet

Petits fours: Les dollars

Vin blanc Gewürztraminer

*T*his Alsatian menu begins with a very old recipe for chicken bouillon that comes from the family of my husband, who were Alsatians; it was created by a rather eccentric aunt, Tante Caroline. In the old version of the recipe, a whole fresh chicken was used, for in those days, of course, chickens simply ran in the yard, and you went out and killed one and put it in the soup. But today, to use a whole chicken only for soup and not for the meat itself seems quite extravagant, and I have found that this soup can be made very well with chicken parts and giblets. It is typically Alsatian—a rich bouillon with a very special taste imparted by the garlic, the herbs, and the beef. The beef is then used to make the *chou en farce*—another creation of the famous Caroline.

She was an Alsatian spinster and what one might call a "case." One of her eccentricities was her resolute insistence on speaking only the Alsatian language, although she spent most of her life in Paris and knew French. A second was her extreme avariciousness, for which she was notorious. A third was her taste for very odd fancy hats and coats—she had no care whatever for how she looked to other people. Be that as it may, she was an extremely interesting cook with a great flair for using herbs, and her cabbage casserole, which has endured in our family through all these years, is inexpensive, can be made with leftovers (almost any kind of meat, but I prefer the combination of beef and boiled ham), and can be prepared ahead of time and reheated. In fact, it is even better when reheated. At the end of the cooking, the cabbage, which is cooked in layers and seasoned with cream, will itself be almost like a cream—smooth and velvety. A *truc* in grinding the meat for the *chou* is to use at the end a small piece of stale bread to help push the last of the meat through the meat grinder.

Raspberries grow in profusion in Alsace, and here their juice is used to make a sherbet. The interesting thing about this sherbet is that it is made only with fruit juice and cooked meringue. Meringue will always produce a light sherbet and will prevent the formation of ice crystals, which is why this type of sherbet can be made in an ordinary ice cube tray. But one day I had the idea that the sherbet would be lighter still if the meringue were cooked, and I found that this was, in fact, very effective in giving the sherbet an elasticity and body that you do not get with un-cooked meringue. I have since applied this idea to other frozen desserts as well.

You can make this sherbet with many different kinds of fruit juice. I have used the juice of oranges, apricots, pineapples, and red currants, as well as applejack and champagne. Lemon and lime juice are too acid to be used alone, but one or the other should always be added to the juice of other fruits to enhance the flavor. Be careful not to make the preparation too sweet; otherwise the sherbet will not freeze properly.

Conseils: Everything in this supper can be made in advance. The longer the bouillon cooks, the stronger and more concentrated it will be. It needs at least 3 hours total cooking; the piece of beef can be removed after 1½ hours for use in the *chou en farce.* This dish can be completely cooked ahead of time and reheated in a 350° oven for a good half-hour. The sherbet is best made a day or two in advance.

Bouillon de poule, comme en Alsace

ALSATIAN CHICKEN BOUILLON

For 6 to 8:

2½ to 3 pounds chicken parts and 1 cup giblets

2 pounds sawed and cracked veal bones or beef bones

4 medium carrots, *cut into quarters lengthwise*

1 stalk celery, *sliced*

2 leeks or scallions, *sliced*

2 to 3 onions, depending on size, *stuck with* 3 to 4 cloves

4 large cloves of garlic, *unpeeled*

Salt

A bouquet garni of thyme, ½ bay leaf, parsley, tarragon, oregano
1 tablespoon peppercorns, *crushed*
1 pound chuck beef, or other cut suitable for pot roast

1 cup bread cubes, *toasted or fried, and/or enough Swiss, or Parmesan cheese, grated, to make ¾ cup*

Rinse the chicken parts and giblets, and the veal or beef bones.

Bring 3 quarts of water to the boil in a large kettle. Put in the bones, bring again to the boil, and skim until the water is clear. Add the carrots, celery, leeks or scallions, onions with cloves, and garlic. When the water returns to a boil, add ¾ teaspoon of salt, the bouquet garni, and the crushed peppercorns. Add more water if necessary to cover the ingredients by at least 2 inches. Simmer gently for an hour.

Add the chicken parts and giblets and the beef, and skim again until the liquid is clear. Cover the pot, leaving the cover askew to allow the steam to escape, and simmer for at least 3 hours. If the beef is to be used in the casserole that follows, remove it after 1½ hours.

Taste, correct the seasoning, and refrigerate until time to serve.

Skim off the fat and rewarm the bouillon. Discard the bones, bouquet, and chicken.

Serve the bouillon accompanied by croutons (p. 320), or some grated Swiss or Parmesan cheese, or a combination of cheese and croutons. (One can serve the vegetables separately, but they won't have much taste.)

Chou en farce Tante Caroline

CASSEROLE OF GREEN CABBAGE, GROUND MEAT,
AND APPLES, WITH CREAM

For 6:

1 medium-sized green cabbage
Salt
Black pepper, *freshly ground*

2 teaspoons cumin, *ground*
1 or 2 yellow onions, *to make ¾ cup, chopped*

2½ tablespoons fresh pork fat, or 4 tablespoons peanut or vegetable oil

Pinch of saffron (*optional*)

½–1 pound boiled beef (left from the bouillon) or fresh country sausage meat

¾ pound boiled ham (with its fat)

3 or 4 slices Canadian bacon or prosciutto (*optional*)

2 large eggs, *lightly beaten*

Allspice

Paprika

Recommended equipment: A 2½-quart casserole, about 4 inches deep, with a lid.

Wash and quarter the cabbage, discarding any tough or wilted leaves. Plunge it into a large quantity of boiling water, add a tablespoon of salt when the water returns to the boil, and boil the cabbage uncovered for about 10 minutes if it is young and tender, slightly longer if less tender. Refresh it in a colander under cold running water; when cool, separate the leaves and spread them out on paper towels until they are thoroughly dry. Season them with a little salt and pepper and about a teaspoon of cumin, and set them aside.

Sauté the chopped onions gently in the fat or oil for about 5 minutes, stirring from time to time. Season with salt, pepper, and saffron if you wish, and continue to cook until the onions are soft and slightly brown. Remove and set aside.

If using sausage meat, brown it in the same skillet, and drain on absorbent paper.

Put the beef, or sausage, the boiled ham, and the Canadian bacon or prosciutto through a meat grinder. (Or, if you prefer, chop the meat into very tiny pieces.) Stir the meat into the onions, and add the beaten eggs. Season highly with allspice, paprika, and the remaining cumin to taste, and set aside.

To assemble, bake, and serve

1½ pounds cooking apples

1 tablespoon lard, melted bacon fat, or oil

8 thin slices prosciutto or Canadian bacon

1¼ cups cream

Canadian bacon, *diced and sautéed* (*optional*)

Preheat the oven to 375°.

Peel and core the apples and cut them into ¼-inch dice.

Rub the casserole with the fat or oil. Line the bottom and sides with a layer of cabbage leaves, and spoon in a little cream. Then put a layer each of apples, cabbage leaves, half the meat mixture, and half the prosciutto or Canadian bacon, spooning some cream between each layer. Finish the casserole the same way, filling it to the top, and finishing with a layer of apples and a layer of cabbage leaves.

Cover the casserole and bake in the preheated oven for ½ hour. Then reduce the heat to 350° and finish cooking for 1¼ to 1½ hours longer. The mixture will be very smooth and tender.

Serve the *chou* in its casserole. If you like, you can garnish it with a sprinkling of diced, sautéed pieces of Canadian bacon.

Sorbet à la framboise (avec meringue cuite)

RASPBERRY SHERBET MADE WITH MERINGUE

For 10 to 12:

3 packages frozen raspberries
Juice of 1 lemon
6 egg whites
Pinch of salt

About 1⅓ cups confectioners' sugar (to taste)
1 tablespoon kirsch (*optional*)
Granulated sugar (*optional*)

Defrost the frozen raspberries, letting the juice drip through a strainer and pressing the berries to extract all their liquid. Reserve berry pulp. You should have 2 cups of raspberry juice; add to it the strained lemon juice and mix well. Pour into an ice cube tray and freeze for about an hour.

Beat the egg whites with a pinch of salt in a nonaluminum heat-proof bowl until they are white and frothy. Gradually beat in 1⅓ cups sugar to make a smooth meringue. Set over barely simmering water (do not let it get too hot) and continue to beat the meringue for about 5 minutes or more until it is quite firm. Then beat over ice cubes until cool, shiny, and thick. Scrape into another ice cube tray and put in the freezer to set. At the same time, chill a mixing bowl.

Combine the frozen raspberry juice and the set meringue in the chilled mixing bowl and beat to combine the two preparations. Pour into a decorative mold, or an ordinary bowl, and freeze again.

To make a raspberry purée to serve with the *sorbet,* simply spin the berry pulp in the blender for 2 minutes. Add a little granulated sugar if needed and a tablespoon of kirsch if you like the flavor.

To unmold the *sorbet,* wrap a wet warm towel around the mold or bowl for a few seconds and reverse onto a serving platter.

Petits fours: Les dollars

See page 221.

9. *Un menu au pili-pili*

A SPICY MENU

Potage mentonnais au fenouil
Purée of fennel soup

Echine de porc au pili-pili/Ragout of
pork with curry, tomatoes, and hot peppers

Riz au safran/Saffron rice

Vin rouge de Beaujolais

Salade d'endives
Endive salad with mustard vinaigrette

Pommes rapées en nougatine
Grated apples baked with nut brittle

*P*ili-pili are tiny peppers about half an inch long, sometimes called "little birds," which are a brilliant crimson and very exciting and beautiful to see if you have the plant in your living room. They have a hot taste that is as pronounced as their bright color, and they give a gay and unusual touch to this dish of diced pork. I have seen these pepper plants in homes in the United States, and I believe you can find the little peppers, dried, in markets as well, especially in Puerto Rican neighborhoods. But if you cannot find them, you can use Tabasco instead. The dish takes its inspiration from the Creole cuisine, which came to France from Guadeloupe and Martinique. It is accompanied by saffron rice, and if you would like to add even more color to this spicy menu, you could add some green peas to the yellow rice.

Conseils: The fennel soup can be made in advance and reheated. The pork can also be made in advance: in that case, cook it for only ½ hour and reheat it for 45 minutes in a 375° oven. If you reheat it you must be very careful with the seasoning; put in only half of the pili-pili or Tabasco during the first cooking and add the rest when reheating. The apple dessert can be prepared just before serving and served warm, or made ahead of time and served cold. Serve it in its baking dish; the juice of the apples will run out if it is unmolded.

Potage mentonnais au fenouil

PURÉE OF FENNEL SOUP, HOT OR COLD

For 8:

1½ pounds fresh fennel bulbs, *trimmed*
Salt
3 medium yellow onions, *to make 1½ cups, sliced*
5 tablespoons olive oil
2 pounds ripe tomatoes, *peeled, seeded, and quartered (technique, p. 325)*, or 3½ tablespoons tomato paste

9 cups good chicken stock
Large bouquet garni of thyme, ½ bay leaf, and savory
Black pepper, *freshly ground*
5 or 6 tablespoons tapioca

Wash, trim, and peel the more fibrous stalks of fennel. Cut the bulbs in half if they are small and into quarters if large. Discard the tops. Blanch for 5 minutes in boiling water to cover with 2 tablespoons of salt. Refresh under cold running water and drain on paper towels.

Remove the fennel hearts and set them aside for decoration. Slice the remaining fennel.

Sauté the sliced onions gently in the olive oil until they are soft and golden. Add the fennel and cook until lightly browned. Add the tomatoes or tomato paste and simmer slowly, stirring occasionally, for 20 to 25 minutes, until the vegetables are tender. Then put them through a food mill to make a fine purée.

Return the purée to the saucepan, add the chicken stock and the bouquet garni, and season with pepper and a little salt. Stir, set over moderate heat, and simmer, uncovered, until the soup has reduced to 7 cups.

Remove the bouquet garni. Pour the tapioca into the simmering soup a very little at a time, stirring constantly while the soup thickens. Taste, correct the seasoning, and remove from the heat.

To serve hot

3 tablespoons butter	About 1 tablespoon fresh dill
Reserved fennel hearts, *chopped*	weed, *chopped,* or 1 teaspoon dried

Stir the butter into the soup and pour it into a heated soup tureen. Serve sprinkled with the chopped fennel hearts and dill weed.

To serve cold

1 cup heavy cream	1 tablespoon fresh dill weed,
Reserved fennel hearts, *chopped*	*chopped,* or 1 teaspoon dried

Chill the soup and fold in the cream. Serve sprinkled with chopped fennel hearts and dill.

Echine de porc au pili-pili avec riz au safran

RAGOUT OF PORK WITH CURRY, TOMATOES, AND HOT PEPPERS, WITH SAFFRON RICE

For 6:

A 3-pound piece of pork, from the butt end or shoulder, *without fat or gristle*

1½ pounds fresh ripe tomatoes, or whole canned Italian plum tomatoes

2 to 4 tablespoons olive oil

1 medium-sized onion, *finely chopped*

1 medium-sized carrot, *finely chopped*

2 or 3 large cloves garlic, *finely chopped*

Bouquet garni of thyme, ½ bay leaf, and a small hot pepper (pili-pili), *crushed* (if pili-pili is unavailable, substitute a few drops of Tabasco)

1 cup beef stock or bouillon

1 teaspoon curry

Salt

Black pepper, *freshly ground*

About 2 tablespoons fresh basil, *chopped* (if dried use less)

Preheat the oven to 375°.

Remove any fat or gristle from the pork and cut it into neat 1-inch dice. Skin and seed the tomatoes if fresh (*technique, p. 325*), and press the fresh or canned tomatoes to remove excess liquid.

Heat 2 tablespoons of the olive oil in a heavy iron pot or skillet. Add the diced pork and sauté over moderate heat, stirring occasionally with a wooden spoon, until the pieces are evenly colored but not browned. Remove them with a slotted spoon and set them aside. Add the chopped onion and carrot, and more oil if necessary, cover, and cook slowly 10 minutes longer. Pour the fat out of the pan. Add the tomatoes, the finely chopped garlic, and the bouquet garni, and simmer for about 5 minutes longer. Return the pork, pour in the beef stock, and stir in the curry. Season very lightly with salt and pepper and bring to a boil.

Cover the pot and set it in the preheated oven for 40 to 50 minutes until the pork is very tender. Serve decorated with chopped basil.

Rice

¼ cup olive oil	3 tablespoons butter
2 cups long-grain rice	2 tablespoons basil, *chopped*
Pinch of saffron	(if dried, use less)
Salt	

Preheat the oven to 350°.

Heat the oil in a heavy-bottomed saucepan. Stir in the rice, and continue to stir with a wooden spatula over medium heat until the rice is a milky color. Pour in 5 cups of water, add the saffron and a little salt, and bring to a boil. Cover the saucepan tightly, and set in the oven to cook for 18 to 20 minutes, until all the water has evaporated and the rice is fluffy and dry.

Mix the butter into the rice, using two forks, and decorate with chopped basil.

—◀●▶—

Pommes rapées en nougatine

GRATED APPLES BAKED
WITH CRUSHED ALMOND BRITTLE

For 6:

Almond nougatine

3 ounces (⅝ cup) whole un-
    peeled almonds

1 tablespoon peanut or vegetable
    oil
½ cup granulated sugar

Preheat the oven to 250°.

Put the almonds to warm in the oven. Oil a baking sheet. Put the sugar and 3 tablespoons of water in an enameled saucepan. Simmer until the sugar has melted, then raise the heat and let the mixture boil slowly until it has turned a golden caramel brown. Immediately add the warmed almonds, stir to distribute them through the caramel, and pour the nougatine onto the oiled sheet, spreading it out into a layer. Set it aside to cool and harden. Then chop it into pieces about ⅛ inch square. *This can be made in advance.*

Almond butter and grated apple filling

1 stick plus 2 tablespoons butter,
    softened
½ cup granulated sugar
2 ounces (about ⅜ cup) almonds,
    pulverized (technique, p.
    317)

1 cup stale biscuit or cookie
    crumbs, or bread crumbs,
    homemade from good bread
2 tablespoons flour
1½ to 2 pounds cooking apples
    (about 4 medium-sized ap-
    ples)
Juice and grated rind of 1 lemon

Cream the butter and sugar. Add the pulverized almonds. Reserving 1 or 2 tablespoons of the biscuit, cookie, or bread crumbs to garnish the top, stir in the rest. Blend in the flour. (The mixture will form a thick mass.) Set aside.

Peel, core, and grate the apples. Stir in the grated rind and juice of the lemon. Set aside.

To assemble, bake, and serve

2 tablespoons butter, *melted*   ¾ cup cream (*optional*)

Preheat the oven to 375°.

Spread half of the almond-butter mixture on the bottom of a serving-baking dish about 8 inches in diameter and 2 inches deep. Fill the dish with alternating layers of grated apples and chopped nougatine, cover with the remaining butter-almond mixture, and sprinkle with the reserved crumbs and the melted butter.

Bake in the preheated oven for 30 to 35 minutes until the apples are soft and tender.

Serve warm or cold, as is, or with fresh light cream.

Do not reheat.

10. *Un menu d'automne Normand*

A NORMANDY DINNER FOR FALL

Soupe de haricots verts et flageolets
Puréed soup of green and dried beans

> *Charlotte Rainfreville au jambon*
> Molded casserole of macaroni, ham,
> and mushrooms

Salade de saison/Green salad vinaigrette

> *Gâteau de pommes, Reinette*/Apple dessert
> with red current or apricot sauce

Fromage de Camembert

Cidre ou Bordeaux rouge/Fresh cider or red Bordeaux

*W*hen I was a young girl in Normandy, we often had this combination of dishes at family suppers. In fact, the *charlotte de jambon* was the first entrée dish that I cooked, alone, at ten years of age, and I remember that I was thrilled by my success in making it and unmolding it. The mixture is like a quiche mixture—the ham, mushrooms, and chopped pasta being bound with eggs and cream. I remember that I made it that first time with leftover noodles, and often I still do. Obviously, it is an easy dish to make.

There was always a jug of cider on our table in my mother's house. But this was not the type of preserved cider usually found in America; it was the dry, sometimes sparkling cider of Normandy, which we drank like wine. If you can get cider pressed from fresh apples—best when it is about a week old and just beginning to bubble—you will have the closest approximation of Normandy cider. Otherwise, it is better to omit the cider and drink wine with this meal.

Flageolets are small, pale green beans (smaller and rounder than lima beans); they are very French—and difficult to find fresh outside of Europe—but you can get them preserved in cans or jars in fine food shops in America. In that case, they will have been precooked and it will not be necessary to parboil them to make them tender. If you cannot get them in jars, you can use the dried variety (which can be purchased through mail order import houses) or substitute pea beans or other small dried white beans. If you use another kind of bean, you will not have the very special delicate flavor of the true flageolets, but you will still have a wonderful soup.

Being Normande, I prefer cheeses made with cow's milk to goat cheese. Camembert is perhaps my favorite of all, and I will tell you an interesting thing that I have discovered about this cheese. When you open a piece of Camembert, there are times when the center is hard and chalky, indicating that the cheese is not yet ripe. This part is not good to eat because it has not developed the proper texture and flavor; and it will never develop once the cheese has been cut into, because at that point the maturing process is arrested. During the war, the Germans often took the good Camembert, and one day I took that hard center and used it in making a Mornay sauce, which turned out to be unusually flavorful. On another day, I was using the chalky center of a Camembert to make a béchamel sauce, and I found that I had made a very, very thick sauce—so thick that it was no longer really a sauce. I took it by spoonfuls, rolled it in bread crumbs, and fried it in deep fat, and it made a wonderful little bouchée to serve with drinks. Since it is difficult to tell from the outside whether or not a Camembert—or a Brie—is completely ripe, and one has to rely on one's cheese vendor—an uncertain enterprise at times—you may find yourself sometime with such a cheese on your hands. If that happens, I recommend these *trucs*.

Conseils: Everything in this menu can be made in advance and reheated. If the soup is made ahead of time, season it very lightly; you can correct the seasoning when reheating it. The charlotte can easily be made a day in advance and reheated for 10 or 15 minutes in a bain-marie. The apple dessert can be cooked the same day and served warm, or made the day before and served cold.

———◄•►———

Soupe de haricots verts et flageolets

PURÉED SOUP OF GREEN BEANS AND DRIED BEANS

For 6:

3 ounces (about ½ cup) flageolets or other dried beans (such as pea beans) about ½ inch long

Bouquet garni of parsley, sprig of thyme, ½ bay leaf, celery stalk

2 pounds green beans, *washed and
  trimmed*
3 cups milk
4½ tablespoons butter
2 tablespoons flour
Salt

Black pepper, *freshly ground*
Nutmeg, *freshly grated*
3 tablespoons fresh chervil or
  parsley, *chopped* (if dried,
  use less)

In a soup kettle, parboil the dried beans for 2 or 3 minutes in about
8 quarts of boiling water. Turn off the heat and let them soak for an hour.
(Do not let them soak longer.)

Pour out the water, leaving 1 inch covering the beans. Add the
bouquet garni, set over low heat, and simmer for about 1¼ hours until
beans are almost tender.

Then bring the water to a full boil, add the green beans and more
boiling water to cover well, and simmer for 12 to 15 minutes longer until
all the beans are tender.

Remove the beans with a slotted spoon and pour out all but 3 cups
of the cooking liquid. Add the milk and bring to a boil. Melt 1½ tablespoons of butter in a large enameled saucepan. Stir in the flour, and
cook, stirring, for a few seconds. Remove from the heat and pour in the
boiling liquid, stirring until smooth. Season highly with salt, pepper, and
nutmeg.

Pour the soup base back into the kettle, return the beans to the kettle, and simmer over medium heat for about 15 minutes until the beans
have almost the texture of a purée. Then put them through a food mill
or into a blender at low speed, to make a very smooth paste. Taste and
correct the seasoning.

Blend half of the chervil or parsley with the remaining 3 tablespoons of butter. Stir into the soup at the very last minute, and serve at
once in a warm soup tureen or individual cups, sprinkled with remaining
herbs.

Optional: For a richer and more elaborate soup, omit the butter and herbs.
Instead, beat 2 egg yolks into ⅔ cup whipping cream, stir in a little of
the hot bean soup, blend thoroughly, and pour back into the soup. Bring
slowly to just under the simmer, stirring constantly, while the soup thickens. Serve immediately, sprinkled with chervil and parsley.

———◆•◆———

Charlotte Rainfreville au jambon

MOLDED CASSEROLE OF HAM AND MUSHROOMS
WITH MACARONI, CHEESE, AND CREAM

For 6:

Butter and stale bread crumbs to
  coat the mold
1 cup macaroni (*to make 2 cups,
  cooked*)
6 ounces boiled ham, *cut into ¼-
  inch dice*
½ pound small white mushrooms
  (or larger ones, *sliced*)
Juice of ½ lemon, *strained*

2 tablespoons butter
¾ cup light cream
4 eggs
1 cup heavy cream
½ cup imported Swiss cheese,
  grated
Salt
Black pepper, *freshly ground*
Nutmeg, *freshly grated*

Recommended equipment: A 2-quart charlotte mold, soufflé dish, or casserole.

Cut a round of waxed paper to fit the bottom of the mold or casserole. Butter the sides of the mold and one side of the paper. Lay the paper, buttered side up, in the mold; then thoroughly coat the paper and the sides of the mold with bread crumbs. Refrigerate.

Cook the macaroni in a large quantity of boiling salted water until barely tender. (It will finish cooking in the oven.) Refresh under cold running water, drain, and dry on towels. Chop the macaroni into ¼-inch pieces and combine with the diced ham.

Clean the mushrooms and sprinkle them with strained lemon juice. Melt the butter in a large frying pan, add the mushrooms, and sauté, stirring, for 2 or 3 minutes. Salt lightly, pour in the light cream, and simmer for 15 to 20 minutes until the mushrooms are tender and the cream has almost evaporated. Drain if necessary.

Beat the eggs thoroughly with the heavy cream and the grated cheese. Add the mushrooms, macaroni, and ham, and season highly with salt, pepper, and nutmeg. Mix thoroughly and fill the mold or casserole.

To bake   *Preheat the oven to 375°.*

Put the mold into a shallow pan and pour about 1½ inches of water into the pan. Bring the water to the simmer on top of the stove. Then cover the mold and put the pan in the preheated oven for 20 to 25 minutes until the mixture has drawn away from the sides of the mold.

To serve

Unmold the charlotte onto a shallow dish and peel off the paper. Coat the charlotte with some of the *sauce Aurore* (following recipe), and serve the remaining sauce in a sauceboat.

Sauce crème Aurore

TOMATO-CREAM SAUCE

For 2½ cups:

2½ tablespoons butter
3 tablespoons flour
1½ cups milk
½ cup cream

1 tablespoon tomato paste
Salt
Black pepper, *freshly ground*
Nutmeg, *freshly grated*

Melt the butter in an enameled saucepan. Stir in the flour, and cook, stirring, for a few seconds. Remove from the heat and pour in the milk, beating vigorously to blend. Return to the heat and continue stirring until the sauce comes to a boil. Add the cream, and a little of the tomato paste and stir again thoroughly. The sauce should be a light golden-rose like the dawn or a tea rose. Add a little more tomato paste if necessary, and let the sauce boil for 2 minutes. Taste, and season highly with salt, pepper, and nutmeg.

———— ◆◆ ————

Gâteau de pommes, Reinette

BAKED APPLE DESSERT WITH RED CURRANT
OR APRICOT SAUCE, HOT OR COLD

This can be served warm, or can be made a day in advance and served cold.

For 6:

½ cup raisins
¾ cup rum, preferably dark rum
1 cup very stale bread crumbs,
    homemade from good bread
About 2 pounds tart, firm apples,
    (*to make about 4 cups,*
    sliced)

3 tablespoons lemon juice,
    strained
4 eggs, *separated*
¾ cup granulated sugar
Rind of 1 orange, *grated*
½ teaspoon vanilla
About 1½ teaspoons cinnamon
Salt

Recommended equipment: A heavy-bottomed enameled ovenproof saucepan with a lid (2½-quart capacity).

Apple mixture

Let the raisins steep in the rum for about 15 minutes, then drain off the rum, add it to the bread crumbs, and mash with a fork to moisten them. Peel and core the apples, cut into slices ¼ inch thick, and sprinkle with the strained lemon juice.

Beat the egg yolks with ½ cup of the sugar until they are a pale creamy yellow. Stir in the raisins, the grated orange rind, the rum-soaked bread crumbs, and the apples. (The mixture will be very thick.) Add the vanilla, and cinnamon to taste.

Beat the egg whites with a pinch of salt until they begin to become white and frothy. Slowly add the remaining ¼ cup sugar, and continue to beat until shiny and firm. Stir a third of the egg whites into the apple mixture to lighten it; then fold all back into the remaining egg whites (*technique, page 321*).

To bake

6 tablespoons sweet butter

Preheat the oven to 375°.

Clarify the butter (*technique, p. 319*); you will have about 3½ tablespoons. Pour it into the enameled saucepan and set over heat. When the butter is hot, pour in the apple mixture to fill the saucepan about ¾ full. Turn up the heat to high and leave the pan on the heat, without stirring the apples, for 2 or 3 minutes. Cover, and bake in the preheated oven for 35 to 40 minutes until the mixture has puffed up and drawn away from the sides of the pan.

To serve

½ cup red currant jelly or strained apricot jam

Raisins or 3 or 4 candied cherries, *diced*

Serve the apple dessert unmolded with a sauceboat of warmed currant jelly or warmed and strained apricot jam. If the dessert is to be served cold, the jelly should be poured over about an hour before serving. Decorate with candied cherries or raisins.

MORE FORMAL
OCCASIONS

———◆·◆——

Six déjeuners

Six Luncheons

Huit dîners priés

Eight Dinner Parties for Eight People

11. *Un petit menu très chic*

A CHIC LITTLE LUNCH

Soufflé roulé farçi aux crabes
Special rolled soufflé filled with crab

Sauce tomate à la provençale/Tomato sauce

Vin blanc sec de la Loire: Pouilly-Fumé

Salade de saison/Green salad vinaigrette

Fromages: Reblochon, le Ste. Maure

Gâteau au chocolat: Le Diabolo/Chocolate cake
or *Fruits de saison*/Fresh fruit

*F*or this little luncheon, especially appropriate for fall or winter, the entrée is a special soufflé that is baked flat, in a large rectangle, spread with filling, then rolled up like a jelly roll, and served with a rich tomato sauce *à la provençale.* The final roll is 3½ to 4 inches high and at least a foot long, so that it is a very beautiful thing. It can be shaped into the form of a fish for an amusing presentation. It can serve as an elegant first course for a formal dinner, and it lends itself to numerous variations.

Although the soufflé may seem a little formidable, I can assure you that it is most easily accomplished with just a little practice. My only caution is not to make it if your oven gives uneven heat. Because the soufflé is baked flat, it will not, of course, rise as high as an ordinary soufflé. The *truc* in making it is to turn it out, as soon as it has been baked, onto a towel that has been dampened with water and wrung out.

Once you have tried this soufflé-roll, you can make it with many other fillings—lobster or shrimp or scallops, for example, or walnuts or *duxelles* (minced mushrooms) with cream.

The soufflé is strongly flavored and filling; followed by a green salad and cheese, fresh fruit, or the *diabolo,* it will constitute a complete lunch. The *diabolo* is a particularly smooth and delicious chocolate cake that came from my mother's old black notebook. It is either served as is or spread with a chocolate butter cream, should you want a very rich finish to this "chic little lunch."

Conseils: The soufflé can wait, wrapped in the foil, from 45 minutes to an hour in the turned-off oven. The sauce can be made in advance and reheated. The cake, of course, can also be made in advance.

———— •••• ————

Soufflé roulé farçi aux crabes

ROLLED SOUFFLÉ FILLED WITH CRAB, TOMATO SAUCE

For 6:

Prepare the tomato sauce, page 301.

Crab filling

10 ounces fresh or canned crab
    meat, *carefully gone over to*
    remove bones and cartilage

Tabasco
1 or 2 tablespoons tomato sauce
    (*above*)

Season the crabmeat nicely with Tabasco. Moisten it with tomato sauce and set it aside.

Soufflé

Butter and flour for the baking
    dish
½ cup flour
2 cups cold milk
4 egg yolks
Salt

Black pepper, *freshly ground*
Nutmeg, *freshly grated*
6 egg whites
½ cup imported Swiss cheese,
    grated
Preheat the oven to 375°.

Recommended equipment: A *lèchefrite:* a shallow enameled metal baking dish with slanting sides—about 12 by 16 inches on the top, and 9 by 13 inches on the bottom, *or* a 9-by-13-inch baking sheet and heavy aluminum foil.

If you have a baking dish as described above, line the bottom and sides with aluminum foil. Otherwise, use a regular baking sheet, and if it has no sides, make them of aluminum foil: cut a piece of aluminum foil 4½ inches broader and wider than the sheet itself; then make slanting sides 1½ inches deep by folding the foil over on itself 3 times, pinching it together, bending it up, and securing it with pins.

Generously butter the foil, sprinkle it with flour, and shake or tap to remove excess flour.

To make the soufflé base or bouillie

Put the ½ cup flour into a heavy-bottomed enameled saucepan. Add some of the milk in small quantities, stirring with a whisk to make a smooth paste. Stir in all the remaining milk and blend well. Set over moderate heat and stir constantly until the *bouillie* has thickened; then remove from the heat and beat vigorously until smooth.

Beat the 4 egg yolks into the *bouillie* one at a time. Season to taste with salt, pepper, and nutmeg, and stir until smooth.

Beat the 6 egg whites with a pinch of salt until they are stiff but not dry. Stir a quarter of the egg whites into the warm *bouillie* to lighten it; then fold all back lightly into the remaining egg whites, at the same time adding the cheese (*folding technique, p. 321*).

Gently pour the soufflé mixture into the shallow dish or baking sheet, spreading evenly, and bake it in the preheated oven for 18 to 20 minutes until it has swelled and lightly browned.

To roll and serve the soufflé

While the soufflé is baking, dampen a dish towel with warm water, wring it out completely, and spread it on a flat surface.

Remove the soufflé from the oven, and immediately invert the baking dish over the towel to unmold the soufflé evenly. Peel off the foil.

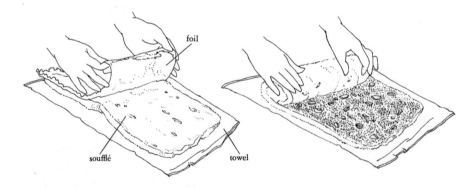

Then spread the soufflé with the crab filling in an even layer and roll it up. Wrap the roll in aluminum foil if you are not going to serve it immediately. *The soufflé can stay in a warming oven for about 1 hour.*

Remove the foil, coat the soufflé with some of the tomato sauce, and serve the remaining sauce in a sauceboat.

———◆●◆———

Gâteau au chocolat: Le Diabolo

CHOCOLATE CAKE GLAZED WITH
CHOCOLATE BUTTER CREAM

For 6:

Butter and flour for the cake pan
¾ cup sugar
4 eggs, *separated*
6 ounces German's sweet choco-
    late, *broken into pieces*
¾ cup butter

4 tablespoons cake flour
2 tablespoons almonds, *blanched*
    and pulverized (*technique,*
    p. 317)
Pinch of salt

Preheat the oven to 375°.

Recommended equipment: A cake pan 8 inches in diameter and 1¾ inches deep.

Cut a round of waxed paper to fit the bottom of the cake pan. Butter the sides of the pan and one side of the paper. Lay the paper butter side up in the pan and flour the paper and the sides of the pan. Set aside.

Beat the sugar with the 4 egg yolks until they are a creamy yellow. Put the chocolate and the butter in an enamel saucepan over simmering water, and stir until the chocolate is smooth. Add the egg and sugar mixture, and continue stirring over low heat until well blended.

Stir in the flour and the pulverized almonds.

Beat the 4 egg whites with a pinch of salt until stiff but not dry. Stir one quarter of the egg whites into the chocolate mixture to lighten it; then fold all back into the remaining egg whites (*folding technique, p. 321*).

Fill the cake pan three-fourths full and tap it gently on the table to distribute the mixture evenly. Bake in the preheated oven for 25 to 30 minutes, watching carefully, until the outside is solid and the center still creamy (not runny and not dry) when tested with a sharp knife. Let the cake cool before unmolding.

To glaze

Chocolate butter cream

3½ ounces German's sweet choco-   2 to 3 tablespoons coffee or water
late, *broken into small pieces*   3 tablespoons butter

Melt the chocolate with the coffee or the water until smooth, remove from the heat, and stir in the butter. Pour on top of the chocolate cake, using a metal spatula (moistened in hot water and dried) to spread.

To decorate

Slivered almonds, *toasted*

Decorate the cake with toasted slivered almonds. Refrigerate before serving.

12. *Un déjeuner sans souci*

A CAREFREE LUNCHEON

Quiche à l'aubergine/Eggplant quiche

La salade de Varengeville: Riz et moules
Salad of mussels and rice

*Fromages: Cantal, Camembert,
ou Tomme de Savoie*

Le gâteau d'Hélène/White cake with
coconut cream and apricot

Vin rosé: Tavel, ou vin rosé de Provence

*H*ere is a *déjeuner sans souci*—gay and carefree—because it can be made completely in advance: a warm Provençal quiche of eggplant, cheese, and tomatoes; a cold salad of mussels and rice in sauce, and a cake —the luscious *gâteau d'Hélène*—which is absolutely white like a virgin with a delicate flavor of coconut and apricot, and completely covered with coconut cream.

I originally made the *salade de Varengeville* with the tiny, sweet and succulent mussels of Varengeville in Normandy. The ravishing commune of Varengeville is situated just below the Falaise Normande, the Normandy Falls, near Dieppe. It was in the rocks below this falls that, in our youth, my older brother Maurice and I used to go to gather those extraordinary little mussels that were to be found there. Leaving from the beach at Quiberville, where our family had a cabin, we would depart in a small canoe, drawing behind us another canoe in which to bring back our catch. Once, surprised by a stormy tide, our canoe filled with mussels was shipwrecked and driven against the rocks. My brother succeeded in rescuing both the canoe and our mussels, but he had to draw it along for several miles, walking barefoot on sharp rocks. This courageous expedition, I am happy to remember, ended well, and for us the best mussels in the world are still those of Varengeville. The mussels, combined with rice and a delicate sauce of cucumbers and soft cream cheese, are decorated with a mimosa—the charming garnish, made of sieved hard-boiled eggs, which evokes the mimosa trees of southern France, whose ethereal yellow flowers are one of the glories of Provence. Frequently, only the yolk of the egg is used for a mimosa, but I prefer to use both the sieved yolk mixed with the finely chopped white, which are then combined with fresh green herbs and sprinkled over the salad.

The eggplant quiche uses a special *truc* that I have developed for making certain quiches or tarts. When one puts pastry into a tart mold and wants to cook it *à blanc*—that is, to bake it without its filling—one generally lines this empty unbaked shell with foil or heavy paper, and then fills the paper either with some little pebbles, or some dried beans, to prevent the pastry from blistering during the baking—which almost always happens. But the following technique can in some cases be used instead. The paper and beans are omitted, and the dough is spread instead with a certain mixture that will prevent it from swelling and at the same time give it flavor. For this eggplant quiche, the pastry is painted with a layer of Dijon mustard, then sprinkled with cheese, and pricked with a fork to allow the steam to escape. It is necessary to watch the pastry closely while it bakes. The oven must not be hotter than 375°, and if by chance it has become too hot and the pastry has succeeded in swelling, immediately remove it from the oven and prick it with a fork before returning it to finish baking. This is more apt to happen with 8-inch molds; with tiny tartlets, it is very rare. The combination of mustard and cheese can be used for many other quiches. For sweet desserts, other glazes obviously are preferable, as I will discuss further on.

Conseils: The quiche can be cooked 2 hours in advance and reheated 15 minutes before serving; it will keep warm in foil for about an hour. The cake should be made ahead and kept in the coolest part of the kitchen, or the least cold part of the refrigerator; if your refrigerator is very cold, the cake should be taken out ahead of time. The salad is to be prepared in advance but should not be combined with the dressing until the last minute; otherwise the watercress will be "cooked" by the action of the vinegar and will wilt.

—●◆●—

Quiche à l'aubergine

EGGPLANT QUICHE

For about 6:

Pastry shell

1 recipe *pâte brisée "A"* (*p. 313*)　　3 tablespoons imported Swiss
3 tablespoons Dijon mustard　　　　　　　cheese, *grated*

Recommended equipment: An 8-inch tart mold.

Make the pastry and put it into the refrigerator to firm.

Roll out the pastry to a thickness of ⅛ inch and line the mold with it (*technique, p. 324*). Brush the bottom of the pastry shell with the mustard, sprinkle with half of the cheese, and prick in several places with a fork. Refrigerate to firm again before baking.

Preheat the oven to 375°.

Partially bake the shell in the preheated oven for about 15 minutes until the pastry is very lightly colored and has drawn very slightly away from the sides of the mold.

Eggplant filling

1½ pounds eggplant　　　　　　　　1½ cups *purée de tomate proven-*
Salt　　　　　　　　　　　　　　　　*çale* (*p. 299*), or canned
⅔ cup olive, peanut, or vegetable　　　Italian plum tomatoes,
　　oil　　　　　　　　　　　　　　*drained and puréed*
Black pepper, *freshly ground*　　　　2 tablespoons basil, *chopped*
¼ pound lean bacon (6 or 7　　　　　2 tablespoons parsley, *chopped*
　　slices of medium thickness)　　　　　(if the herbs are dried, use
3 eggs　　　　　　　　　　　　　　　less)

Peel the eggplant and dice it into ½-inch pieces. Spread out on paper towels, sprinkle with salt, and leave for about 15 minutes, turning and salting once more, while the eggplant disgorges its liquid. Then rinse and pat dry.

Heat the oil in a frying pan, and sauté the eggplant over moderate heat for about 10 minutes until it is soft and lightly browned. Then drain it on paper towels, season with salt and pepper, and set aside.

Pour out the oil, and put the bacon to fry in the same pan. Also drain and set aside. When it is cool, crumble it.

Beat the eggs in a mixing bowl. Add the eggplant, the bacon, the tomato purée or tomatoes, and the chopped herbs, and season with pepper and a little salt.

To bake and serve   *Preheat the oven to 375°.*

Fill the tart shell with the eggplant mixture, and sprinkle with the remaining cheese. Bake in the preheated oven for 18 to 25 minutes or until the top is set.

Let the quiche cool briefly before unmolding it. Serve it warm.

La salade de Varengeville: Riz et moules

SALAD OF MUSSELS, SHRIMPS, AND PEAS WITH
SAFFRON RICE WITH SAUCE ROSY

For 6:

About 6 pounds of fresh mussels in the shell (small ones, if possible)

Black pepper, *freshly ground*

Juice of ½ lemon

About 1 cup *sauce rosy (p. 307)*

½ cup tiny shrimps (fresh, frozen, or canned), *cooked and shelled*

1 cup sweet small green peas, *cooked and drained*

1 cup cooked saffron rice *(p. 310)*

6 ounces small mushroom caps, prepared in oil and vinegar *(optional)*

2 tablespoons parsley, *chopped*

2 eggs, *hard boiled*

Bunch of watercress

Thoroughly wash and scrub the mussels in several changes of water to remove all grit. Put them without liquid into a heavy pot, cover, and set over quite high heat for 5 minutes, shaking the pot every 2 minutes or so until all the mussels have opened; discard any that don't open. Drain and cool them. (Reserve their cooking juices, which can be saved for another preparation such as a fish fumet).

Shell the mussels, sprinkle them with pepper (but not salt), and some lemon juice, and set them aside.

In a large mixing bowl, combine the cooked rice, mussels, shrimp, and peas with the optional mushroom caps and some of the chopped parsley. Mix in half of the sauce. Refrigerate until time to serve.

To serve

Line a salad bowl with the watercress. Put the salad mixture in the middle, coat with the remaining sauce, and sprinkle with the remaining parsley and the hard-boiled eggs, pressed through a food mill to make a "mimosa."

Gâteau d'Hélène

WHITE CAKE FILLED AND ICED WITH
COCONUT CREAM AND APRICOT

For about 8:

The cake should be made a day ahead of time; it is best when it is slightly stale.

Grated coconut

2–3 cups grated canned coconut,
   preferably unsweetened

The day before making the cake, spread out the coconut to dry on a tray.

Génoise cake

Butter and flour for the cake pan	3 eggs
12 tablespoons (1½ sticks) sweet butter	1 cup cake flour
	1⅓ tablespoons baking powder
1 cup sugar	Pinch of salt
1 orange	

Preheat the oven to 375°.

Recommended equipment: A round cake pan approximately 8½ inches wide and 1½ inches deep.

Heavily butter the cake pan, and line the bottom with buttered waxed paper (buttered side up). Sprinkle the pan with flour, and shake off the excess.

Cream the butter and sugar, and beat until smooth and pale yellow. Grate the peel of the orange, and juice the orange. Add the peel to the butter and sugar and set aside ¼ cup of the juice for the filling. Beat the eggs into the creamed butter one at a time. Sift the flour with the baking powder and salt, and add to the batter, beating until smooth.

Pour the batter into the cake pan and bake in the preheated oven for 35 to 40 minutes.

Let the cake cool on a rack, unmolding it after about 20 minutes.

Apricot-coconut filling and icing

¼ cup orange juice (*above*)	1 teaspoon vanilla extract
½ cup rum (preferably dark rum)	⅓ cup sugar
	2 cups grated dry unsweetened co-
½ cup apricot jam, *strained*	conut (*above*)
1½ cups heavy cream	

Mix the orange juice and the rum.

Slice the cake into 3 layers, and lay the layers on a board. Prick each layer with a fork in several places. Sprinkle each layer with ⅓ of the rum and orange juice mixture and then spread two layers with some apricot jam, reserving some of the jam for the top layer.

Whip the cream over ice and add the vanilla; when the cream is almost firm, add the sugar and continue to whip until stiff.

Place about 4 tablespoons of the whipped cream in another bowl, and stir in about 5 tablespoons of the coconut to make a thick mixture.

Build the cake, spreading the coconut cream on the first and second layers. Cover the top layer with the remaining apricot jam. Then neatly coat the top and sides of the cake with the remaining whipped cream, making a dome on the top. Sprinkle the entire cake with the remaining coconut; it will stick to the frosting.

Put the cake in a cool place until time to serve.

13. *Déjeuner "au manoir"*

LUNCHEON AT A COUNTRY HOUSE

Le pain manoir/Molded salad
of beets and potatoes

ou Asperges vertes en vinaigrette "mimosa"
Cold asparagus vinaigrette "mimosa"

Filets de poisson florentine
Fish fillets on a bed of creamed spinach

Salade de romaine et Roquefort
Green salad with Roquefort vinaigrette

Fromages: Excelsior ou Vacherin

Le croquant aux prunes
Plums baked with sweet almond-butter crust
or *Fruits frais*/Fresh fruit

Vin de Champagne blanc de blancs

*T*his lunch, typical of one that might be served at a country house in France, begins either with a dish called the *pain manoir*—a familiar dish of my childhood—or, if fresh asparagus is in season, with *asperges en vinaigrette.* The word *pain* here does not mean "bread," but rather something that is molded and formed into a round shape—in this case it is a molded salad of sliced potatoes and beets marinated with shallots and mixed with a light and creamy cold sauce with grated raw cucumbers.

This style of serving cold asparagus—seasoned with a simple vinaigrette and covered with a mimosa of finely sieved hard-boiled eggs and minced herbs—is certainly the most popular in France. There is an essential difference to be observed in the method of cooking asparagus when it is to be served cold. Asparagus tends to contract in the cooling, and thus the skin often becomes wrinkled. This can be prevented by cooking it in what is called a *blanc*—which means that the water in which it is boiled should contain flour. Thus the asparagus will have a smoother and more velvety quality.

The word *croquant* has the same derivation as the word *croque* in the sandwiches *croque-monsieur* and *croque-madame.* It means something hard and crunchy when you bite into it, but softer inside. The *croquant* is an informal pastry made with equal parts of flour, butter, pulverized almonds, and sugar. They are mixed lightly together and, after having been chilled, are crumbled and spread on fruit or fruit tarts which are then baked in the oven. A very versatile preparation, and so easy to do. When making it with plums, I prefer the large violet ones, very sweet and juicy, that ripen in the fall. One can also use the type called Reine Claude, the green ones; they are much more tender and require less cooking time. It helps to peel the plums before cooking them because they will be just that much more tender and will absorb the flavor of the syrup. A variety of other kinds of fruit can be used instead, either fresh or canned: apricots, peaches, pears, raspberries, strawberries, blueberries, pineapple—or any good combination. Fresh apricots or peaches should be sprinkled with lemon juice and poached, in their skins, in a syrup of water and sugar; when they are tender they are removed from the syrup and peeled. Pears are simmered with water, sugar, and white wine. Raspberries, strawberries, blueberries, or sliced bananas can be used raw. The *croquant* mixture can be frozen.

Conseils: The *pain manoir* is best when made two or three days in advance so that the vegetables have time to be imbued with the marinade. If you are serving asparagus instead, it should be cooked long enough in advance so that it will be thoroughly cool when served. The fish fillets and the *croquant aux prunes* can be partially prepared ahead (see the recipes), but both should be completed just before the luncheon.

Le pain manoir

COLD MOLDED SALAD OF MARINATED POTATOES
AND BEETS, WITH SAUCE ROSY

The vegetables for this salad should marinate for two days. They can, if necessary, marinate for only one day, but the salad will not be quite as good. They should not marinate longer than three days.

For 6:

¾ pound boiling potatoes	Black pepper, *freshly ground*
¾ pound beets	2½ cups *sauce rosy* (*p. 307*)
6 shallots, *minced*	3 tablespoons mixed parsley,
¾ cup dry white wine	chives, and tarragon, *minced*
2 tablespoons wine vinegar	1½ tablespoons if dried)
Salt	

To marinate the potatoes and beets

Boil the potatoes. Boil or bake the beets until tender. Peel both potatoes and beets and cut into slices about ¼ inch thick. Combine them in a bowl with the minced shallots, the white wine, and the vinegar, season with salt and pepper, and let marinate for about 48 hours in the coolest part of the kitchen, turning occasionally. The potatoes should turn a nice pinkish color.

Prepare the *sauce rosy.*

To assemble and serve

Line a 1½-quart bowl with slices of beets and potatoes, making an even outside layer that will show when the salad is unmolded. Cut the remaining potatoes and beets into small dice or chop them roughly. Combine them with 1½ cups of the sauce and 2 tablespoons of the fresh herbs, reserving about 1 cup of the sauce to coat the *pain manoir.* Pack the salad tightly in the bowl and refrigerate for at least half an hour.

Unmold the salad on a serving dish, coat it with the remaining sauce, and serve it sprinkled with the remaining herbs.

Asperges vertes en vinaigrette "mimosa"

COLD ASPARAGUS VINAIGRETTE "MIMOSA"

For 8:

4 pounds very fresh tender green asparagus
½ cup flour
3 tablespoons white wine vinegar

1 tablespoon salt
About 1 tablespoon melted butter to brush the cheesecloth

To cook the asparagus

Break off the fibrous root of each piece of asparagus, leaving only the tender green, then peel off the outside skin. Wash the stalks well and tie them together into eight bundles.

Boil 3 quarts of water in a pot that will comfortably hold the asparagus. Meanwhile blend the flour with a little cold water and the white wine vinegar, and then add this paste to the boiling water along with the salt. When it is boiling hard again, add the asparagus bundles to the water, covering them with cheesecloth that has been brushed with melted butter. Cook the asparagus 10 to 15 minutes until the tips are tender. Remove the bundles carefully and spread out to dry on a towel, then chill in the refrigerator while making the sauce.

Sauce vinaigrette "mimosa"

To make 1¼ cups sauce:

2 eggs, *hard boiled*
About 3 tablespoons mixed chervil, parsley, and chives, *minced* (if using dried herbs use 1 teaspoon of each)
3 tablespoons wine vinegar

1½ tablespoons Dijon mustard
About 10 tablespoons olive oil or 12 tablespoons peanut oil
Salt
Black pepper, *freshly ground*

Put the hard-boiled eggs through a food mill to obtain a "mimosa." Mix the mimosa with the herbs, and set aside.

In a bowl blend the vinegar and the mustard, then very gradually beat in the oil, using a whisk. Season highly with salt and pepper.

When the asparagus is cold, pour part of the dressing over it, and sprinkle the tips with the reserved mimosa and herbs. Serve the remaining dressing, chilled, in a sauceboat.

———◄•►———

Filets de poisson florentine

FISH FILLETS ON A BED OF
CREAMED SPINACH, MORNAY SAUCE

For 6 to 8:

Bed of creamed spinach

4 pounds fresh spinach
Salt
5 tablespoons butter

6 tablespoons heavy cream
Black pepper, *freshly ground*
Nutmeg, *freshly grated*

Trim and wash the spinach. Blanch it for 5 minutes in about 8 quarts of boiling salted water. Refresh it in a colander under cold running water. Squeeze it to extract as much water as possible, and chop it roughly.

Warm the butter in a skillet, add the spinach, and cook it slowly for 5 to 6 minutes, stirring from time to time. Add the cream, a spoonful at a time, season highly with salt, pepper, and nutmeg, and set aside. *The recipe can be made in advance to this point.*

Fish fillets

About 4 tablespoons butter	Salt
3 pounds fillets of sole, lemon sole, whiting, flounder, cod, or red snapper	Black pepper, *freshly ground*
	2 cups dry white wine

Preheat the oven to 375°.

Liberally butter a 10- to 12-inch shallow baking and serving dish. Season the fish fillets lightly with salt and pepper, and arrange them in the dish in one layer, overlapping slightly. Pour in the wine, which should barely cover the fillets, and dot them with the remaining butter.

Set the dish over moderate heat and bring the wine to the simmer. Lay a piece of buttered waxed paper neatly over the fish (buttered side down). Then set in the preheated oven to cook for 8 to 10 minutes until the flesh is milky and can easily be pierced with a fork. Do not overcook. Maintain the liquid almost at the simmer, regulating the heat if necessary.

Remove the fish from the pan with a slotted spoon and set aside. Place the pan over high heat, and boil down the liquid to make 1 cup of fish fumet.

Sauce Mornay

2½ tablespoons butter	Black pepper, *freshly ground*
3 tablespoons flour	Nutmeg, *freshly grated*
1 cup of fish fumet (*above*)	⅔ cup imported Swiss cheese, *grated*
About 1⅓ cups cream	
Salt	

Melt the butter in an enameled saucepan. Stir in the flour, and cook, stirring, for a few seconds. Remove from the heat. Pour in the cup of fish fumet, stirring thoroughly until smooth. Then add 1 cup of the cream, return to the heat, and beat vigorously until it comes to a boil. When smooth, season highly with salt, pepper, and nutmeg.

Remove from the heat, stir in half of the grated cheese, and add the remaining cream a spoonful at a time, until the sauce has the desired consistency. Taste, and correct the seasoning if necessary. *The recipe can be made a few hours in advance to this point.*

Final assembly   *Preheat the oven to 400°.*

If the sauce is cold, bring it slowly to a simmer. Reheat the spinach. Spread the spinach in one layer in the dish in which the fish fillets were cooked. Arrange the fillets on the spinach, and cover all with the hot sauce. Sprinkle with the cheese and dot with butter.

Put in the preheated oven for 5 or 6 minutes, until very lightly browned.

Serve at once, in the baking dish.

Le croquant aux prunes

PLUMS STEWED WITH SUGAR AND LEMON
JUICE AND BAKED WITH AN
ALMOND-SUGAR-BUTTER CRUST

For 6:

Le croquant

½ cup almonds, *blanched and finely chopped*
⅓ cup sugar
½ cup flour

Pinch of salt
4 tablespoons (½ stick) cold sweet butter
1 teaspoon vanilla extract

This mixture may be made in advance, like a pastry, and set aside in a cool place.

Mix the almonds with the sugar, the flour, and a pinch of salt. With a fork, two knives, or a pastry blender—never with your hands—work in the cold butter by bits. Add the vanilla. Do not moisten the mixture or overwork it: it should remain crumbly. Set the *croquant* mixture aside in a cool place.

Plums

2 pounds plums, fresh or canned
About ½ cup sugar

Juice of 1 lemon, *strained*
Butter for the baking dish

For fresh plums: Peel and pit the plums and put them in an enamel saucepan. Add the sugar and the strained lemon juice, and let the plums macerate for about 1 hour. Set the pan over moderate heat, bring to a boil, then turn the heat down and simmer, uncovered, for about 20 minutes or less time if the plums are very ripe and tender.

For canned plums: Peel and pit the plums if necessary, sprinkle with lemon juice, warm briefly in their syrup, and then proceed.

Remove the plums to a buttered baking dish. Strain the juice, return it to the pan, and reduce it over heat to a thick heavy syrup. Pour the syrup over the plums and set them aside to cool.

To bake   *Preheat the oven to 400°.*

Spread half of the *croquant* mixture over the plums. Bake in the preheated oven for about 10 minutes until the *croquant* is golden and crunchy. Again, spread with the remaining *croquant* mixture, making a dome toward the center, and return to the oven to bake for about 10 minutes longer until nicely golden brown. Set on a rack and cool slightly before serving.

14. *Un menu délicat*

A DELICATE MENU

Soufflés d'Alençon, en timbales
Individual cheese soufflés

*Salade verte, composée de chicorée,
endives, et betterave rouge*/Salad of chicory,
endive, and beets, vinaigrette

*Plateau de fromages variés: Camembert
et Pont-l'Évêque ou Petit Suisse*

Tarte de Nancy (aux amandes)/Almond tart

Vin rouge de Bordeaux: St.-Émilion

*T*he entrées for this luncheon are delicate little individual cheese soufflés, called *soufflés d'Alençon* after a small town in Normandy. They are served, unmolded, in a sauce that is characteristically Normand in that it is nothing but fresh cream simmered with tarragon. They are a special kind of soufflé that bakes in individual molds and rises very, very slowly in the oven in a bain-marie. Their consistency is consequently more dense than that of the typical highly inflated soufflé and they will keep their shape when unmolded. These soufflés have an extraordinary attribute that I discovered quite by chance in the course of my last visit to the United States.

In the past few years I have made these soufflés—as I do all cheese soufflés—without butter. This idea originally occurred to me a few years ago when I was trying to develop a light chocolate soufflé for students in my cooking classes—chocolate soufflés always tending to be heavier than any other kind. Since butter in a soufflé sometimes melts and pushes the whites down—with a consequent heaviness—I decided to omit it. The result was the special chocolate soufflé to be found on page 289 in which only cold milk and flour are used in the base. I later extended the idea to other soufflés.

During my last visit to the United States, I stayed for a time with a friend in Virginia, and we had the opportunity to do a great deal of cooking together. One day she asked me to make some soufflés for guests who were expected for dinner that night, so that she might learn the process, and I chose these *soufflés d'Alençon.* I cooked them about two hours in advance with the idea of rewarming them for dinner. But just as I was about to put them back into the oven, there was a telephone call to say that the guests would not be coming. We set them aside and forgot them completely. They stayed in the kitchen, not in the refrigerator, just sitting in a corner, and no one—not even the dog, a funny little bulldog who was very well behaved—thought to eat them. Two days later, my friend said suddenly: "The soufflés!" We looked at them, and they had deflated completely; they looked to be fit for neither man nor dog. On an impulse, however, I put them into a bain-marie and popped them into a moderate oven. And we were astounded to find that they puffed up again to fill the molds. We then unmolded and gratinéed them with their cream sauce, they turned out to be as delicious as they would have been the day they were made. So you can see that I find these soufflés remarkable in every respect—another instance of the phenomenon, which has occurred over and over again in the history of cuisine, of an oversight or accident leading to a fortuitous discovery. This experience only reinforces my French instinct that one must never throw anything away!

Conseils: If you make the soufflés in advance, they will deflate as they cool. About half an hour before serving them, reheat them in a bain-marie; then turn them out upside down in a gratin dish, pour the sauce around them, and put the dish in the oven until they rise again. They will not rise quite as high as the first time they were baked, but the taste will be as good. The tart can be made a day in advance.

Soufflés d' Alençon, en timbales

INDIVIDUAL CHEESE SOUFFLÉS, TARRAGON CREAM SAUCE

For 6:

2½ tablespoons butter for the
    ramekins
5 level tablespoons all-purpose
    flour, *tapped to settle the*
    flour
1 cup cold milk
3 egg yolks

4 egg whites
½ cup imported Swiss cheese,
    grated
Salt
Black pepper, *freshly ground*
Nutmeg, *freshly grated*

Recommended equipment: 12 half-cup ramekins or timbale molds.

Heavily butter the ramekins or timbale molds and set them in the refrigerator to chill until they are to be used.

Make the bouillie: Put the flour into an enameled saucepan, and very gradually add the cold milk, a little at a time, stirring with a whisk or spatula to make a smooth paste. Pour in the remaining milk and stir thoroughly. Add a pinch of salt and season highly with pepper and nutmeg. Set over medium heat, and stir continuously for several minutes until the mixture is quite smooth and thick. Remove from the heat and continue to stir for a few seconds to cool the *bouillie* slightly. Set aside.

Separate four eggs, dropping the whites into a mixing bowl and three of the yolks, one by one, into the warm *bouillie,* stirring to incorporate each yolk thoroughly before adding the next.

Beat the egg whites with a pinch of salt until they are stiff but not dry. If the *bouillie* has cooled, return it to the heat and warm it gently (it should be warmed only enough so that you can still put your finger into it). Then fold it into the stiffly beaten egg whites (*technique, p. 321*), gradually sprinkling on the grated cheese at the same time.

To cook the soufflés   *Preheat the oven to 375°.*

Fill the ramekins or timbale molds two-thirds full of the soufflé mixture. Set them in a shallow pan, and pour water into the pan to come two-thirds of the way up the sides of the molds. Bring the water to the simmer on top of the stove. Then very carefully set the pan with the molds into the preheated oven to cook the soufflés for 12 to 15 minutes until they have risen a good ¾ inch above the edges of the molds. (The water in the pan must not boil; if it does, regulate the oven temperature.)

When you remove the soufflés from the oven they will deflate a little, but do not worry. They may be served immediately, or they may be held for 24 hours or more before serving. If held, reheat in a bain-marie, 6 to 8 minutes, in a 350° oven.

Final cooking, serving, and sauce

Twenty minutes before serving the soufflés, butter a flat ovenproof dish and unmold the soufflés upside down onto the dish. Prepare the sauce.

Tarragon cream sauce

1½ to 2 cups heavy cream

3 to 4 tablespoons fresh tarragon, *minced* (if dried use less)

Salt

Pepper, *freshly ground*

Bring the cream to the boil with the tarragon and seasoning and let it simmer slowly for several minutes until it takes on the taste of the tarragon. Pour the boiling sauce over and around the soufflés and return them to the oven for 10 to 12 minutes or until they swell and absorb almost all the cream.

Serve immediately in the baking dish.

Note: To make this recipe for 8 people, use exactly the same ingredients but add 1 extra egg.

———●◆●———

Tarte de Nancy (aux amandes)

ALMOND TART

For 6 to 8:

Pastry shell

1 recipe *pâte sablée* (*p. 314*)

5 heaping tablespoons apricot jam

Recommended equipment: An 8-inch tart mold.

Make the pastry and put it into the refrigerator to firm.

Preheat the oven to 375°.

Roll out the pastry to a thickness of ⅛ inch. Line the tart mold with the dough (*technique, p. 324*), and refrigerate to firm again before baking.

Warm and strain the apricot jam. Spread it on the bottom of the tart shell and prick in several places with a fork. Then bake in the middle level of the preheated oven for about 10 minutes. (If the center rises a little during the baking, prick the bottom again, to let the steam escape.) While the crust is baking, prepare the filling.

Almond-cream filling

2 eggs

1 cup sugar

¾ cup almonds, *blanched and pulverized* (*technique, p. 317*)

¼ teaspoon vanilla extract

3 tablespoons milk

Pinch of salt

Separate the eggs, putting the whites in a mixing bowl and the yolks in an enameled saucepan. Gradually beat the sugar into the yolks, waiting each time until the mixture is runny before adding more sugar. When all of the sugar has been incorporated and the mixture is a pale creamy yellow, beat in the pulverized almonds, the vanilla, and the milk. (The mixture will be *very thick.*)

Set the pan over low heat, stirring constantly for a few minutes until the sugar has thoroughly melted.

Immediately beat the egg whites with a pinch of salt until they are stiff but not dry. Stir 1 or 2 tablespoons of the egg whites into the warm egg yolk mixture to lighten it. Then lightly fold all back into the remaining egg whites (*folding technique, p. 321*).

Final baking and serving

About 2 tablespoons confectioners' sugar

Fill the tart shell with the almond cream and return it to the level of the oven farthest from the source of heat to bake the filling for about 15 to 18 minutes, until the top is puffed and browned.

Remove the tart from the oven and sprinkle it with 2 tablespoons confectioners' sugar. Turn the oven up to 425°. Return the tart to the 425° oven to bake for 5 minutes longer until the sugar is lightly caramelized.

Just before serving sprinkle with confectioners' sugar. This tart is good served tepid or cold (I prefer cold).

15. Un déjeuner de dames, pour six à huit

A LADIES' LUNCHEON FOR SIX TO EIGHT

Apéritif: Vin d'orange de Bramafam
White wine with essence of orange

Les amuse-gueule/Small cocktail delicacies

Brouillade d'oeufs "mystère"
Eggs with mushrooms and Mornay sauce

Salade de haricots verts provençale
Green bean salad Provençal

Gâteau au chocolat: Le Doris/Chocolate cake
with almonds, raisins, and whiskey

*Vin rouge léger de Touraine: Bourgueil,
ou vin rouge de Bordeaux*

*L*adies' luncheons were not known in France until very recently because the men, as my husband still does, came home for lunch every day. But as times are changing, the idea is coming more and more into vogue.

This luncheon begins with a special apéritif, *le vin d'orange,* a lovely and refreshing drink—often made in Provence—of white wine that has been imbued with a taste imparted by the rind of oranges. In Provence, in the springtime, the orange trees are in bloom everywhere. These trees are grown not for their oranges, but for their blossoms, which are gathered and used in making essence for perfume. The oranges of these trees, which are used in making the special *vin d'orange,* have a taste different from that of all other oranges; the fruit juice is a little bitter. But since these oranges are not to be found in the United States, it occurred to me to try to make this wine in a different way, using ordinary oranges, and only the rinds. If you have only a short period of time in which to make the wine, use only the *zeste,* because the white part of the rind will give an unpleasantly bitter taste. But if you completely dry the rind for half a month or even more, you can use the white part as well, for its bitterness will diminish with the passage of time.

The "mystery" in the scrambled eggs *"mystère"* is the creamy mushrooms that are concealed between the layers of eggs. The mushrooms are cooked in a manner that resulted, once again, from an accident. Instead of cooking them in milk, a procedure I often use, I took by mistake a liter of cream from the refrigerator and poured it over the mushrooms. The result was superb: the mushrooms were very, very creamy, and became a very, very pale golden—so pale that they were still almost white. I have since experimented with evaporated milk, which I sometimes use as a substitute for cream, since it is so much cheaper and will keep so much longer, and it also gives very satisfactory results.

The recipe for the mushrooms is a complete recipe in itself. This is equally true of the recipe for the scrambled eggs, which are done according to the procedure that I always follow. I beat the eggs just long enough for the whites and yolks to be blended, but not long or hard enough to create foam, for foam tends to burn when the eggs cook. I always add a tablespoon of water at this point; it is a *truc* that helps them to blend nicely. Then, after the eggs have finished cooking, especially a large number of eggs, I always beat in one raw egg, which stops the cooking and gives the finished eggs a very smooth consistency.

The cold salad of green beans, with the flavor of Provence, will give a fresh interlude between the richness of the eggs and the chocolate cake.

Conseils: Everything but the *brouillade d'oeufs* can be made in advance. The eggs themselves can be done 25 minutes before serving time and can wait, covered, in a warm place, before the final step, which is to brown them in the sauce for about 10 minutes in a moderate oven. The mushrooms can be cooked several hours in advance. The *sauce Mornay* can be made in advance up to the point where the cheese should be added, but it is preferable to add the cheese when the sauce is reheated; otherwise the sauce will become stringy and salty. The salad must be prepared at least two or three hours in advance. The chocolate cake should be prepared a day in advance. It can be decorated with candied flowers.

Apéritif: Vin d'orange de Bramafam

White Wine with Essence of Orange. See page 240.

Les amuse-gueule

For small cocktail delicacies, I suggest the *canapés basques* made with sardines (p. 238) or the little onion quiches (p. 231).

Brouillade d'oeufs "mystère"

EGGS WITH SAUTÉED MUSHROOMS, CHEESE, AND MORNAY SAUCE

For 6 to 8:

1 pound of white mushrooms
Juice of 1 lemon
2 tablespoons shallots or scallions, *minced*
2 tablespoons butter

1 cup light cream or unsweetened evaporated milk
Salt
Black pepper, *freshly ground*

Wipe the mushrooms and separate the stems from the caps. Cut both into thin slices, then sprinkle with lemon juice to keep them white. In a large frying pan, cook the minced shallots or scallions in the butter for 2 minutes, stirring until tender. Add the sliced mushrooms and sauté for 2 or 3 minutes, stirring occasionally. Cover with the cream or evaporated milk, season with salt and pepper, and let simmer slowly, uncovered, until the mushrooms have absorbed the cream. *The recipe can be made several hours in advance to this point.*

Mornay cream sauce

2 cups milk
6 tablespoons butter
8 tablespoons flour
2 tablespoons Parmesan cheese, or mixed Parmesan and Swiss, *grated*

½ cup heavy cream
Salt
Black pepper, *freshly ground*

Bring the milk to the boil. At the same time, melt the butter in a heavy-bottomed enameled saucepan, stir in the flour, and continue to stir while the mixture bubbles for a few seconds. Remove from the heat and pour in all the boiling milk, whipping vigorously until smooth. Set back over the heat and stir in the cheese and the cream. Season with salt and pepper and set aside while scrambling the eggs.

Scrambled eggs

12 eggs   Black pepper, *freshly ground*
Salt   5 tablespoons butter

Very lightly beat 10 of the eggs with 1 tablespoon water, and season them with salt and pepper. Melt 3½ tablespoons of the butter in a heavy-bottomed enameled saucepan. Pour the eggs into the hot butter, and stir them continuously over a low flame with a wooden spoon until they are creamy. As soon as the eggs begin to scramble, remove them from the heat and stir them very vigorously until smooth. Then immediately add the two remaining raw eggs, and beat until smooth again. Stir in the remaining butter, taste and correct the seasoning; the eggs should be highly seasoned.

To assemble and serve

½ cup heavy cream   2 tablespoons Parmesan cheese, or
1½ tablespoons butter   mixed Parmesan and Swiss,
                                                   grated

Gently reheat the Mornay sauce, and stir in the cream. Butter a shallow baking dish. Sprinkle the bottom with 1 tablespoon of cheese, and pour in half of the sauce. Cover evenly with the sautéed mushrooms, and then with the scrambled eggs. Cover with the rest of the sauce, sprinkle with the remaining cheese, and dot with remaining butter. *The dish can wait, covered, in a warm place for about a half-hour before the final step.*

Just before serving, put into a 400° degree oven for 8 to 10 minutes until the cheese has melted and the top is very lightly browned.

Serve immediately in the same dish.

———◆•◆———

Salade de haricots verts, provençale

GREEN BEAN SALAD PROVENÇALE

This salad should be prepared two or three hours in advance.

For about 6:

1½ pounds tender young green
  beans
1 large or 2 small very tender fennel bulbs, *washed and
  trimmed*
4 small, ripe tomatoes, *peeled and
  seeded (technique, p. 325)*
Handful of fresh chervil (½ teaspoon dried)

6 ounces (about 1 cup) small
  Mediterranean-type black
  olives, *pitted*
12 to 18 anchovy fillets (packed
  in oil)
3 medium-sized eggs, *hard boiled*
1½ tablespoons fresh basil,
  chopped (if dried, use less)

Slice the beans into halves lengthwise. Cook them in a large quantity of boiling salted water until they are tender but still a little firm. Refresh thoroughly under cold running water, drain, and set aside.

Thinly slice the fennel and quarter the tomatoes, and assemble them
with the beans, chervil, and olives in a salad bowl. Add the dressing (*below*) and mix thoroughly.

Drain the anchovy fillets and wipe them on paper towels. Decorate
the salad with quartered hard-boiled eggs and rows of anchovy fillets,
sprinkle with the chopped basil, and refrigerate for 2 to 3 hours before
serving.

Garlic-basil vinaigrette

3 large cloves garlic, *peeled*
6 to 8 fresh basil leaves, *washed
  and patted dry*
¼ cup olive oil

3 tablespoons wine vinegar
Salt
Black pepper, *freshly ground*

Smash the peeled garlic with the side of a heavy knife or a bottle; then pound it with the basil, adding the olive oil, drop by drop, to make a fine paste. Add the vinegar and season with salt and pepper.

Gâteau au chocolat: Le Doris

CHOCOLATE CAKE WITH ALMONDS, RAISINS,
AND WHISKEY; CHOCOLATE ICING

This cake is best when made a day in advance.

For 6 to 8:

Butter and flour for the cake pan	⅔ cup granulated sugar
¼ cup raisins	4½ tablespoons cake flour
¼ cup Scotch whiskey	⅔ cup almonds, *blanched and*
7 ounces German's sweet choco-	*pulverized* (*technique,*
late, *broken into small pieces*	*p. 317*)
½ cup butter	Pinch of salt
3 eggs, *separated*	

Preheat the oven to 375°.

Recommended equipment: A cake pan 8½ inches wide by 2 inches deep.

Cut a round of waxed paper the size of the bottom of the cake pan. Butter the sides of the pan and one side of the paper. Then lay the paper butter side up in the pan and flour thoroughly.

Put the raisins to steep in the whiskey. Place the chocolate in the top of a double boiler with 3 tablespoons of water and stir until smooth. Remove from the heat and stir in the butter in small pieces, thoroughly incorporating each piece before adding the next.

Beat the egg yolks with the sugar until the mixture is a pale creamy yellow. Combine with the chocolate and stir in the flour, mixed with the almonds. Then stir in the raisins and whiskey.

Whip the egg whites with a pinch of salt until they are stiff but not dry. Stir a third of the egg whites into the chocolate to lighten it; then fold all back into the remaining egg whites (*folding technique, p. 321*). Pour the cake mixture into the pan.

Bake the cake in the middle level of the preheated oven for 20 minutes; the outside should be firm, but the center should remain moist.

Let the cake sit for 10 minutes; then unmold it on a cake rack and let it cool for a few hours or overnight. Peel off the paper before icing it.

Chocolate-butter icing

3 ounces German's sweet chocolate, *broken into small pieces*

3 tablespoons confectioners' sugar
3 tablespoons butter

Melt the chocolate in the top of a double boiler. Stir in the confectioners' sugar and then the butter a little at a time. Blend well and spread immediately on the cake. Allow the icing to set for about half an hour before serving the cake.

16. Un menu de gala pour un dimanche

A GALA SUNDAY LUNCH

Truites grillées à la normande
Broiled trout with tarragon cream sauce
or *Truites normandes de la Saane*
Sautéed trout with almond cream sauce

Vin blanc de Bordeaux: Graves

Pièce de boeuf farçie provençale
Stuffed beef Provençal

Tomates grillées/Small whole broiled tomatoes

Salade de saison/Green salad vinaigrette

*Plateau de fromages: Sancerre, La Bouille,
St. Florentin, Beaufort ou Comté, Emmenthal*

Tarte à l'orange à la Valenciana/Orange tart

Vin rouge de Provence ou la Sangría de Bramafam

*T*his is a very substantial lunch in the grand old tradition of French Sunday lunches. It will be a beautiful lunch—the trout with their bright green tarragon, the beef with a garnish of small red tomatoes, and the brilliant orange tart. With green salad and cheese to complete it, it will be a full *repas*. It is the kind of lunch that I might serve for a very special occasion: perhaps someone has been promoted to a high position, or received a *Légion d'honneur,* and one wants to say, "Congratulations! Happy to know that this has happened to you!"—and so we invite the person to a gay Sunday lunch. Or we might have such a lunch for a birthday. In that case I always serve champagne.

In the summer, when the tarragon leaves are full and fresh, you can prepare *truite à la normande,* the perfect Normand way with trout, cream, and tarragon. Chicken with tarragon is traditionally done the same way—the tarragon simmering slowly with the cream. The alternative trout recipe, for the wintertime when there is no fresh tarragon, is done completely differently, the trout being sautéed rather than broiled and completed with cream and almonds. This second recipe comes from a little restaurant near my childhood home at Rainfreville in Normandy, and in that connection, there is a point I might mention. In little bistros in France, when they sauté a fish and later complete it with a sauce, they don't always remove the butter in which the fish was sautéed; they put the almonds in the same butter. I say, "No!" It is much better to clean the pan and add fresh butter. It should also be noted that in sautéing a fish one must almost always cut off the end of the tail; not only will this thin part of the tail absorb too much of the butter—which would be a waste —it will also burn.

Either of these trout dishes is substantial enough to serve as a main course in a lighter menu. Here, for this "gala Sunday lunch," it comes first. It is followed by a rich braised beef that is sliced almost all the way through and filled with a *farce* of spinach, bread crumbs, and chicken livers, with a Provençale complement of garlic and herbs, and surrounded by small ripe red tomatoes, broiled. If you cannot get really fine tomatoes, I think it would be better not to serve them. You could substitute instead some broccoli, or asparagus sautéed in butter.

The *tarte à l'orange à la Valenciana* is named for the Valencia oranges of Spain. It can be made with any type of oranges, but for the finest orange glaze try to find oranges with a hard pulp, not too juicy or watery. The tart is very sweet; except for people who are exceptionally fond of sweet things, the servings should be small. Here is another instance of the *truc* mentioned on page 81 for coating unbaked tart shells; in this case the shell is coated with apricot jam.

Conseils: The grilled trout can be fully prepared and placed in their cooking dish so that nothing remains but to cook them—10 minutes at the most; the sautéed takes only about 15 minutes. The sauce can also be prepared ahead; it will only be better when reheated, because it will have a stronger taste of tarragon. The beef requires 1¾ to 2 hours cooking in the oven. To make it in advance, take 40 minutes off the cooking time and finish cooking it the next day in a 375° oven. The tomatoes can be cooked and the salad prepared while the beef waits after having been taken from the oven. Preferably, the orange tart should not be made much longer than 2 or 3 hours before serving, so that the crust will be very fresh and flaky. But if you must make it further in advance, it will still be very good.

———◆•◆———

Truites grillées à la normande
(à la crème et à l'estragon)

BROILED TROUT WITH TARRAGON CREAM SAUCE

For 6 to 8:

6 to 8 trout, about ½ pound each,
   cleaned
Salt
Black pepper, *freshly ground*
9 fine branches tarragon (4 or 5
   leaves apiece)

¼ cup peanut oil
1 teaspoon cornstarch
1¼ cups heavy cream
1 tablespoon butter for the pan
1 or 2 tablespoons fresh tarragon,
   minced

Preheat the broiler.

If possible have your fish man gut the trout through the gills so that the backs needn't be opened.

Thoroughly rinse and dry the trout, and cut off a bit of the tail and the fins, which burn easily. Sprinkle the inside of each trout with salt and pepper, and put in each a branch of tarragon to perfume the flesh. Slash the skin of the trout in 2 or 3 places with the point of a sharp knife. (This will facilitate the serving and prevent the skin from bursting under the heat of the broiler.) Then paint the fish with oil.

Arrange the trout on an oiled shallow baking dish, and set them under the broiler for about 5 minutes on one side and about 3 minutes on the other.

In a saucepan dissolve the cornstarch in the cream, then season highly with salt and pepper. Add the remaining branch of tarragon. Bring to just below the simmer, stirring constantly until smooth. Immediately remove from the heat and set aside.

Take the dish from the broiler, set the fish aside, and pour off the cooking oil. Lower the oven to 375°. Wipe the dish, butter it, and replace the trout. Discard the branch of tarragon from the cream and pour the cream over the trout.

Finish cooking the trout about 5 minutes longer. Serve them in their cooking dish, sprinkled with minced tarragon.

————•━•————

Truites normandes de la Saane

SAUTÉED TROUT WITH ALMOND CREAM SAUCE

For 6 to 8:

6 to 8 trout, about ½ pound each, *cleaned*
¾ cup flour
10 tablespoons butter
3 to 4 tablespoons peanut oil

¾ cup almonds, *slivered*
1 to 1¼ cups heavy cream
Juice of 1 lemon
Salt
Black pepper, *freshly ground*

Thoroughly rinse and dry the cleaned trout, and cut off a bit of the tail and the fins (which may absorb too much butter and burn). Sprinkle them with salt and roll them in flour, shaking off the excess flour.

In a large heavy frying pan set over high heat, melt 6 tablespoons of the butter and add the peanut oil. Add the trout, in one layer if possible, and cook them for 7 or 8 minutes until they are golden. Then turn them carefully and brown them on the other side. Cover the pan and cook the trout 4 or 5 minutes. Remove, then clean the pan.

Put the remaining butter into the pan and heat it until it is on the point of coloring. Add the slivered almonds, and toss and shake the pan until they are very lightly browned. Pour in the cream, just heating it, and deglaze the pan. Season with lemon juice, salt, and pepper to taste.

Coat the trout evenly with some of the hot almond cream sauce. Serve the rest of the sauce in a sauceboat.

———— •◆• ————

Pièce de boeuf farçie à la provençale

BRAISED BEEF STUFFED
WITH SPINACH AND CHICKEN LIVERS

For 8 to 10:

A 4-pound piece of beef, top of the rump, or chuck roast, *well marbled and cut into as neat a rectangle as possible*

3 pounds sawed veal bones

Trim the beef if necessary, carefully removing all gristle, and set aside.

Clean the bones, parboil them for 5 minutes, drain, dry well, and set aside.

Stuffing

2 pounds spinach or Swiss chard
⅔ cup stale bread crumbs, *homemade from good bread*
⅓ cup beef stock or bouillon
2 tablespoons olive oil
4 tablespoons butter
4 tablespoons shallots or scallions, *minced*
2 slices bacon, *blanched (technique, p. 317), to make ⅓ cup, minced*

2 large cloves garlic, *minced*
½ pound chicken livers
2½ tablespoons anchovy paste
1 egg yolk
Salt
Black pepper, *freshly ground*
Nutmeg, *freshly grated*
Tabasco (*optional*)
2 tablespoons mixed oregano, basil, thyme, *minced* (if dried, use less)

Thoroughly wash and trim the spinach or Swiss chard. Blanch the spinach for 5 minutes or the chard for 10 minutes in boiling salted water. Refresh thoroughly in a colander under cold running water and drain; then squeeze by handfuls to remove as much moisture as possible. Set aside.

Combine the bread crumbs with the beef stock and mash with a fork to make a purée.

Heat the oil and 2 tablespoons of the butter in a large heavy skillet. Add the minced shallots or scallions and cook, stirring, for about 2 minutes; add the minced bacon and garlic, and cook 2 minutes longer. Then add the spinach or chard and the rest of the butter, and continue to cook for 4 or 5 minutes, stirring from time to time. Remove from the heat and set aside for a few minutes to cool.

Purée the chicken livers by putting through the fine blade of the meat grinder or food mill. Then mix them with the soaked bread crumbs, the anchovy paste, and the egg yolk. Season with salt, pepper, nutmeg, and, if you like, a dash of Tabasco (be careful not to oversalt, since the anchovy paste and the bacon are already salty). Stir the mixture into the spinach or chard, taste, and correct the seasoning. Add the herbs and blend again thoroughly. If you have time, refrigerate the stuffing to firm.

To stuff and cook the beef

A thin piece of fresh pork fat
    (caul fat) large enough to
    cover the top of the meat
    (*optional*)
About 1 pound pork fat (*to yield*
    4 tablespoons rendered)

4 tablespoons flour
About 2 cups light beef stock or
    bouillon to come halfway up
    the stuffed piece of meat
Butter for the waxed paper
Salt

Recommended equipment: A heavy ovenproof cooking pot, preferably oval, with a lid, just wide enough to hold the meat.

Place the piece of beef (*above*) on a board. Using a good sharp knife, make vertical slices about ⅓ inch thick, coming within only ¾ inch of the bottom, being very careful not to cut all the way through. The sliced beef should be like an open book with thick leaves. Spread about 2½ tablespoons of chilled stuffing between each slice. Spread the remaining stuffing on the top of the meat.

If you have a strip of fresh pork fat, lay it on top of the meat. Then wrap the meat in a double thickness of cheesecloth. Tie it up with kitchen string, making rows every ⅓ inch and taking special care that it is tightly closed at the end so that no stuffing will escape during the cooking.

Preheat the oven to 350°.

Cut the pound of pork fat into small pieces and put it into the cooking pot over heat to render. Put the wrapped meat and the veal bones into the fat, and brown them evenly on all sides. Remove the meat and the bones and stir in the flour, stirring constantly until it is nicely brown. Remove from the heat and add the stock or bouillon. Then return to the heat and stir thoroughly until thick and smooth. Return the meat to the pan, put in the bones, cover with buttered waxed paper (buttered side down), and bring to a boil on top of the stove. Then put the lid on the pot and finish cooking in the oven for 1¾ to 2 hours. Halfway through the cooking salt and turn the meat.

To serve

Remove the strings, the cheesecloth, and the layer of fat from the meat, and keep it warm on a board.

Strain the sauce and carefully remove the fat (*technique, p. 320*). Correct the seasoning.

Finish cutting the slices of beef all the way through and arrange them with their stuffing, overlapping each other, on a heated serving dish. Arrange broiled tomatoes (*following recipe*) around the beef, coat the meat slices with some of the sauce, and serve the rest in a sauceboat.

—◆—

Tomates grillées

GARNISH OF SMALL
WHOLE BROILED TOMATOES

For 6 to 8:

20 to 24 small or medium-sized
plum tomatoes, well ripened,
of uniform size
Salt
Black pepper, *freshly ground*

Olive oil
2½ tablespoons mixed parsley,
chervil, and tarragon, *minced*
(if dried, use less)

Preheat the broiler.

Wash and dry the tomatoes. Trim the stem ends evenly so the to-matoes can stand, and sprinkle with some salt and pepper. Brush the to-matoes with olive oil and put them, stem end down, in an oiled roasting pan just large enough to hold them easily. (Do not crowd them.)

Set them under the broiler 3½ to 4 inches from the source of heat for about 10 minutes. Watch them carefully: they will be done when the skin begins to break a little, and they should not be baked longer, or the skin will burst.

Baste them with the pan juices, season again lightly, and sprinkle with minced herbs. Serve them immediately, around the meat.

———— •◦• ————

Tarte à l'orange à la Valenciana

ORANGE TART

For 8:

Tart shell

1½ recipe *pâte sablée* (*p. 314*)   4 tablespoons apricot jam

Recommended equipment: An 8-inch or 9-inch tart mold or ring.

Make the pastry and set it into the refrigerator to firm.

Preheat the oven to 375°.

Warm and strain the apricot jam. Roll out the pastry to a thickness of ⅛ inch. Line the mold with the pastry (*technique, p. 324*), prick the bottom with a fork, and spread with the apricot jam. Refrigerate to firm again before baking.

Bake tart shell for 12 to 15 minutes until it has drawn away slightly from the sides of the mold and is very lightly colored. Set it aside to cool.

Orange glaze

1 cup orange juice, or half orange and half lemon juice	1 cup granulated sugar
	2 large thick-skinned oranges

Make a syrup by slowly boiling the sugar with the orange juice or orange and lemon juice for about 20 minutes. Wash and wipe the 2 oranges and cut them, unpeeled, into neat, thin slices. Add them to the syrup and simmer them for 10 or 15 minutes until they are well glazed. Spread them out to dry on a rack, reserving the syrup. When they are dry, cut them into quarters.

Almond cream filling

2 egg yolks	2 ounces almonds (⅜ cup),
6½ tablespoons sugar	*pulverized (technique, p.*
½ stick sweet butter	*317)*

Beat the egg yolks with 3½ tablespoons of the sugar until they are a pale yellow. Cream the butter and the remaining sugar. Blend with the egg yolks and add the pulverized almonds.

To assemble,
bake, and decorate
¼ cup orange liqueur   *Preheat the oven to 400°.*

Fill the cooled tart shell with the almond cream and bake in the preheated oven for 8 to 10 minutes until the center is set and golden brown. Let cool for about 10 minutes.

Boil down the orange syrup until it has the consistency of a glaze. Remove it from the heat and immediately stir in the orange liqueur.

Arrange the quartered orange slices on the tart in overlapping circular rows. (If less taste of rind is desired, use fewer orange slices.) If the glaze has cooled, reheat it to make it fluid. Pour it over the oranges.

Let the tart cool completely before unmolding and serving it.

17. Un dîner chic en hiver

A CHIC WINTER DINNER

Couronne rose de l'océan
Rose-colored ring of fish mousse

Vin blanc: Chablis ou Muscadet

Pigeons ou pintades, sauce "tortue"
Cornish hens or squabs in "turtle" sauce

Riz au blanc/Buttered rice

Salade de saison/Green salad vinaigrette

Mousse ou glace au chocolat, sans oeufs
Frozen chocolate mousse

Petits fours: Petits sablés de Melanie

Vin rouge de Bourgogne: Beaune ou Beaujolais

Sauce tortue, or turtle sauce, is the classic sauce for *tête de veau,* calf's head. In my mother's house, calf's head with turtle sauce was often served for hunt lunches. The taste will be more familiar to Americans as that which is found in snapper soup. The flavor derives from a combination of four herbs with other ingredients that traces back to the English, who invented turtle soup. In the nineteenth century, *consommé tortue,* made from the turtles that were brought from India, was considered *le potage aristocratique par excellence;* it was served at all great diplomatic dinners and meals of ceremony. The "turtle herbs" are thyme, oregano, basil, and marjoram. The sauce, as served with *tête de veau,* traditionally includes either tomato or Madeira, which I prefer, and green olives, and the dish is accompanied by large croutons—slices of sautéed bread—and poached eggs. But I have omitted the poached eggs in this adaptation of the recipe for pintades, squabs, or Cornish hens.

The pintade, which is very close to the pheasant, is a bird rarely found in the United States. It is not a wild bird, but the meat is dark like that of pheasant, and the flavor is about the same. In fact, some restaurants in Paris serve pintade and call it fresh pheasant. If you have the luck to have some pheasant, by all means use it, but the recipe is also valuable in giving extra flavor to Cornish game hens, which do not always have as much as they should. The recipe is not difficult to execute, and the turtle sauce is pungent, robust, and delicious.

A classical entrée for this dinner would be smoked salmon, oysters, caviar, or foie gras. But since these are either extraordinarily expensive or unavailable in some parts of the United States, I have suggested the alternative of *couronne rose de l'océan,* a highly seasoned purée of fish and tomatoes, molded, and served cold with a green mayonnaise or a mustard sauce. Frozen fish can well be used in making it. For a festive presentation, the purée can be baked and served in scooped-out tomatoes, three-fourths filled with the fish purée, cooked for about 20 minutes in a 375° oven, and served cold, each tomato garnished with the slice taken from the top and a branch of parsley.

Conseils: The *couronne rose* could be made well ahead and unmolded, whenever convenient, before serving. The Cornish hens can be made a day in advance; in fact, the flavor improves on reheating. If doing them in advance, cook them for only 30 minutes, and the next day finish cooking them very slowly, adding 2 or 3 tablespoons of water, or, if not too highly seasoned, ¼ cup of chicken broth. Reheat them well for about 20 minutes and meanwhile prepare the rice. In making the croutons, remember that it is best always to start with stale or dried-out bread, as discussed in the *aide-mémoire*—a *truc* that prevents them from absorbing too much butter. The chocolate dessert can be made a day in advance.

Couronne rose de l'océan

A ROSE-COLORED RING OF FISH MOUSSE

For 6–8:

Enough court-bouillon to cover fish (p. 298)
1 pound cod, scrod, halibut, or whiting, fresh or frozen
1 pound fresh tomatoes
1½ tablespoons butter
2 cloves garlic
1 tablespoon tomato paste
½ teaspoon *quatre épices* (a mixture of ground pepper, clove, ginger or cinnamon, and nutmeg)

Salt
Black pepper, *freshly ground*
Tabasco to taste
4 extra-large eggs
5 tablespoons heavy cream
2 tablespoons fresh herbs, *minced* —tarragon, chervil, parsley, chives (if dried, use less)
1 cup green mayonnaise (p. 306)
1 dozen tiny shrimp and additional fresh herbs (*optional*)

Recommended equipment: A ring mold of 4½ to 5-cup capacity, lined with buttered waxed paper.

Following the directions on page 298, prepare enough court-bouillon, if you do not have some on hand, to cover the fish generously. Add the fish and simmer 15 minutes—20 if frozen. Remove the fish and let it cool sufficiently so that you can remove any bones or skin.

While the fish is cooking, peel and seed the tomatoes (*technique, p. 325*), chop them roughly, and let them cook in the butter, stirring and mashing them for about 10 minutes. Press 2 cloves of garlic and add the pulp, some of the tomato paste if the tomatoes are pale, and the seasonings. Purée the tomato and the fish in an electric blender, adding a little of the fish stock if the mixture is too dry. You should have about 3 cups of a smooth purée, not too thick.

Preheat the oven to 375°.

Beat the eggs with the cream and add the fish-tomato purée. Mix in the fresh herbs, taste and correct the seasoning (it should be highly seasoned because chilling tends to dull the flavor), and add a little more tomato paste if the color is not rosy. Scrape the mixture into the ring mold lined with waxed paper, set into a pan of boiling water that will come about halfway up the mold, and bake in a 375° oven for 30 minutes. Remove from the oven, and leave the fish mousse in the mold to chill.

Meanwhile prepare a green mayonnaise (see p. 306), using the same herbs you have used for the fish ring. When the fish is cold, unmold it onto a serving platter, peel off the waxed paper, pile the green mayonnaise in the center, and garnish, if you like, with a dozen or so tiny shrimp and a sprinkling of fresh herbs.

———•••———

Pigeons ou pintades, sauce "tortue"

CORNISH HENS OR SQUABS, MUSHROOMS, AND OLIVES
IN A RICH HERB SAUCE, WITH CROUTONS

This is at its best when made a day in advance and reheated. It can, of course, be made and served the same day.

For 8:

To cook the game hens or squabs

1 stick (¼ pound) butter
2 tablespoons olive oil
½ pound lean bacon, *cut into 1-inch dice*
4 Cornish game hens, *quartered,* or 6 to 8 squabs, *halved*
8 shallots or scallions, *minced*
1 large or 2 medium yellow onions, to make 1 cup, *sliced*
2 carrots, *sliced*
5 tablespoons flour
2½ cups dry white wine
2 to 2½ cups chicken stock
5 tablespoons Madeira wine

⅓ teaspoon fennel seeds
2½ tablespoons "turtle herbs" (equal amounts of thyme, oregano, basil, and marjoram, *minced*); if dried use less
¾ cup green olives, *pitted*
1 pound small white mushrooms (or larger ones, *stemmed and quartered*)
Salt
Black pepper, *freshly ground*
Additional chicken stock, if necessary

Recommended equipment: A heavy cooking pot with a lid, just large enough to hold the hens or squabs.

Heat 3 tablespoons of the butter with the oil in the heavy pot. Add the bacon and sauté it over moderate heat until it is nicely browned. Remove it with a slotted spoon and drain on paper towels.

Dry the pieces of fowl, sprinkle them with pepper and a little salt, and brown them in the same fat. When they are evenly browned on all sides, remove them with a slotted spoon and set them aside.

Put the minced shallots or scallions, onions, and carrots into the pot and cook, stirring occasionally, until they are lightly colored. Remove and set aside. Sprinkle the flour over the same fat and stir until brown. Add the wine and continue to stir while the mixture thickens and comes to a boil. (The sauce will be very thick.) Still stirring, add 2 cups of chicken stock. Remove from the heat and stir in half of the Madeira wine, the fennel seeds, and 2 tablespoons of the "turtle herbs." Return to low heat to simmer for about 3 minutes longer, stirring occasionally. Add the sautéed vegetables, the fowl, and the bacon, cover with the sauce (if there is not enough, add some chicken stock), and continue to simmer, covered, for about 40 minutes, stirring from time to time, until the birds are cooked through. (If the sauce is too thick, add some chicken stock.)

Parboil the olives for about 15 minutes in a quart of water, rinse, and set aside.

Melt the remaining butter in an enameled saucepan, add the mushrooms, ¼ cup of water, and a pinch of salt, and simmer for about 10 minutes. Strain, reserving the cooking juices.

Remove the pieces of fowl from the pot with a slotted spoon and keep them warm. Strain the sauce, pressing thoroughly with a pestle or wooden spoon, and remove the fat (*technique, p. 320*). Add the cooking juices from the mushrooms. (There should be about 1½ cups of sauce; if not, add a little more stock.)

Clean and wipe the pot and return the sauce. Bring to the boil, stir thoroughly, add the fowl, bacon, olives, and mushrooms, and simmer very gently for a few minutes before serving. *If the dish has been made in advance and is to be reheated, it may be necessary to thin out the sauce with some chicken broth. Bring very slowly to the simmer and simmer very gently with the remaining Madeira for about 10 minutes.*

Croutons

The croutons, which should be made from slices of stale or dried-out bread cut diagonally in halves, should be sautéed at the last minute (see p. 320).

To serve

½ tablespoon "turtle herbs"   About 1 tablespoon parsley, *finely chopped*

Arrange the hens or squabs on a warm serving platter. Serve them coated with the sauce, sprinkled with the parsley and the remaining "turtle herbs," and surrounded with the lemon quarters and the croutons.

Riz au blanc

Buttered rice. See page 309.

Mousse ou glace au chocolat, sans oeufs

FROZEN CHOCOLATE MOUSSE

For 8:

10 ounces semisweet chocolate, *broken into small pieces*	¾ cup sugar
4 tablespoons strong coffee	2½ cups heavy cream
	¾ teaspoon vanilla

Put the chocolate and the coffee into the top of a double boiler, place over heat, and stir until the chocolate is melted and smooth. Set aside and keep warm.

In an enameled saucepan boil the sugar with ½ cup of water over high heat until the syrup forms a soft ball when dropped from the tip of a spoon into a bowl of cold water, or reaches a temperature of 238°. Pour the syrup immediately into the tepid chocolate, mix thoroughly, then set the pan over a bowl of ice cubes and stir until cold and very stiff.

Whip the cream with the vanilla in a chilled bowl set over the bowl of ice cubes. Stir the whipped cream, a spoonful at a time, into the chocolate until the mixture is fluid; then beat all into the remaining cream and continue to beat until the mixture is very smooth.

This mousse can be poured into an ice cube tray, frozen for only 1 hour, and served in individual sherbet dishes. But it is best when frozen for several hours—long enough to become a real ice cream—in which case freeze in a decorative mold or bowl and serve unmolded.

Serve with *les petits sablés de Mélanie* (p. 217).

18. *Un dîner insolite au printemps*

A DINNER FOR EARLY SPRING

Bouchées demi-lune aux crustacés
Small shellfish pastries

Vin blanc sec d'Anjou

Poulet au beurre "d'escargot"
Roast chicken stuffed with
bread crumbs, herbs, and garlic butter

Pommes de terre rissolées Jeanette
Potatoes sautéed with unpeeled garlic

Purée d'asperges tourangelle, gratinée
Asparagus purée with cheese

Vin rouge, Côtes-du-Rhône:
Hermitage ou Châteauneuf-du-Pape

Soufflés à l'orange dans les écorces
Orange soufflés in orange shells

*M*y *poulet au "beurre d'escargot"* draws its inspiration from a classic dish of the *haute cuisine, poulet au truffes,* in which one perfumes and flavors the flesh of the chicken by sliding sliced truffles beneath the skin. Of course, truffles, magnificent as they are, are exorbitant in price; yet I liked very much the idea of a *farce* that would give flavor to the flesh of the chicken. In France, as elsewhere, chickens are no longer so flavorful as they once were, since (with the exception of the *poulet de Bresse*) they are now raised en masse. So I have tried instead this stuffing *à l'escargot,* the traditional accompaniment for snails, based on garlic, chives, fines herbes, shallots, and thyme, worked with butter. To keep the stuffing from being too oily, I have also added some bread crumbs. And I think the results are very interesting.

Do not be in the least alarmed by the idea of stuffing the chicken beneath the skin. This is very easily accomplished. Once a cut has been made through the membrane, the skin draws smoothly away from the meat when you gently insert your fingers.

Other stuffings might also be used in the same way. Garlic does not suit everyone, and one could easily omit it; the result would be a *poulet insolite aux herbes.* Other stuffings are also promising: *poulet en duxelles,* a stuffing based on mushrooms, for instance, one might want to investigate; in this case, it would be necessary to first cook the mushrooms to a purée. *Poulet aux écrevisses* would be sublime: the great gastronome Curnonsky once observed that the combination of crayfish and poultry is the best of all.

I think the asparagus purée a very elegant accompaniment, easily made, and prepared ahead of time. Again it is named in honor of the beautiful asparagus of the Touraine. This purée also goes well with leg or shoulder of lamb, veal scallops, and other meat or poultry dishes.

It is always difficult to find a wine to serve with a sweet dessert such as the orange soufflés in orange shells. But should you wish to serve a third wine with this dinner, you might consider the *vin d'orange* to be found in the cocktail section. The orange soufflé is a classic. Served in a shell it is a little more *insolite*—unusual—and much more spectacular than when presented in one large soufflé dish. Each orange shell comes to the table with its little puff of soufflé, sitting on a saucer made of a slice from the top of the orange to keep it nicely balanced.

Conseils: This is not a dinner that can be made completely in advance, but a great many of its elements can be. The bouchées can be baked ahead and then reheated. The chicken cannot be reheated, but it can be completely prepared for cooking and set aside in a cool place; it will only be better this way, for the flesh will have time to become impregnated with the perfume from the snail butter. The cooking will require about 1 hour and 15 minutes, the *déglaçage* a few minutes at the end, and the potatoes will cook along with the chicken. The *purée d'asperges* can be prepared ahead of time and browned at the last minute. Put it in a 350° oven for 15 minutes; then place the dish under the broiler to brown for 4 or 5 minutes. For the soufflés, everything can be prepared ahead of time except beating and folding in the egg whites, which should be done only when you are ready to place the soufflés in the oven, in their warmed shells.

Bouchées demi-lune aux crustacés

Small pastries filled with shrimp, crabmeat, and apples. See page 235. The recipe there calls for 60 small bouchées, but to serve them as a first course you might want to make them somewhat larger, using a cutter about 6 inches in diameter, and serve only one per person. You will have extra pastry and filling so it would be wise to make also some small bouchées and freeze them to use on an occasion when you have unexpected guests for cocktails.

———— •◆• ————

Le poulet au beurre "d'escargot"

ROAST CHICKEN STUFFED BENEATH
THE SKIN WITH CHICKEN LIVERS, BREAD CRUMBS,
HERBS, AND GARLIC BUTTER

For 8:

Chickens and fresh chicken bouillon

2 roasting chickens, 3½ pounds each
2 cups chicken bouillon, *made from the necks, gizzards, and* *wing tips simmered with a sliced carrot, an onion, and a bouquet garni for one hour* (or canned chicken broth)

Garlic and bread crumb stuffing

½ pound plus 2 tablespoons butter
4 large cloves garlic, *minced or grated*
8 to 10 shallots or scallions, *minced*
2 tablespoons *each* chives, chervil, and parsley, *minced* (if dried, about ½ teaspoon each)

1 teaspoon dried thyme
The 2 chicken livers
3 or 4 tablespoons Cognac
2 cups stale bread crumbs, *homemade from good bread*
Salt
Black pepper, *freshly ground*

Cream the butter in a mixing bowl with the garlic, shallots or scallions, and herbs, working thoroughly to make a homogenous mixture. Season with salt and pepper.

Chop the raw chicken livers, combine them with the Cognac, and blend thoroughly with a fork. Add half of the bread crumbs, blend in the herb butter, and add the remaining bread crumbs. Taste, and correct the seasoning. Set aside.

To prepare and stuff the chickens

1½ tablespoons cooking oil

Turn the chickens breast side up.

Lightly loosen the skin of both chickens so that the stuffing can be inserted: first detach the skin on either side of the tail with the point of a knife. Then, dip your fingers into the oil and gently insert them under the skin of the breast. (If you have long fingernails, put on rubber gloves, so as not to pierce the skin.) Push your fingers gradually farther under the skin to loosen it as much as possible. In the same way, loosen some skin along the thighs and legs and a little on the back.

Carefully fill the areas between the flesh and the loosened skin with the stuffing (do not put in too much) and pat to distribute the stuffing evenly. Sprinkle the chickens inside with salt and pepper and fill them with the rest of the stuffing. Sew up all the openings, and truss the chicken (*technique, p. 319*).

To roast and serve   *Preheat the oven to 375°.*

   2 or 3 tablespoons butter

Remove the grease from the chicken bouillon (*technique, p. 320*). Put the chickens into the broiler pan or a shallow roasting pan. Set the pan over medium heat, and brown the chickens on each side. (If some of the stuffing escapes, don't worry.) Pour ⅔ cup of the chicken bouillon into the pan. Then turn the chickens on their sides and set them into the preheated oven to cook for about 45 to 50 minutes until they are tender. Turn them halfway through the cooking.

Remove the chickens and keep them warm while completing the sauce.

Add about 1⅓ cups of chicken bouillon to the liquid in the roasting pan, set over heat, and deglaze the pan, scraping the bottom with a fork to collect all the sediments. Strain, return to the saucepan, set over heat, and let the sauce boil for about 3 minutes. Remove from the heat and swirl in 2 or 3 tablespoons of butter.

To serve, coat the chickens with some of the sauce, and serve the rest in a sauceboat.

Pommes de terre rissolés Jeanette

Potatoes sautéed with unpeeled garlic. See page 48; note that the recipe serves 6 and the ingredients should be increased to serve 8.

———◆•◆———

Purée d'asperges tourangelle, gratinée

ASPARAGUS PURÉE WITH CHEESE

For 8:

3½ pounds fresh asparagus
Salt
6 tablespoons butter
1½ tablespoons flour
1¼ cups heavy cream
Black pepper, *freshly ground*

Nutmeg, *freshly grated*
Butter for the baking dish
3 tablespoons stale bread crumbs,
    homemade from good bread
1½ tablespoons Parmesan cheese,
    grated

Wash and trim the asparagus. Put the stalks into a large quantity of boiling water and add about 1½ teaspoons of salt per quart when the water returns to the boil. Boil the asparagus for 12 to 15 minutes until a stalk can be easily pierced with a fork; do not overcook. Refresh in a colander under cold running water, drain well, and purée by putting the asparagus through a food mill. *The recipe can be prepared in advance to this point.*

Melt 4 tablespoons of the butter in a skillet, add the asparagus purée, and cook over medium heat, stirring often, for about 5 minutes. Sprinkle with the flour, and cook, still stirring, for about 2 minutes longer. Gradually stir in the cream and season very highly with salt, pepper, and nutmeg.

Put the asparagus into a shallow buttered baking dish, sprinkle with the bread crumbs mixed with the grated cheese, and dot with the remaining butter. Keep warm.

Preheat the broiler.

Just before serving, run under the preheated broiler for 3 or 4 minutes until the top is brown.

Serve in the baking dish.

———— •◦• ————

Soufflés à l'orange dans les écorces

ORANGE SOUFFLÉS WITH
ORANGE LIQUEUR IN ORANGE SHELLS

For 8:

8 large navel or Temple oranges	8 lumps of sugar plus enough granulated sugar to make ½ cup

Preheat the oven to 350°.

Wash and wipe the oranges and rub each one with a lump of sugar to absorb the orange essence contained in the rind. Add enough granulated sugar to the lumps to make ½ cup and set aside in a small enameled saucepan.

Slice off 1-inch circles from one end of each orange; grate the orange rind from them and discard.

Squeeze 4 tablespoons of orange juice and reserve for the soufflé. Then, using a small spoon, scoop out all the flesh from each of the oranges, being very careful not to damage the skin. Put the orange shells in the oven to dry out for 10 minutes.

Orange soufflé

4 egg yolks
¼ cup orange liqueur or
    Benedictine

½ teaspoon vanilla
6 egg whites
Salt

Put the 4 egg yolks in a saucepan. Set aside.

Add 4 tablespoons of orange juice and the grated orange peel to the reserved sugar (*above*), set over heat, and boil to the soft ball stage or a temperature of 230°. Immediately pour the syrup in a thin stream into the egg yolks, beating vigorously with a whisk until smooth and creamy. Add the liqueur and the vanilla, return to the saucepan, and heat, beating with the whisk, for a good 2 minutes to *lightly* thicken the mixture. Remove from the heat and continue to beat until cool. Set aside.

Beat the 6 egg whites with a pinch of salt until they are stiff but not dry.

Fold a quarter of the egg whites into the yolk mixture to lighten it; then lightly fold all back into the remaining egg whites (*technique, p. 321*).

To assemble and bake

Confectioners' sugar

1 or 2 extra oranges (*optional*)

Preheat the oven to 425°.

Fill the orange shells two-thirds full with the soufflé mixture. (A *truc:* If some of the oranges are not steady, you can make little "saucers" for them by cutting ½-inch slices from an extra orange or two and scooping out the pulp to make hollow circles on which to set the unsteady oranges.) Bake for 12 to 15 minutes. After about 8 minutes dredge them with confectioners' sugar and return them to the oven. A few minutes later, when the soufflés will have risen well above the edge of the oranges, dredge them once again with sugar.

After they have risen about a half-inch above the edge of the orange and the sugar on the top has caramelized, remove them from the oven. Place each orange on the "saucer" cut from the top, which will keep the orange steady. Serve at once.

19. Un menu de panache au Champagne

A SPECTACULAR DINNER WITH CHAMPAGNE

Saumon ou "bass" en brioche/Whole stuffed
salmon or striped bass in brioche

Quasi de veau à l'anchois en gelée
Jellied rolled roast of veal with anchovies

Vin blanc sec de Bourgogne: Meursault

Salade de laitue/Lettuce salad vinaigrette

*Plateau de fromages: Boursin,
Münster, Beaufort ou Compté*
Assorted cheeses

Le doyenné: Bavarois aux poires
Bavarian cream with pears and sauternes,
raspberry sauce

*Champagne demi-sec
ou Tout au Champagne brut*
(or champagne, brut, throughout)

*I*f you would like to dazzle your friends by presenting them with a dish that we would say in France would *leur en jeter plein la vue* (knock them right between the eyes), you could choose no more wonderful and spectacular a dish than this *saumon ou "bass" en brioche.* It is a whole fresh salmon or striped bass, filled with a mushroom stuffing and baked in a brioche crust, which seals in the natural flavor of the good fish with the mushrooms and, baked golden in the shape of the fish, makes a beautiful presentation. It can be served with a *sauce hollandaise* or with the very interesting sauce recommended here, *beurre mousseux.*

This dish was the inspiration for all the dishes *en croûte* in Volume II of *Mastering the Art of French Cooking,* after Julia Child and I discovered it one day in a restaurant near Cannes. We ultimately decided not to develop a section on fish for that volume, and the recipe was, in the end, left out, surviving only in its adaptations. But I have made it many times since then, with great success. The fish is covered with a special brioche made with oil, very easily accomplished, and the sugar in the pastry will help the crust to brown. The whole dish, once you have made it successfully, is so easy to do that you will want to make it again and again. However, it requires a little practice, and I suggest that before serving it for company you might want to try a small version of it first with your family, using a trout.

Completed by a cold roll of veal stuffed with anchovy and garlic paste, accompanied by vegetables *en gelée,* and finished with a great entremets, *le doyenné,* this menu will constitute a perfect harmony of dishes —the kind of dinner with which, in France, we might honor a *ministre,* a *diplomate,* or some other important personage *en grand tralala.*

The *veau à l'anchois* was created especially to be served cold. The butt end that it requires is not the most expensive cut of veal; the important thing is to try to get a very good young, pale piece of veal, as uniform as possible in texture and shape. The meat is sliced, stuffed, and rolled, and cooked with carrots and onions, allowed to cool completely, and then covered entirely with a light aspic. There is a strong, but not too strong, flavor of the garlic and anchovies with which the veal is stuffed. When it is sliced, the design of the roll will show attractively, and each slice will be garnished with some minced herbs and some of the cold jelly.

For me, Sauternes is like a jewel—the first-class French sweet white wine. In this Bavarian cream, the *doyenné,* it combines with pears in a custard to produce a very, very delicate frozen dessert, served with a cold raspberry sauce. This entremets is named after a special juicy melt-in-your-mouth variety of pear found in France. But other types of pears will also give a perfect result.

Conseils: The veal and the dessert are made at least a day ahead. The brioche dough, of course, is also made in advance. The fish must be made the day of the dinner itself, but after it has cooked it can wait for at least half an hour, wrapped in foil, in a turned-off oven. The *beurre mousseux* must be made at the last minute.

Saumon ou "bass" en brioche

WHOLE SALMON OR STRIPED BASS
IN BRIOCHE WITH MUSHROOM STUFFING

For 8:

Brioche crust

The day before this dish is to be served, prepare the brioche dough, page 315, using only 2 tablespoons of sugar.

Salmon or striped bass

A 4-pound salmon or striped bass

If possible, have the fish cleaned by cutting through the side and pulling out the guts rather than slicing open. Do not remove the backbone. Thoroughly wash and dry the cleaned fish, patting dry any surplus moisture. Cut off the fins and a little of the tail (which would otherwise be too long).

Mushroom stuffing

½ cup stale bread crumbs, *home-made from good bread*

2 to 3 tablespoons chicken bouillon or fish stock

3 shallots or scallions, *minced*

3 tablespoons butter

1 pound mushrooms, *cleaned and minced*

2 tablespoons mixed parsley and chervil, *minced* (if dried, use less)

1 egg yolk

Salt

Black pepper, *freshly ground*

Mix the bread crumbs with the bouillon or stock and mash them with a fork.

Cook the minced shallots or scallions gently in the butter for 1 or 2 minutes until they are soft but not colored. Add the minced mushrooms and sauté them until the moisture is cooked out. Combine them in a bowl with the bread purée, the herbs, and the egg yolk, and blend well; the mixture should be quite stiff. Taste, and season with salt and pepper.

Fill the fish with the stuffing, packing it in very firmly. Then sew up the side opening (or if it has been sliced open sew along the length of the fish).

To assemble

2 small eggs, *beaten in* 1 tablespoon water

1 olive or caper

Lightly beat the eggs with the water. Cover a baking sheet with foil.

Divide the brioche pastry in half, and roll out a piece about ⅓ inch thick and 1½ inches longer and wider than the fish. Put the pastry onto the baking sheet. Place the fish carefully in the center of the pastry on the diagonal. With a brush dipped into the beaten egg, paint the exposed surface of the pastry. Fold the edges of the pastry up the sides of the fish, pressing the edges so that they will adhere to the fish. Then paint the outside surfaces of the pastry with egg yolk.

Roll out the remaining pastry in exactly the same way. Place it on the fish, press it down and tuck it under so that it will neatly mold the shape of the fish. Again paint the surface with egg, and press the overlapping pieces of pastry firmly together.

Lightly draw the line of the fish's head on the pastry and put a slice of olive or a caper for the eye. Then make a pattern of the fish's scales. (This is easily accomplished by nicking the pastry at intervals with the circular end of the nozzle that fits on a pastry bag, or with a round melon cutter or a tiny spoon.)

Again brush the pastry with egg, and refrigerate on the baking sheet until firm again. (Save the remaining beaten egg.)

To bake   *Preheat the oven to 375°.*

Remove the fish from the refrigerator and glaze it once again with beaten egg. Bake for about 45 minutes, until the pastry is a rich golden brown. Look at the fish from time to time; if the dough gets too brown during the cooking, cover it with a piece of wrapping paper. *When it is done, the fish can rest a good half-hour in the turned-off oven with the door ajar, while you have your drink before dinner.*

Prepare the *beurre mousseux avec crème* (page 302—the variation) using fish fumet for the liquid. If you prefer a very generous amount of sauce, double the recipe.

To serve

Lemon wedges   Bunches of watercress

Surround the fish with wedges of lemon, and put bunches of watercress under the head and tail. Remove the top of the crust in one piece by carefully cutting all around along the line that will show between the top and bottom layers of pastry, and lay the top aside. Portion off the fish, cutting through to the backbone, according to the number of guests. Slice off equal portions from the piece of crust. The bottom crust is not served. (Return to warming oven. The backbone should be removed before the dish is brought back to the table for further servings.)

Serve the *beurre mousseux* in a sauceboat.

———•◦•———

Quasi de veau, à l'anchois en gelée

JELLIED ROLLED ROAST OF VEAL, WITH ANCHOVIES

This recipe can be made two days in advance.

For 10 to 12:

Filling

3 cans anchovy fillets in oil (1¼ ounces per can)
4 large cloves garlic
7 tablespoons butter

2 heaping tablespoons mixed basil, parsley, and chervil, *minced* (if dried, use less)
Black pepper, *freshly ground*

Vegetables

2 tablespoons olive or peanut oil
4 medium onions, *sliced*

10 to 12 medium carrots, *sliced*

Veal

A 5-pound roast of veal from the butt end in a "loaf" shape as solid as possible, about 12 inches long x 4 inches wide
Lard or cooking oil, *melted*
1 tablespoon olive or peanut oil
2 pounds veal knuckles, *sawed in half*

1 cup chicken bouillon or veal stock
Bouquet garni of thyme, ½ bay leaf, and parsley
Salt
Black pepper, *freshly ground*

Mince the anchovy fillets and the garlic and pound them into a smooth purée, adding the butter by tablespoons. When thoroughly blended, add the minced herbs and pepper (salt will probably not be needed) and refrigerate to firm.

Heat the oil in a heavy skillet, add the sliced onions, and lightly

brown them over moderate heat for 12 to 15 minutes, turning them frequently until they are evenly browned on all sides. Remove from the pan,
set them aside, and repeat the process with the carrots. Remove the carrots from the skillet and set them aside with the onions. (Do not clean
the pan.)

Trim the veal if necessary, removing any fat and particles of gristle,
and set it on its side on a board. With a sharp knife pointing straight
downward, cut a spiral in the meat, beginning at the outer edge and
spiraling toward the center, not cutting all the way through, and leaving
½ inch uncut on the under side.

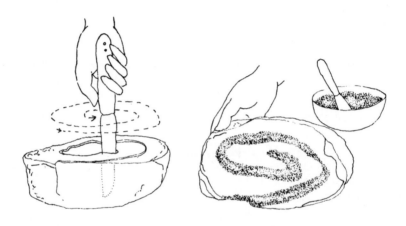

Stuff most of the filling carefully between the cuts, reserving the
rest. Tie the veal thoroughly at intervals with string and spread the remaining filling over the uncut side of the meat. Wrap the veal in cheesecloth dipped into melted lard and tie it again with string but this time
not so tightly and the strings not so close together.

To cook the veal   *Preheat the oven to 375°.*

Heat 1 tablespoon of olive or peanut oil in the skillet in which the
vegetables were cooked. Add the veal and the veal knuckles and sauté
them for about 15 minutes over moderate heat, turning them to brown
evenly on all sides.

Return the vegetables to the skillet, placing the onions around the
meat and the carrots on top. Pour in the stock or bouillon, add the bouquet garni, cover, set over heat, and bring to a simmer. Then finish cook-

ing in the preheated oven for about 1 to 1½ hours, depending on the tenderness of the veal. Check after an hour and season with salt and pepper. When the veal is done, set it aside to cool thoroughly in the pan. *The veal can be made 2 days in advance to this point and refrigerated.*

To serve

1 package gelatin	Salt
3 tablespoons port or sherry	Black pepper, *freshly ground*
2½ cups good beef or chicken bouillon	Lettuce leaves
	Parsley, *minced*
1 branch tarragon (or about 1 teaspoon dried tarragon)	

Remove the veal from the pan and place it on a board. Cut off the cheesecloth and all of the strings. With a good sharp knife, cut the meat into even slices about ⅓ inch thick. Remove the hardened fat from the vegetables. Arrange the slices of veal on a shallow serving dish, slightly overlapping, with some of the vegetables between the slices and the rest arranged around.

Heat and strain the cooking juices (which, if cold, will have jelled). Soften the gelatin in the chosen wine. Pour the bouillon into the cooking juices, add the tarragon, and bring to a boil, then season with salt and pepper. Stir in the softened gelatin and wine, bring to the boil again, and strain. Let cool a little, but do not wait until the gelatin mixture is set. Pour it over the meat and vegetables to cover them entirely, and refrigerate to set.

Serve surrounded by lettuce leaves and sprinkled with minced parsley. Separate the slices a little to help in the serving.

---•◆•---

Le doyenné: Bavarois aux poires

BAVARIAN CREAM WITH PEARS AND
SAUTERNES, RASPBERRY SAUCE

For 8 to 12:

¼ cup raisins
At least ¼ cup pear liqueur
  (*alcool de Poires, William,*
  is very fine) or kirsch
1 pound fine brown winter pears
  (about 2 large pears), ripe
  or almost ripe

1½ cups Sauternes or a good
  sweet white wine
1 cup granulated sugar
2 envelopes gelatin
10 egg yolks
1 cup heavy cream
½ teaspoon vanilla
2 tablespoons confectioners' sugar

It is important to assemble all the materials and equipment needed for this recipe before beginning.

Recommended equipment: A 3-quart charlotte mold, ring mold, or other mold.

Put the raisins to steep in the pear liqueur or kirsch. Peel, core, and quarter the pears. Put the Sauternes and the sugar into an enameled saucepan and boil until the mixture forms a syrup. Turn down the heat, add the pears, and poach them gently until they are tender—5 to 8 minutes according to their degree of ripeness. Remove them from the syrup with a slotted spoon (reserving the syrup) and purée them through a food mill. There should be 1 cup of pear purée. Drain the raisins (reserving the liqueur) and add the raisins to the puréed pears. Soften the gelatin in the liqueur, adding more liqueur if necessary.

Boil down the pear syrup to slightly less than 1½ cups. Add the softened gelatin and stir over heat until it is thoroughly dissolved. Keep the syrup warm over a low flame or warm water to prevent the gelatin from setting.

Put the egg yolks into a large (nonaluminum) heatproof mixing bowl or saucepan. Set into barely simmering water (the water should be warm but not boiling; you should be able to put your finger in it), and beat the egg yolks for one minute. Beat in the hot pear syrup a little at a time and continue to beat vigorously for about 5 minutes. Remove the bowl from the water and continue to beat until the mixture has doubled in volume and is thick and creamy. Stir in the pear purée and raisins and let cool while whipping the cream.

Put the cream and the vanilla into a mixing bowl and set over a bowl of ice cubes. Whip the cream until the beater leaves marks on the surface; then add the confectioners' sugar and continue to beat a few seconds longer. Remove the bowl of whipped cream from the ice cubes and replace it with the bowl or saucepan containing the pear mixture. Beat until the mixture is cool but not cold (the gelatin will set if it is completely cold). Fold in the whipped cream.

Cut a piece of waxed paper to fit the bottom of the mold. Dampen the paper, shake it to remove excess water, and place it in the mold. Fill the mold with the Bavarian mixture, cover it with a second piece of waxed paper resting lightly on the top of the mold, and refrigerate for at least 3 or 4 hours.

Raspberry sauce

2 cups raspberry jelly or 2½ cups
    raspberry jam

2 or 3 tablespoons of the liqueur
    used above

If using raspberry jam, warm and strain it.

Just before serving time, melt the raspberry jelly or strained jam with 2 tablespoons of water and 2 or 3 tablespoons of the liqueur.

To serve

Unmold the *doyenné* onto a round serving dish and peel off the paper. Coat it with a little of the sauce, and serve the rest in a sauceboat.

20. Un dîner canaille pour joyeux amis

AN EARTHY DINNER FOR HIGH-SPIRITED FRIENDS

Coquilles St. Jacques nantaise (au naturel)
Scallops in scallop shells or ramekins

Vin blanc sec: Muscadet ou Vouvray, non-mousseux

Canards en cassoulet
Cassoulet with duck and hot sausages

Vin rouge de Bourgogne: Pommard

*Asperges vertes en vinaigrette "mimosa" ou
Salade d'endives en vinaigrette à base
de moutarde*
Cold asparagus vinaigrette "mimosa"
or endive salad with mustard vinaigrette

Fromage: St. Marcellin, Maroilles, ou Livarot
A strong cheese

*Le Talleyrand: Cerises en crème meringuée
et flambée/*Dark cherries in custard with
meringue, flamed with Kirsch or rum

This is a gay menu, full of *saveur,* to share with friends who love to eat, to laugh easily, to savor together the strong sensations of life. The word *canaille* means something with a very highly developed, very pronounced flavor. For example, there is a seasoning for oysters, called *canaille,* that is only vinegar and raw shallots sprinkled over the oysters. The word has another connotation, and in this sense it is perhaps best translated by the British expression "racy"—a little fast, a little spicy, a little "low."

The scallops, well seasoned with shallots, have a distinctive lusty taste of the sea—that is why they are *canaille.* They are cooked *au naturel,* in butter, with some bread crumbs sprinkled on top only to preserve the moisture of the scallops while they are in the oven. They are served simply decorated with parsley. For me, this method is best—no rich ingredients to interfere with the natural succulent flavor of the scallops. I like to serve them in scallop shells, but they can be as successfully made in individual ramekins or baking cups.

The cassoulet with its white beans, garlic, tomatoes, and duck is also a strong, earthy dish, and with its hot sausages, also very pungent, *canaille.* It might be called a *cassoulet bâtard,* because it differs considerably from the traditional cassoulet, which is most commonly made with lamb or goose and is often days in the preparation. This recipe is extremely simple for a cassoulet—made in an afternoon. The pork rind is used here not only for flavoring but also for the gelatinous syrup it will render, which will give a silky consistency to the sauce. The smaller you cut the pieces, the more gelatin they will give. A *truc* in rendering the fat is always to add a little bit of water to the pan. The pork and duck will yield as much as 2 or 3 cups of fat at the end of the cooking, for American ducks are much fatter than French ones. However, this can easily be removed before serving, and the dish will not be rich or greasy.

The dessert is warm and is served flaming. I think the technique of flaming dishes has been overdone in restaurants in recent years: game, meat, shellfish—all are served with great bursts of flame, and while spectacular, the drama tends to lose its charm. In some dishes, such as fish, the flaming even kills the flavor. But for desserts, especially crêpes, or dishes covered with meringue, I think flaming gives a warm *saveur* that is infinitely pleasing, and certainly points up the taste. This dessert is beautiful to see, brought flaming to the table, and delicious with cherries, *crème frangipane,* and liqueur. It is named for Talleyrand, whose fame as the greatest and most distinguished host of his era has come down through the centuries. He entertained royally, like a king, like a poet, ruining himself by the splendor of his table, and he was especially fond of sweet and spectacular desserts.

A little *truc* is the eggshell, which is buried in the meringue and will serve as a cup into which the liqueur will run when the dessert is flamed.

Conseils: The ducks are best cooked a day in advance so that the fat can be more easily removed, then reheated. If doing them ahead, cook them for a shorter time so that the beans will not be overdone when the dish is reheated, and be careful not to overseason after the first cooking. Correct the seasoning when the dish is completely cooked. The *coquilles St. Jacques* cannot be made in advance but require only about 15 minutes in the oven and can cook while the ducks are reheating. The dessert can be prepared ahead up to the point when it is spread with the meringue, sprinkled with almonds, and set in the oven to brown.

———•◦•———

Coquilles St. Jacques nantaise (au naturel)

SCALLOPS IN SCALLOP SHELLS
OR RAMEKINS WITH BUTTER AND SHALLOTS

For about 8:

Butter for the ramekins
2 to 3 dozen scallops, depending
    on their size
Salt
Black pepper, *freshly ground*
About 8 shallots or scallions,
    minced

1 stick plus 2 tablespoons butter
⅔ cup stale bread crumbs, *home-
    made from good bread*
3 tablespoons parsley, *chopped*
    (if dried use less)

Recommended equipment: 8 scallop shells, Pyrex cups, or ramekins, buttered.

Preheat the oven to 375°.

Wash the scallops and keep them in fresh water until ready to be cooked.

Dry the scallops on paper towels. Cut them in half if they are small, or into 3 pieces if they are large. Season them with salt and pepper and put them into the buttered shells or cups.

Cook the minced shallots or scallions in 2 tablespoons of the butter until they are soft. Melt the remaining butter. Distribute the shallots or scallions in the shells or cups, and sprinkle them with the melted butter and the bread crumbs.

Arrange the cups on a tray and set them in the preheated oven for 12 to 15 minutes until the scallops are tender when pierced with a pointed knife.

Serve them in the shells or cups, boiling hot, sprinkled with minced parsley.

———•◆•———

Canards en cassoulet

SPECIAL CASSOULET WITH DUCK AND HOT SAUSAGES

For 8:

2 pounds (5½ cups) dry white
  beans (Great Northern)
½ pound pork rind
1 onion, *peeled and stuck with 2
  cloves*
4 medium carrots, *sliced*
Bouquet garni of 1 sprig thyme, 2
  bay leaves, parsley stalks, and
  3 large cloves garlic
A 2½-pound chunk of bacon or
  salt pork: 1½ pounds to
  make lardons and about 1
  pound to yield 4 tablespoons
  rendered fat

2 ducks, about 4½ pounds each
1½ pounds hot Italian or Spanish sausage
1 large or 2 medium yellow
  onions, to yield 1 cup, *sliced*
Chicken bouillon or stock to cover
  the ducks (about 3 cups)
About 5 tablespoons tomato paste
3 additional large cloves garlic
Black pepper, *freshly ground*
Salt
1 or 2 tablespoons parsley,
  chopped

Recommended equipment: A 6- to 8-quart heavy casserole or cast-iron
pot, about 6 inches deep.

Fill a large kettle with tepid water, drop in the beans, set over heat,
and bring slowly to the boil. Remove from the heat and let the beans soak
for about 1½ hours.

Put the pork rind into a pot of cold water, bring to the boil, and boil
for 20 minutes. Rinse under cold water and cut into pieces about 1 inch
square. Wrap in cheesecloth, tie into a bundle, and set aside.

When the beans have finished soaking, add the bundle of pork rind,
the onion stuck with cloves, the sliced carrots, and the bouquet garni. Add
more water if necessary to cover the beans well, bring to a boil, and simmer, uncovered, for about 1½ hours or until the beans are tender but still
slightly firm. From time to time remove the scum that will rise to the
surface of the water.

Cut 1½ pounds of the bacon or salt pork into lardons 1 inch by ½ inch and blanch them for 10 minutes (*technique, p. 317*).

Cut the ducks into large serving pieces with poultry shears, cleaver, or heavy sharp knife. Cut the sausage into thick slices.

Put the remaining salt pork or bacon and 1 tablespoon of water into the heavy pot or casserole and set over heat to render about 4 tablespoons of fat. Discard the pork and leave the fat in the pot.

Thoroughly dry the pieces of duck and add them to the pot with the sausage and the prepared lardons of salt pork or bacon, and brown the duck evenly on all sides (about 15 minutes). (If the pot is not large enough to brown the meat without crowding, use a second pot or heavy skillet.) Add the sliced onions. When everything is browned, cover with chicken stock, stir in the tomato paste, and bring to a boil, stirring. Smash the 3 cloves of garlic, and add to the pot. Sprinkle with pepper, turn down the heat, and simmer for about 45 minutes until the duck is tender. If the duck is cooked before the beans, turn off the flame and let it wait, covered.

When the beans have finished cooking, discard the pork rind and the bouquet garni, and add the beans and their cooking juice to the duck. Simmer all together until the flavor is nicely blended.

With a spoon or bulb baster, remove as much as possible of the liquid fat that will have risen to the surface. Remove the beans to a warm serving platter with a slotted spoon, and arrange the duck, bacon, and sausage on top of them.

Boil down the cooking liquid to 2 cups and strain. Taste, and correct the seasoning.

Pour the sauce over the meat and beans, sprinkle with chopped parsley, and serve.

———————•◦•———————

Le Talleyrand: Cerises en crème meringuée et flambée

CHERRIES IN CUSTARD WITH MERINGUE,
FLAMED WITH KIRSCH OR RUM

For 8:

2 one-pound cans dark cherries,
   pitted
¼ cup granulated sugar (for the
   cherries)
⅓ cup kirsch or dark rum
4 egg yolks
¾ cup granulated sugar (for the
   custard)

About ⅔ cup almonds, *pulverized*
   (*technique, p. 317*)
4½ tablespoons flour, preferably
   cake flour
⅔ cup heavy cream
5 tablespoons confectioners' sugar
1¼ teaspoons vanilla extract
7 egg whites
Pinch of salt

Recommended equipment: An oval baking dish about 8 by 12 inches and 2 inches deep.

Put the cherries into a bowl with ¼ cup sugar and the kirsch or rum, and ¾ cup of the juice from one of the cans of cherries, and let them macerate for at least half an hour, stirring once or twice.

Put the 4 egg yolks into an enameled saucepan with ¾ cup granulated sugar. Save the neatest empty eggshell, trimming its edges neatly with scissors.

Beat the egg yolks with the sugar until they are smooth and a pale creamy yellow. Strain in the maceration liquid from the cherries and stir to blend well. Stir in the pulverized almonds and the flour. Set over low heat and stir constantly for 5 to 10 minutes until the mixture forms a thick, smooth custard. Remove from the heat and stir for a minute or two to cool; then set the custard over ice cubes to become very cold.

Whip the cream in a bowl set over ice until the beater leaves light traces on the surface of the cream. Beat in 2 tablespoons of the confectioners' sugar and ½ teaspoon of the vanilla, and set aside.

Beat the 7 egg whites with a pinch of salt until they are stiff but not dry. Fold half of the egg whites into the whipped cream until thoroughly mixed. Stir 2 or 3 tablespoons of the cream and egg whites into the cold custard to lighten it; then fold all back into the remaining cream and egg whites (*folding technique, p. 321*). Set aside.

Add the remaining confectioners' sugar and the remaining vanilla to the remaining egg whites, and beat to make a kind of meringue.

To assemble

Butter for the baking dish

Butter the baking dish. Spread the cherries on the bottom of the dish and pour the custard over them. Spread the meringue neatly over the custard, leaving a small border all around and making a dome of meringue toward the center. Press the eggshell into the meringue so that it shows only as a well in the center. *The dessert can be made ½ to 1 hour in advance to this point, and set aside in the coolest part of the kitchen.*

To brown and serve

3 tablespoons almonds, *slivered*   ¼ cup kirsch or rum
4 to 5 tablespoons confectioners'
     sugar

Preheat the oven to 425°.

Sprinkle the meringue with the slivered almonds, then the confectioners' sugar. Set into the preheated oven for about 5 minutes until the meringue is lightly browned.

Heat the kirsch or rum.

Remove the dessert from the oven, pour some of the kirsch or rum into the eggshell, letting the rest run over the meringue, and set aflame. Bring flaming to the table, spooning the liqueur over the top of the meringue to caramelize the sugar, until the flames goes out.

21. *Un dîner d'automne à la campagne après une journée sportive*

AN AUTUMN DINNER AFTER A DAY IN THE FRESH AIR

Soupe de Bramafam
Chicken soup with garlic, cream, and basil

Porc sylvestre/Braised pork stuffed
with ham and mushrooms

Choux brocoli sautés/Sautéed broccoli

Salade de saison/Green salad vinaigrette

*Plateau de fromages: Fourme d'Ambert
ou fromage de Monsieur, Livarot, Valençay*
Assorted cheeses

Soufflé meringué à la liqueur
Soufflé with orange liqueur or Benedictine

Vin rouge de Bordeaux: St.-Émilion

*I*n the autumn, when the last of the fresh basil still lingers, it can be used to make this *soupe de Bramafam,* a good Provençal chicken soup with garlic. It is nourishing but light, a little tapioca gives the ingredients the necessary liaison, and cream and egg yolks complete the ensemble. After half an hour's simmering, the cloves of garlic will have lost their strong taste, to leave only a delicate and subtle residue of flavor. But since much of the garlic flavor is contained in the hard outer skin as well as the clove (something that is not always realized), the garlic is used unpeeled, in order to extract as much flavor as possible.

The *porc sylvestre*—named for the woodland mushrooms—is an unusual dish, with a lovely harmony of flavors. It is cooked in a heavy pot, tightly covered, so that it will be very juicy. Note that good "country" ham, Canadian bacon, or prosciutto is recommended for inserting between the slices rather than ordinary boiled ham, which really does not have enough flavor.

The dinner is completed by a simple soufflé made with liqueur—a lovely warm ending for a fall evening.

Conseils: The pork can be made completely in advance and gratinéed at the last minute. The broccoli can be blanched ahead and completed before serving. If the soup is made ahead, the egg yolks and cream should not be added until after it has been reheated. The soufflé can wait, assembled, for almost 2 hours before being placed in the oven. It requires 25 to 30 minutes' cooking time.

———◆•◆———

Soupe de Bramafam

CHICKEN SOUP PROVENÇALE
WITH GARLIC, CREAM, AND BASIL

For 8:

12 large cloves garlic
10 cups good chicken bouillon,
    preferably but not neces-
    sarily homemade
2 to 2½ tablespoons tapioca
2 egg yolks

¼ cup heavy cream or unsweet-
    ened evaporated milk
For garnish: 6 or 7 branches fresh
    basil, *chopped* (or 1 tea-
    spoon dried), with 2 table-
    spoons parsley, *chopped*

Crush the cloves of garlic roughly with a bottle or the bottom of a pan, and remove the papery outer skin, but not the hard skin. Put the garlic in a saucepan with half of the chicken stock, set over low heat, and simmer, uncovered, for 25 to 30 minutes until tender. Remove the garlic cloves with a slotted spoon and purée them by putting them through a food mill or garlic press.

Add the remaining chicken stock to the stock in the pan, and reduce it over high heat to about 7 cups. Turn down to a simmer, add the garlic purée and 2 tablespoons of the tapioca, and cook, stirring constantly, until the soup is lightly thick and perfectly smooth. Add ½ tablespoon more tapioca if not thick enough.

Beat the egg yolks with the cream. Stir half of the chopped basil (or the teaspoon of dried basil) into the soup. Pour a little of the hot soup into the cream mixture to warm it; then pour it back into the soup, stirring constantly over heat until the soup is smooth again, without letting it come to the boil.

Pour the soup into a heated soup tureen, and put some fresh basil (or the chopped parsley) into each soup plate before serving.

Porc sylvestre

BRAISED PORK STUFFED WITH
HAM AND MUSHROOMS

For 8:

5 tablespoons rendered pork fat,
    lard, or cooking oil
A 4-pound boneless roast of pork
    in a loaf shape, well tied
3 tablespoons butter
2 tablespoons cooking oil
3 medium onions, *peeled*

2 carrots, *sliced*
½ cup beef bouillon
3 large cloves garlic, *unpeeled*
A bouquet garni of ½ bay leaf,
    4 to 6 parsley sprigs, a small
    branch of thyme
Salt

This dish can be made in the morning for the evening, but it is even better when made one or two days in advance; the pork and stuffing are even better when reheated; and the leftovers better still, reheated again.

Melt the fat, lard, or oil in a heavy ovenproof cooking pot over moderate heat. Dry the tied pork, and brown it in the pot on all sides for about 15 minutes.

Preheat the oven to 375°.

Remove the pork and set it aside. Pour out the fat and rinse and dry the pot. Melt the butter and oil in the same pot, and when the butter foam begins to subside, stir in the onions and carrots. Continue to stir until the vegetables are beginning to brown.

Return the pork to the pot; add the beef bouillon, the unpeeled garlic, and the bouquet garni, and bring to the simmer. Add ¼ teaspoon salt, cover with a piece of waxed paper and a lid, and set into the lower third of the preheated oven.

After ½ hour, turn and baste the meat, sprinkle it with ¼ teaspoon salt, and reduce the heat to 350°. Continue to cook for 2 to 2½ hours longer, turning and basting the meat every half-hour (always returning the waxed paper to the pot).

Sylvestre filling

3 tablespoons butter
1½ tablespoons oil
4 tablespoons shallots or scallions,
    minced
1½ pounds mushrooms, to make
    4 cups, *minced*

1 cup heavy cream or unsweetened
    evaporated milk
Salt
Black pepper, *freshly ground*

While the pork is cooking, prepare the filling and the Mornay sauce. Melt the butter and oil in an enameled skillet. Add the minced shallots or scallions and let them sauté for 2 to 3 minutes; add the minced mushrooms and sauté for 3 to 4 minutes longer, stirring constantly. Season lightly with salt and pepper. Then pour in the cream or milk, which should just cover the mushrooms and let them cook slowly while the cream evaporates and the mushrooms and the cream become a golden thick mixture, not runny (about 15 to 20 minutes).

Pour off the excess cream, if any. Season the mushroom mixture well, and set aside while making the sauce.

Sauce Mornay

3½ cups milk
5 tablespoons butter
7 to 8 tablespoons flour
½ cup imported Swiss cheese,
    coarsely grated

Salt
Black pepper, *freshly ground*
Nutmeg, *freshly grated*
½ to ⅔ cup heavy cream
    (*optional*)

Bring the milk to just under the boil. In a 2-quart enameled saucepan set over heat, melt the butter. Stir in the flour, and cook, stirring, for a few seconds. Remove from the heat and pour in the hot milk all at once, stirring vigorously with a wire whip until smooth; then return to the heat and bring to the boil, stirring constantly until very thick and smooth. Season highly with salt, pepper, and nutmeg. Remove from the heat. When tepid, add the grated cheese.

Add about 1½ cups of the sauce bit by bit to the mushrooms. The mixture should be thick, but if it is too thick, add some of the cream. This is the *sylvestre* filling, and it should be of the right consistency to make the ham adhere to the pork slices.

Reserve the rest of the Mornay sauce to coat the pork.

Final assembly

About ¾ pound good country ham, or Canadian bacon, or prosciutto, *cut into thin slices and then into pieces about ½ inch square*	¼ cup good brown stock or beef bouillon Heavy cream remaining from sauce ¼ cup imported Swiss cheese, grated

Recommended equipment: An ovenproof serving platter about 1½ inches deep and 15 inches long.

When the pork is done, remove it from the pot, let it cool, and cut off the string. Reserve and chill the juices in the pot. Carve the pork into at least 24 neat serving slices about ⅓ inch thick, piling them in the order in which they were sliced so as to be able to re-form them into a neat pattern of overlapping slices.

Place the last slice on the ovenproof platter. Using a spatula, spread a little less than a tablespoon of the Mornay sauce over the slice in a very thin layer. Press on enough pieces of sliced ham to cover the slice of pork; then spread on about 2 tablespoons of the mushroom filling. Place the next slice of pork against the filled piece so that it overlaps, and garnish it in the same way (a thin layer of Mornay sauce, slices of ham, a layer of mushroom filling). Continue thus until all of the pork has been used. Neatly fill in the gaps in the top and sides of the pork with the remaining mushroom filling.

Preheat the oven to 350°.

Remove the fat from the chilled cooking juice and boil the liquid. Strain to remove the vegetables and the bouquet garni, bring again to the boil, scraping the brown bits from the bottom of the pan. Taste, and correct the seasoning. Spoon this sauce over the pork to baste it; then cover the dish with aluminum foil and reheat slowly for about 30 minutes in the preheated oven.

Put the reserved Mornay sauce over moderate heat, stir in the remaining cream by spoonfuls (you want to thin it a little, but the sauce should not become runny), and continue to stir until smooth.

About 20 minutes before serving, remove the pork from the oven and turn the oven up to 375°. Coat the pork generously with the Mornay sauce, sprinkle with the cheese, and return it to the upper level of the oven until the top has lightly browned. If the pork has to wait, leave it in the oven with the heat turned off; it can stay easily 40 to 50 minutes covered with a foil and still be perfect.

If you have some leftovers, reheat in the same way—but make some additional Mornay sauce to coat the pork again before reheating.

Choux brocoli sautés

Sautéed broccoli. Prepare the recipe on page 280 for *brocoli en purée* up until the broccoli is puréed. Serve in a warm vegetable dish.

------◆●◆------

Soufflé meringué à la liqueur

SOUFFLÉ WITH ORANGE LIQUEUR
OR BENEDICTINE

For 8:

Butter and confectioners' sugar
    for the soufflé dish
5 egg yolks
1⅓ cups granulated sugar
½ teaspoon vanilla extract

¼ cup orange liqueur or
    Benedictine
8 egg whites
Pinch of salt

Recommended equipment: A 2-quart soufflé dish.

Put a collar of buttered aluminum foil around the soufflé dish. Butter the insides of the mold and collar, and sprinkle with confectioners' sugar.

Beat the egg yolks with half of the sugar until the mixture is smooth and a pale creamy yellow. Beat in the vanilla and the liqueur.

Whip the egg whites with a pinch of salt until they are white and frothy; gradually pour in the remaining sugar and continue to beat to make a meringue-like mixture, very white, shiny, and firm.

Stir a quarter of the egg whites into the egg yolk mixture to lighten it; then fold all back lightly and evenly into the remaining egg whites (*folding technique, p. 321*).

Fill the prepared soufflé dish. *The recipe can be made up to 2 to 3 hours in advance to this point if the egg whites have been properly beaten and folded.*

To bake and serve   *Preheat the oven to 375°.*
2 tablespoons confectioners' sugar

Bake the soufflé in the oven for 25 to 30 minutes. Sprinkle it with confectioners' sugar just before serving.

22. *Un dîner élégant de fin d'eté sur la terrasse*

AN ELEGANT SUMMER DINNER ON THE TERRACE

Tourtes de fruits de mer à la dieppoise
Shellfish in velouté sauce baked in pastry

Vin blanc fruité: Sancerre au Sauvignon

Terrine de volaille panachée (sans croûte)
Terrine of chicken with
chicken livers, prosciutto, and curry

Vin rouge de Bordeaux: St-Émilion

Salade de saison avec pommes et Gruyère
Chicory and lettuce salad
with diced Gruyère and apples

Nougatine glacée au café
Frozen coffee mousse with nut brittle

Petits fours: Les rosetta

ou Tout au Champagne blanc de blancs
(or champagne throughout)

*T*his is an attractive and pleasant dinner to eat out of doors. The warm dish comes first, so that you will need have no concern for a cooling breeze. The rest of the dinner can be served and enjoyed with complete ease, because it is all cold and can be entirely prepared in advance.

The *tourte* is a Normand dish. It differs from a classic French tart or quiche in that a *tourte* is covered with a pastry lid, whereas French tarts or quiches are always open-faced. It is very likely that the pie, which came to America via England, had its origins in the Normand *tourte.*

The word *tourte* has a rather droll sense in Normandy because it is often used to describe someone who is a little dull, stupid, or, as we say, *"zin-zin."* This may be because a *tourte* with its cover of pastry is a bit heavier in appearance than an ordinary decorated French tart.

In this menu I specify fresh mussels for the *tourte.* But other shellfish could be substituted if you cannot find mussels: oysters, pieces of lobster, crab, or scallops—all would lend themselves well to this treatment.

I offer this recipe for the *terrine de volaille panachée* because it is one that I often make and serve. It is a typical French terrine, in this case a mixture of ground chicken and meat interspersed with layers of prosciutto, chicken breast, and chicken livers, wrapped in the skin of the chicken. I have called it *panachée,* which indicates a variegation of colors, because each piece will be a mosaic of pink, brown, and white when it is sliced. I have not given instructions here for the process of skinning and boning a chicken, because the description is quite lengthy and is to be found in other books, particularly explicitly in our *Mastering the Art of French Cooking,* Volume II. If you have never done it and are alarmed by the thought, you may wish to substitute another dish—for example, the *terrine de porc en verdure,* on page 198.

The dinner concludes with an elegant entremets, the *nougatine glacée au café,* a soft coffee ice cream made with crushed nougatine, which can be served with a cold chocolate sauce.

Conseils: The two *tourtes* can be made several hours in advance and re-heated for about 20 minutes. When reheating them, wrap them in foil; the crust will remain mellower that way. The terrine should be made at least 2 days before it is served. The dessert is best when prepared a day or two in advance, or at the very least, the evening before the day of the dinner.

———— ·•• ————

Tourtes de fruits de mer à la dieppoise

MUSSELS, SHRIMPS, AND MUSHROOMS
IN VELOUTÉ SAUCE BAKED IN PASTRY

For 8:

Two pastry shells

3 recipes *pâte brisée "A"* (p. 313)

Make the pastry and set it in the refrigerator to firm.

Shellfish-mushroom filling

2 pounds fresh mussels
Black pepper, *freshly ground*
2 cups dry white wine
½ pound small fresh shrimps, *cooked* (or equivalent amount canned)

1 pound small white mushrooms (or larger ones, *stemmed and quartered*)
Salt

Wash and scrub the mussels thoroughly in several waters to remove all sand. Put them into a heavy skillet and sprinkle them with pepper. Cook them over high heat for about 5 minutes, shaking the pan two or three times until all the mussels have opened. Discard any that do not open. Line a strainer with cheesecloth, set over a bowl, and pour the mussels through the cheesecloth to collect the liquid from the mussels and to remove any remaining sand.

Let the mussels cool. Return the liquid to the pan. Add the white wine and the shrimps and set over moderate heat for about 5 minutes.

Shell the mussels and discard the hard part from each mussel.

Remove the shrimps from the cooking liquid, add the mushrooms, and cook them for 8 or 9 minutes until just tender. Remove them and set them aside with the mussels. Boil down the liquid to 3 cups. (If there is not enough liquid, add some bottled clam juice or some water.) Season with more pepper and a little salt to taste, and set aside.

Velouté sauce

4½ tablespoons butter
6 tablespoons flour
The 3 cups of shellfish-mushroom
    stock
1¼ to 1½ cups heavy cream

Lemon juice to taste (*optional*)
Salt
Black pepper, *freshly ground*
Nutmeg, *freshly grated*

Melt the butter in an enameled saucepan. Stir in the flour, and cook, stirring, for a few seconds. Remove from the heat and stir in the shellfish-mushroom stock. Then return to the heat and stir vigorously until smooth. Let cool a few minutes before adding the cream, by tablespoons, until the sauce is velvety. Add lemon juice if you wish, and season with salt, pepper, and nutmeg.

To assemble the tourtes

1 egg *beaten in* about ½ table-
    spoon of water

Recommended equipment: Two 8-inch tart molds.

Mix the shellfish into the velouté sauce. (If there is too much sauce, remove a little and set it aside.)

Divide the pastry into 4 pieces. Roll out one piece into a circle about ¼ inch thick and fit it into one of the tart molds (*technique for tourtes, p. 324*). Fill the shell three-fourths full with the filling. Roll out a second piece of pastry to the same size and thickness and lay it over the filling. Repeat to fill the second tart mold.

Press down lightly around the rim to seal the two pieces of pastry, and remove the excess dough with the back of a knife. Brush with beaten egg to glaze the pastry. Make a little flower-like design on the top layer of pastry and 2 or 3 small gashes in the middle of the design through which steam will escape. Then refrigerate to firm again before baking. *The recipe may be made several hours in advance to this point.*

To bake and serve   *Preheat the oven to 375°.*

Again brush beaten egg over the *tourte,* and bake in the preheated oven for 20 to 25 minutes until the crust is nicely browned.

Serve unmolded on a platter.

———— •••• ————

Terrine de volaille panachée (sans croûte)

TERRINE OF CHICKEN WITH CHICKEN LIVERS, HAM OR PROSCIUTTO, COGNAC, AND CURRY

Make at least 2 days before serving.

For 10 to 12:

A 4½ to 5-pound roasting chicken, with its giblets
10 ounces lean bacon
10 ounces ham
4 extra chicken livers
2 tablespoons butter
½ teaspoon dried thyme
Salt
Black pepper, *freshly ground*
½ cup Cognac or Madeira wine
1 large egg
Nutmeg, *freshly grated*
¼ teaspoon ground coriander
2 tablespoons mixed tarragon, thyme, oregano, ½ bay leaf, *pulverized*

Recommended equipment: A 2½-quart terrine with a lid.

With a sharp knife, very carefully remove the skin of the chicken in one piece and set the skin aside.

Next, bone the chicken.

Cut half of the breast meat into strips and set it aside.

Put all of the rest of the chicken meat through the finest blade of the meat grinder, with the bacon, ham, and the chicken gizzard. Combine in a mixing bowl and set aside.

Clean the chicken livers and cut each into 4 pieces. Heat the butter in a frying pan, add the livers, and sauté them for 2 or 3 minutes; then sprinkle with some thyme, salt, and pepper, pour in half of the Cognac or Madeira, and set aflame.

When the flame goes out, remove the livers with a slotted spoon and set them aside. Add their cooking juices to the ground chicken meat along with the egg and the remaining cognac or Madeira. Mix thoroughly, and season highly with nutmeg, coriander, the aromatic herbs, salt, and pepper.

To assemble, bake, and serve

½ pound Virginia ham or prosciutto, *cut into 3 thick slices*

1 cup flour, to seal the terrine

Preheat the oven to 375°.

Cut the ham or prosciutto into strips slightly thinner than the strips of chicken breast.

Line the terrine with the chicken skin. (If there are too many holes in the chicken skin, line the terrine first with cheesecloth.) Spread a third of the chicken mixture over the chicken skin, moistening your hand to make it spread evenly. Cover with layers of ham or prosciutto, strips of chicken breast, and chicken livers, and repeat with a second layer of the chicken mixture and then a second layer of ham or prosciutto, chicken breast, and chicken livers. Cover with the remaining chicken mixture, and if some ham or prosciutto strips are left press them into the top. Cover all tightly with the chicken skin.

Make a thick paste of the flour and ¼ cup cold water, adding more water if necessary. Put the lid on the terrine and press the paste around the lid to seal it thoroughly.

Put the terrine in a shallow pan, pour 1½ inches of water into the pan, and bring the water to the boil on top of the stove. Then set the pan into the preheated oven to cook the pâté for 1½ to 2 hours.

Remove the flour paste. Test the terrine by pricking; it will be done when the juice runs clear like bouillon. If the juices are still rose-colored, reseal the terrine and return it to the oven.

Remove the lid, and place a smaller lid, or a plate or small board, on top of the pâté with a weight on top of that. Let the terrine stand with its weight for 48 hours, refrigerating it after 12 hours.

To serve in the French manner, cut slices inside the terrine, removing the first piece to make it easier to extract the remaining pieces neatly; these should then be sliced and piled on top of the uncut pâté.

———— •=• ————

Nougatine glacée au café

FROZEN COFFEE MOUSSE WITH NUT BRITTLE

This dessert is even better when made the day before.

For 8:

Nougatine (*nut brittle*)

½ cup any mixture almonds, wal-
    nuts, hazelnuts, filberts

⅓ cup sugar
Cooking oil for baking sheet

Let the nuts warm (but not brown) in a moderate oven. Put the sugar
and 3 tablespoons of water into an enameled saucepan and boil to form
a light caramel syrup. Immediately add the warmed nuts, stir over the
heat for a few minutes to distribute the nuts through the syrup, and pour
the nougatine onto an oiled metal sheet, spreading it out into a layer. Set
it aside to cool and harden. Then chop it into small pieces. *The nougatine
can be made in advance.*

Frozen coffee mousse

4 eggs
Pinch of salt
6 tablespoons sugar
3 teaspoons powdered instant
    coffee

1 cup heavy cream
¼ teaspoon vanilla
2 tablespoons confectioners' sugar

Separate the eggs, putting the yolks into a heatproof (nonaluminum) mixing bowl.

Whip the egg whites with a pinch of salt until they are white and
frothy. Then beat in 2 tablespoons of the sugar to make a kind of meringue.

Beat the egg yolks with the remaining sugar until they are a pale creamy yellow. Set over barely simmering water and continue to beat until thick and smooth. Add the instant coffee, stirring to dissolve it well. Remove from the heat and stir in the nougatine.

Mix in one-third of the meringue to lighten the mixture. Then fold all back into the remaining meringue (*technique, p. 321*). Set over ice cubes and beat until cool.

In a separate bowl whip the cream and vanilla over the ice cubes until almost firm. Then beat in the confectioners' sugar.

Fold the whipped cream into the cold mousse mixture.

To serve

Shaved chocolate, sweet or semi-
    sweet (*optional*)

The mixture can be poured into an ice cube tray and the mousse served in individual chilled dessert dishes after freezing for about an hour. But if it is made in advance, it can be frozen in a bowl or decorative ice mold and served unmolded as an ice cream. It can be decorated with some shaved chocolate, or, for a very rich dessert, served with chocolate sauce.

Chocolate sauce

5 ounces German's sweet choco-
    late, *broken into small pieces*

5 tablespoons strong coffee
3 tablespoons butter

Stir the chocolate with the coffee and ¼ cup water over heat until smooth. Let cool to tepid. Add the butter, by bits, stirring thoroughly to incorporate each piece before adding the next.

Spread some of the sauce over the dessert and serve the rest in a sauceboat.

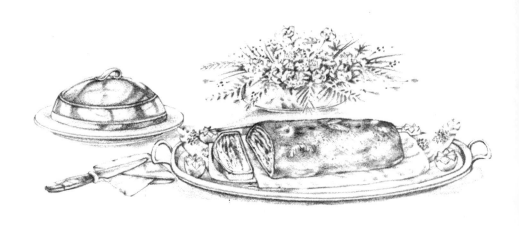

23. *Une reception en hiver avec dîner buffet*

A WINTER SIT-DOWN BUFFET

Timbales de purée d'artichauts
Timbales of artichoke purée

Pâté de saumon, Olga, en croûte
Pâté of salmon and rice in brioche

Salade de saison/Green salad vinaigrette

*Plateau de fromages: Coulomniers ou Brie,
Reblochon ou Demi-Sel, et Selles sur cher*
Assorted cheeses

Glace Caroline aux marrons
Chestnut ice cream

Sauce au chocolat/Chocolate sauce

Petits fours secs: Les rosetta

Vin de Champagne rosé (*brut*)

*T*his is the kind of buffet dinner that I have served in Paris on occasion to the Cercle de Gourmettes. The group was founded in the year 1929, and the story might be of some interest to proponents of "women's liberation." One day an American woman, a charming Mme. Etlinger, who was married to a Frenchman, was invited to a wives' dinner given by the Club des Cents, an exclusive dining club in Paris which has as its members only men, and never more than one hundred. At the end of the dinner, which had been truly extraordinary, the president, Louis Forest, rose to give a toast, saying "There is not a woman in the world who would be able to serve a dinner such as we have had in this club this evening!" Mme. Etlinger's reaction was furious and instantaneous. The next morning she called on all the wives of the members of the Club des Cents, and the Cercle de Gourmettes was formed. The Cercle is partly a school of cuisine and partly a dining club. We have an extremely gifted chef, Mms. Cassiot, as good as any male chef I have ever known, from whom I have learned a very great deal. We hold luncheons twice a month, and each of us is responsible once a year for planning the menu. Our president is Mme. Poussard, an extraordinary woman who, at the age of eighty-three still has a grand lunch and a grand dinner every day. The vice-president is Mme. Françoise Régnier, who is responsible for the sauce, *beurre mousseux,* used in this menu.

This menu begins with individual timbales of artichoke purée, very fresh and delicate, which can be set out on the dining table before the guests sit down. The pâté that follows, *pâté de saumon, Olga,* will be very beautiful on the side table. It has a Russian name because it is an adaptation of a Russian dish called *coulibiac,* the pie made in Russia with fish, usually salmon or pike, and hard-boiled eggs, in brioche. This recipe, not as rich as *coulibiac,* includes, in addition to the salmon and hard-boiled eggs, rice, dill, and pulverized almonds, which give a very subtle taste and make an extremely pretty dish—all encased in parsley with the green dill, the white and yellow of the hard-boiled egg, and the pink salmon—spectacular when you slice it. Like all pâtés, it is served tepid, and so it can wait on the table while the guests finish their entrée.

The dessert, a chestnut ice cream, is the result of many years of work. Julia Child and I tried on numerous occasions to make a light dessert with chestnuts, but they were all quite heavy, and we were never absolutely satisfied with our results. When I began to work on this book, she insisted that I must finally arrive at a successful chestnut ice cream! The first one I tried after that was too thick, the next one too runny, a third too strong with liqueur. I finally hit on the idea of using a *crème anglaise*—egg yolks, sugar, and milk, with a little butter—instead of the heavier cream. I also decided to use a cooked meringue, which gives more lightness than the usual raw meringue. We were finally both happy with the result, which is not a hard ice cream, but a soft one, served coated with a chocolate sauce.

Conseils: Like all timbales, the artichoke timbales can be made in advance and reheated in a bain-marie on top of the stove for about 12 minutes. The *pâté de saumon* should be assembled the same day so that the crust will stay firm, but the pastry dough can be made well ahead. The cooked, finished *pâté* can be kept, well wrapped in foil, in a turned-off oven several hours. The *beurre mousseux* should be made just before serving. The ice cream should be made a day ahead of time, if possible; but it could be made a little as 2 or 3 hours in advance if you have a very cold freezer.

———•—•

Timbales de purée d'artichauts, Sauce crème à l'estragon

INDIVIDUAL MOLDS (OR ONE LARGE MOLD)
OF ARTICHOKE PURÉE WITH TARRAGON CREAM SAUCE

For 8:

8 large, fresh artichokes, or 2
    packages frozen artichokes
⅓ cup heavy cream
Salt
¾ to 1 cup stale bread crumbs,
    homemade from good bread

⅓ cup cold milk
5 shallots, *minced*
4 tablespoons butter
5 medium-sized eggs
Black pepper, *freshly ground*
Nutmeg, *freshly grated*

Recommended equipment: 16 half-cup ramekins or a 2-quart charlotte
mold or other baking dish.

To make the artichoke purée

If using frozen artichokes cook them according to the package directions. To purée, spin briefly in the blender with ⅓ cup cream until
smooth.

If the artichokes are fresh, bring about 8 quarts of water to the boil.
Drop them in the boiling water and add 2 to 3 tablespoons of salt when
the water returns to the boil. Cover the artichokes with a double thickness of cheesecloth to keep them down in the water, and weight them
with a plate if necessary. Cook them for 40 to 50 minutes until a leaf can
easily be removed. Drain, refresh under cold running water, and drain
again thoroughly.

With a teaspoon scrape the pulp of each leaf into a bowl. Remove
the chokes, and purée the hearts by putting them through a food mill or
spinning in a blender, adding ⅓ cup of cream.

Soak the bread crumbs in the milk and mash them with a fork. Then
squeeze through cheesecloth to remove the moisture.

Sauté the minced shallots in the butter until they are soft but not colored. Add the artichoke purée and stir for a few minutes. Then stir in the bread.

Beat the eggs in a mixing bowl, add the artichoke purée, and season highly with salt, pepper, and nutmeg.

To bake and serve   *Preheat the oven to 375°.*

Butter

Cut a round of waxed paper to fit the bottom of the mold or molds. Butter the sides of the mold and one side of the paper. Lay the paper butter side up in the mold and flour thoroughly. Fill with the artichoke purée.

Set the mold or molds into a shallow pan. Pour water into the pan to come about ⅓ of the way up their sides. Bring the water to the simmer on top of the stove; then set the pan into the oven to bake the artichoke purée for 15 to 20 minutes for small molds, 25 to 30 minutes for a large one—or until the mixture has drawn away from the sides and the top is set.

Prepare the tarragon cream sauce, page 99.

Unmold and serve with the sauce.

Pâté de saumon, Olga, en croûte

PÂTÉ OF SALMON AND RICE IN BRIOCHE

The brioche should be made a day in advance, but the pâté itself should be made on the day it is to be served. It can be made 1 or 2 hours in advance and kept warm, wrapped in foil, in the turned-off oven.

For 8:

Pastry

1 recipe *pâte à brioche à l'huile*
   p. 315)

Make the brioche.

Salmon-rice filling

¼ cup uncooked rice
Pinch of saffron
2 pounds fresh salmon steaks,
  poached, or ¾ pound canned
  salmon, free of skin, bones,
  and cartilage
1 to 2 tablespoons olive oil
½ cup shallots or scallions,
  minced
2 tablespoons butter
¾ cup milk
1½ tablespoons tapioca

1 egg yolk
3 tablespoons cream
3 tablespoons almonds, *pulverized*
  (*technique, p. 317*)
Cumin
Paprika
1 teaspoon fresh dill, *chopped* (or
  ½ teaspoon dried)
Cayenne pepper
Salt
Black pepper, *freshly ground*
½ cup vodka

Boil the rice with the saffron (see p. 310). Refresh under cold running water, dry thoroughly on towels, and set aside.

Reserve two nice pieces of salmon for the filling, painting them generously with olive oil. Purée the rest in a food mill.

Cook the minced shallots or scallions gently in the butter until they are tender and translucent.

Bring the milk to the boil, add the tapioca, and stir for a few minutes until the paste is smooth.

Lightly beat the egg yolk with the cream; then combine with the salmon, shallots or scallions, and tapioca paste. Add the pulverized almonds and season highly to taste with cumin, paprika, dill, cayenne pepper, salt, and freshly ground black pepper. Stir in the vodka.

To assemble

3 eggs, *hard boiled and sliced*
1 egg, beaten

Leaves of Boston or Bibb lettuce
Fresh watercress

Divide the brioche pastry in half. Return one piece to the refrigerator. Roll out the other piece and shape it into a neat rectangle 7 by 11 inches. Put the rectangle of pastry on a baking sheet and refrigerate to firm again.

Spread half of the rice evenly onto the firm pastry, leaving a 1-inch border of pastry all around. Spread half of the salmon filling evenly on top of the rice, and cover with half of the sliced hard-boiled eggs, then with the reserved pieces of salmon. Cover with the remaining hard-boiled eggs, salmon filling, and rice, making each layer very neat. Brush the exposed pastry with beaten egg, fold up the borders of pastry squarely against the filling, and brush the outer sides with beaten egg.

Roll out the second strip of pastry and shape it into a rectangle 9 by 13 inches. Lay it evenly on the filling; then tuck it neatly under the pâté, brushing it with beaten egg to help it stick.

Make two holes in the top of the pastry through which steam can escape. Cut out two small rounds of pastry from the remaining pastry, flute their edges with a fork, and brush them with beaten egg. Set one round on top of each hole, and push your finger through to make a corresponding hole in the middle of each round. Roll a small cylinder of cardboard or foil and put it into the hole to keep it open while baking. (If you like, further decorate the top with fluted strips made from any remaining pastry.)

Brush the entire pâté with beaten egg, and put it into the refrigerator until the pastry is firm again.

To bake and serve   *Preheat the oven to 375°.*

Bake the pâté in the preheated oven for 35 to 40 minutes, until it is nicely browned. Prepare the *buerre mousseux de Françoise* (page 302), using fish fumet.

Serve lukewarm, sliced and placed on a napkin on an oval serving platter, surrounded with lettuce leaves and bouquets of watercress. Serve the *beurre mousseux* in a sauceboat.

———◆•◆———

Glace Caroline aux marrons
Sauce au chocolat

CHESTNUT ICE CREAM WITH CHOCOLATE SAUCE

For 10 to 12:

Chestnut purée

2 pounds unsweetened chestnut
purée, canned or fresh

Beat the chestnut purée with an electric beater for about 5 minutes, until it is very smooth.

Crème anglaise

6 egg yolks
1 cup sugar
2 cups milk
1 teaspoon vanilla

½ pound butter
5 to 6 tablespoons rum, preferably
    dark rum

Beat the egg yolks with the sugar until the mixture is a pale creamy yellow.

Put the milk into a heavy-bottomed enameled saucepan, stir in the vanilla, and bring to a boil. Slowly stir the hot milk into the egg yolks and sugar. Pour back into the saucepan and set over simmering water. Stir constantly with a wooden spoon until the foam has disappeared, and the mixture has thickened slightly, coating the spoon.

Remove the saucepan from the heat and let cool a little, then add the butter to the mixture by bits, waiting until each piece has been incorporated before adding the next. Stir in the chestnut purée and the rum. Set the saucepan over a bowl of ice cubes and continue to stir until the mixture is cool. Scrape into two ice cube trays and freeze for 30 to 40 minutes.

Cooked meringue

12 egg whites
Pinch of salt

2⅔ cups confectioners' sugar

Beat the egg whites with the pinch of salt until they are frothy; gradually stir in the confectioners' sugar, continuing to beat until the meringue is white and shiny. Set over simmering water, and beat for about 5 minutes until the meringue is thick and firm. Then set over ice cubes and beat to cool the meringue completely.

Put the meringue into ice cube trays and freeze for about 45 minutes. At the same time, chill a mixing bowl and a mold if you will be using one.

Turn the two preparations into the chilled mixing bowl (let soften slightly if necessary) and beat together vigorously for 10 seconds. Then pour into the chilled ice cream mold or leave in the mixing bowl, and put into the freezer to set again for at least 2 hours.

Chocolate sauce

8 ounces German's sweet choco-   3 tablespoons butter
    late, *broken into small pieces*

Melt the chocolate in a double boiler with 5 or 6 tablespoons of water. Let cool a little. When smooth and slightly cooled, stir in the butter by bits, blending well and waiting until each piece of butter is thoroughly incorporated before adding the next. Let cool.

To serve

Serve the ice cream unmolded, coated with the chocolate sauce, and accompanied by *les rosetta,* page 216.

24. *Un menu somptueux pour recevoir Mr. Knopf*

A DINNER TO HONOR MR. KNOPF

Mousseline de poisson/Molded fish mousse

Vin blanc sec: Pouilly-Fumé de la Loire

Gigot d'agneau de pré-salé à la bourgeoise
Leg of lamb on a bed of
creamed spinach with Madeira

Les pommes de terre en lichettes (fines herbes)
Baked pancakes of potatoes puréed with herbs

Vin rouge de Bordeaux: Médoc: Château Margaux

Salade de saison/Green salad vinaigrette

Plateau de fromages: Livarot ou Münster;
Brie ou Coulomniers; Valençay ou Ste. Maure
Assorted cheeses

Le "Mont Blanc" en surprise
Snow mousse with walnut brittle or rum

Petits fours: Les dollars

Champagne demi-sec
ou tout au Champagne blanc de blancs
(or champagne throughout)

Once in a while one has the opportunity to receive for dinner a great gourmet, such as our publisher Alfred Knopf. I have been well entertained by Mr. Knopf when in New York but have never had the pleasure of receiving him in France. This is a menu that I might serve on such an occasion.

It begins with a *mousseline de poisson*—a delicate molded mousse of puréed fish served with a *sauce velouté suprême* made from the good stock of the bones of the fish and completed with egg yolks and cream. That is accompanied by a dry white wine.

The *plat de résistance,* the main course, is not a dish from the *haute cuisine,* but a very special and savory leg of lamb *à la bourgeoise,* which is cooked with a mirepoix—finely chopped carrots, onions, and celery—seasoned with Provençal herbs and garlic and served on a bed of creamed spinach with an unusual flavor imparted by the cream and Madeira wine. For the most elegant presentation, the leg of lamb is boned when it is served, but it is not necessary to do so. It is best accompanied by a red Bordeaux wine—a Médoc such as Château Margaux, perhaps my favorite wine of all.

The word *lichette* means a thin slice of bread that is often served, buttered, with cheese. In this potato dish, *pommes de terre en lichettes,* the potatoes are puréed and combined with eggs, butter, herbs, and finally some flour to form a kind of dough, then later rolled out to form large *lichettes* about one-third inch thick. The *lichettes* are baked, then brushed with butter and herbs, and put under the broiler to make them brown and bubbling. They can be served in slices or wedges, as suggested in this recipe, or you could cut out smaller rounds of dough to make individual *lichettes.*

The dessert is a frozen mousse, almost a soft ice cream, very, very light, made with whipped cream and meringue. All white, and decorated with a ring of crystallized violets, it is very beautiful and spectacular, and when you cut into it, it will reveal a softer inner center of an unctuous cream mixed either with crushed nougatine and coffee or with rum and raisins. I call the latter filling the "Corinthe" after the type of yellow raisins that I prefer to use; I recommend them, but only if you can be sure they have not been chemically treated. This dessert is the kind of thing I like very much because you can vary indefinitely the soft inner filling, the "surprise." Chocolate, fruit *sorbet,* many different kinds of filling lend themselves to this sort of presentation. This entremets is best accompanied by champagne.

Conseils: The entrée, the fish mousse, can be made in advance and kept in a cool place until it is to be baked. You can cook it about an hour before serving and leave it covered with wax paper in a bain-marie, renewing the hot water from time to time. The sauce is easily reheated, but the egg yolks and cream should be added only at that time. The lamb must be cooked the day it is to be served; it will not be as savory if reheated. But it will keep warm for up to an hour if made in a heavy enough cooking pot. The *pâte* for the potatoes can be prepared the day before, just as for a pastry, and the recipe completed while the lamb cooks or stays warm. The dessert is best when prepared a day ahead of time. The petits fours can of course be made in advance; afterward they should be kept tightly sealed in a metal box, where they will keep well for about a week.

Mousseline de poisson

MOLDED FISH MOUSSE

For 8:

Butter for the mold
2½ pounds salmon, trout, or pike, *cleaned and boned*
Bones, skin, and trimmings from the fish

2½ cups dry white wine
Bouquet garni of thyme, ½ bay leaf, and parsley
Salt
About ½ teaspoon paprika

Nutmeg, *freshly grated*   1 egg white
Black pepper, *freshly ground*   2 cups heavy cream, *chilled*

Recommended equipment: A 4½-cup ring mold, or a fish design mold or other mold, buttered and lined with buttered waxed paper (buttered side up).

Fish fumet

Put the bones, skin, and trimmings of the fish into a large saucepan. Pour in the white wine and, if necessary, water to exactly cover. Add the bouquet garni, ¼ teaspoon of salt, and a pinch of freshly ground pepper. Stir and set over low heat to simmer for 25 minutes.

Strain the liquid; pour it back into the pan and reduce it over high heat to 2 cups. Taste, correct the seasoning, and let cool. (The fish fumet will be used in the velouté sauce.)

Fish mousseline

Roughly chop the fish. Rub it first through the medium disk and then through the fine disk of a food mill to obtain a very fine texture. (A food mill will give the best result, but if you do not have one, a blender can be used. If you use a blender, run it at low speed, use a small amount of liquid, if necessary, and repeat the process several times, until the fish is absolutely smooth and homogenous.)

Put the fish purée into a mixing bowl and season it with paprika, freshly grated nutmeg, salt, and pepper. Set the bowl into a bowl of ice cubes and beat thoroughly with a spatula or fork or an electric beater until it forms a cohesive mass. (This step must not be omitted, because if not worked over ice cubes, the mousseline will not keep its shape.) Add the unbeaten egg white and continue to work until the purée is very, very smooth and firm. Add the chilled cream, stirring it by spoonfuls into the mixture, still over ice. Taste, and correct the seasoning if necessary. *The mousseline may be made in advance to this point and refrigerated.*

To cook the mousseline   *Preheat the oven to 375°.*

Fill the lined mold with the mousseline mixture and cover it with buttered waxed paper (buttered side down). Set the mold into a shallow pan, pour about an inch of water into the pan, and bring the water to a simmer on top of the stove. Then set the pan into the oven to cook the mousseline for 15 to 20 minutes until it is firm to the touch. *It can be kept warm over hot water for 25 to 30 minutes.*

To serve

While the mousseline is poaching, prepare the velouté sauce (*following recipe*).

Unmold the mousseline onto a warmed serving dish. Drain any surplus cooking juices into the sauce, and heat thoroughly. Coat the mousseline with some of the sauce, and serve the rest in a sauceboat.

———— •◦• ————

Sauce velouté suprême

VELOUTÉ SAUCE SUPREME

2½ tablespoons butter	½ cup cream
3½ tablespoons flour	Salt
2 cups fish fumet	Black pepper, *freshly ground*
3 egg yolks	Lemon juice

Melt the butter in an enameled saucepan. Stir in the flour, and cook, stirring, for a few seconds. Remove from the heat and pour in the 2 cups of fish fumet, stirring vigorously. Return to the heat and continue to stir until the mixture becomes thick and smooth and begins to boil. Set aside.

Beat the egg yolks with the cream. Pour in 2 or 3 tablespoons of the sauce to warm the eggs. Then blend all together in the saucepan, return to moderate heat, and stir continuously until the sauce is perfectly smooth, being careful not to let it boil.

Taste, and season with salt, pepper, and lemon juice to taste.

———◆●◆———

Gigot d'agneau de pré-salé à la bourgeoise

LEG OF LAMB ON A BED OF CREAMED SPINACH WITH MADEIRA

For 8:

Recommended equipment: A heavy ovenproof cooking pot, preferably oval, with a lid, large enough to hold the leg of lamb.

To cook the lamb and vegetables

A 6-pound leg of spring lamb, *trimmed*
5 large cloves garlic
½ pound fresh pork rind
1½ tablespoons olive oil, *or* 2½ tablespoons vegetable oil
2 tender stalks of celery, *finely diced*

2 medium carrots, *finely diced*
About 2 medium yellow onions, to make 1 cup, *finely diced*
Bouquet garni of thyme, oregano, savory, basil, and parsley
½ cup beef, chicken, or lamb bouillon

A few hours before cooking the lamb, cut 2 of the garlic cloves into slivers and insert them here and there along the bone and under the skin, pushing them well inside. Do not refrigerate.

Put the pork rind into a saucepan of cold water and bring the water to the boil. Blanch the pork rind for 5 minutes; then rinse and dry it, and cut it into one-inch strips.

Preheat the oven to 400°.

Heat the oil in the heavy pot. Arrange the strips of pork rind in the oil, fat side down. Mince 2 or 3 cloves of the remaining garlic (according to your taste). Add it to the pot with the diced celery, carrots, and onions, and cook gently for about 5 minutes until the vegetables are almost tender but not brown. (Shake the pan a few times, but do not stir, in order to not disturb the pork rind, which should remain on the bottom of the pan.) Add the bouquet garni and set aside.

Put the lamb into a roasting pan and set it into the preheated oven for about 15 minutes to brown it evenly on all sides.

Remove the roasting pan from the oven, and turn the oven down to 375°. Take the lamb out of the pan and set it on top of the minced vegetables. Pour the ½ cup of bouillon into the roasting pan, set over heat, and bring the liquid to the boil, stirring to deglaze the cooking juices. Then pour the juices over the lamb and vegetables, cover the pot, and set it into the oven. For *saignant* (very rare)—the French style—cook it for about 1 hour and 35 minutes. For pink, cook it for about 1 hour and 50 minutes.

To cook the spinach

5 pounds fresh spinach	Nutmeg, *freshly grated*
Salt	2 egg yolks
3 shallots or scallions, *minced*	⅔ cup heavy cream
3½ tablespoons butter	2 tablespoons lemon juice
Black pepper, *freshly ground*	½ cup Madeira wine

Wash and trim the spinach. Put it into a large quantity of boiling water, add a handful of salt, and boil for 5 minutes.

Pour the spinach into a colander and refresh it thoroughly under cold running water. Then take it by handfuls and squeeze out as much water as possible. Chop it and set it aside.

In an enameled saucepan, cook the minced shallots or scallions gently in the butter, stirring occasionally, for about 3 minutes until tender. Add the chopped spinach, stir thoroughly to blend in the butter, and cook, stirring, to dry out the spinach. Season highly with salt, pepper, and nutmeg, and keep warm under a lid or foil.

Beat the egg yolks with the cream, the strained lemon juice, and the Madeira. Set the spinach over medium heat and pour in the cream mixture, stirring constantly, watching carefully, and moving the pan back and forth over the heat to keep the egg yolks from scrambling. Remove from the heat and correct the seasoning if necessary.

To assemble and serve

¼ cup beef bouillon	1½ to 2 tablespoons butter
¼ cup Madeira wine	

Remove the lamb from the pot and keep it warm under foil while finishing the sauce. Strain the cooking liquid into a bowl, pressing the vegetables to extract all the juices, and remove the fat (*technique, p.*

320). Return the cooking juice to the pot, and stir in the bouillon, scraping the bottom with a fork to dislodge all the sediments. Bring to the simmer, stir in the Madeira, and simmer briefly. Taste and correct the seasoning. Finish the sauce by swirling in 1½ to 2 tablespoons of butter.

Spread the spinach on a warm serving dish, and keep it warm while carving the lamb. Cut half of the lamb into thin slices and arrange them, overlapping, over the spinach. Serve the sauce separately.

Pommes de terre en lichettes (fines herbes)

BAKED PANCAKES OF POTATOES WITH BUTTER AND HERBS

For 8:

2 pounds boiling potatoes or 3½ cups leftover mashed potatoes

Salt

4 egg yolks

¼ pound butter

1¼ tablespoons *each* tarragon, parsley, and chervil, *minced* (if dried, use less)

Black pepper, *freshly ground*

Nutmeg, *freshly grated*

½ to ¾ cup flour, depending on the dryness of the potatoes

To make the potato purée   *Preheat the oven to 375°.*

Peel the potatoes. Boil them for about 20 minutes in salted water until they are tender. Drain them, spread on a baking sheet, and put into the preheated oven for about 10 minutes to dry. Then put them (or the leftover mashed potatoes) through a food mill or ricer to make a purée.

Mix the egg yolks, half of the butter, and half of the herbs into the puréed potatoes, and season with salt, pepper, and nutmeg.

Spread about half of the flour onto a board and knead with the potato mixture until homogenous. Taste, correct the seasoning, and refrigerate until firm.

To bake and serve   *Preheat the oven to 375°.*
Butter for the cake pans or baking sheet, *softened or melted*

Recommended equipment: Two 8 or 9-inch cake pans, or a baking sheet.

Turn the cake pans upside down and butter the bottoms, or butter the baking sheet. Divide the potato mixture into two pieces. Using as much of the remaining flour as necessary, roll out each piece into a rough circle about ⅓ inch thick. Roll the dough carefully; it is delicate. Lay the circles of dough on the bottoms of the cake pans, and flick or trim off the excess dough all around with the back of a knife. (Or trim them into neat circles and lay them on the baking sheet.) Prick in several places.

Heat the remaining butter until it is nut brown, and pour it over the potatoes. Bake in the preheated oven about 20 minutes until browned.

Brush the softened or melted butter over each "pancake" or *lichette,* sprinkle with the remaining herbs, and serve immediately. Slice at the table into triangles or strips.

———•◦•———

Le "Mont Blanc" en surprise

SNOW MOUSSE: FROZEN MOUSSE WITH
CRUSHED WALNUT BRITTLE OR RUM

For 10:

Snow mousse

2 cups heavy cream, *chilled*
½ teaspoon vanilla extract
3½ tablespoons confectioners' sugar

3 egg whites
Pinch of salt
¾ cup granulated sugar

Recommended equipment: A 2-quart charlotte mold or bowl.

Pour the cream into a chilled bowl, set it into a bowl of ice cubes, and whip the cream until it is almost firm. Beat in the vanilla and the confectioners' sugar and set aside.

Beat the egg whites with a pinch of salt until they are stiff but not dry. Put the granulated sugar and ¼ cup cold water into an enameled saucepan, set over heat, and boil to form a thick syrup. Pour immediately, a little at a time, into the egg whites, beating vigorously until smooth. Set the bowl into the ice cubes and continue to beat until the mixture is thick and cool. Then lightly fold it into the whipped cream.

Spoon the mixture into the mold or bowl and freeze for 2 or 3 hours until the mousse has set around the edge to a thickness of about ½ inch. Set two other empty bowls in the freezer to be used later.

To make the surprise:

While the cream is setting, prepare the nougatine or the Corinthe.

Nougatine (*crushed walnut brittle*)

½ cup walnuts
½ cup granulated sugar

1 to 1½ teaspoons powdered
    instant coffee

Corinthe (*rum and raisins*)

⅔ cup raisins

¼ cup dark rum

For the nougatine: Put the walnuts into a moderate oven to warm but not brown. Put the sugar and 3 tablespoons of water into an enameled saucepan, set over heat, and boil to form a light caramel syrup. Immediately add the warmed walnuts, stir over the heat for a few seconds to distribute the nuts through the caramel, and, being careful of the hot caramel, pour it onto an oiled pan, spreading it out into a layer with a spatula. Set aside to cool and harden. Then chop into pieces about ⅛ inch square.

For the Corinthe: Steep the raisins in the rum for 30 minutes.

When the mousse has set around the edges, take the mold and the two empty bowls from the freezer. Scoop out 1 cup of the unset cream from the center into one of the chilled bowls and return it to the freezer while making the "surprise" or center. Then scoop out all but an inch of the remaining unset cream into the other chilled bowl. For the nougatine surprise, beat the dry coffee and then the chopped nougatine into this cream. For the Corinthe, stir in the raisins and rum.

Pour the surprise back into the mold, pour the reserved cup of unset cream on top, level off, and return to the freezer for 2 or 3 hours. The center should not be as hard as the edges and should remain a little creamy.

To serve

15 to 20 crystallized violets or
    other candied flowers or fruit

Turn the *Mont Blanc* onto a chilled serving platter and decorate its top with a ring of crystallized flowers or fruit.

SPECIAL
OCCASIONS

———◦—◦———

25. *Une collation d'un jour de chasse*

A HUNT BREAKFAST

Les oeufs "à la tripe"/Hard-boiled eggs
with onions in cheese sauce or

Rognons à la Madras/Curried lamb kidneys

Salade verte vinaigrette
Green salad vinaigrette

Plateau de fromages:
Roquefort, Brie, Petit Suisse
Assorted cheeses

Deux tartes aux fruits: aux poires,
aux prunes et bananes
Pear tart and plum tart with bananas

Vin rouge léger: Beaujolais

*A*s a little girl and young woman in Normandy, I hunted on horseback with my father, who was an extraordinary sportsman as well as a very elegant and wonderful man. He died in 1933, at the age of 57, and after that I never really wanted to hunt again.

But my husband hunts, and in the wintertime on most Sundays I accompany him with a group of friends to Sologne, about two hours from Paris, where they hunt for small game. At about 10 o'clock in the morning, we have a hunt breakfast, the main dish most often served being an omelet of ham or mushrooms. The more substantial type of hunt breakfast that follows is also served on some occasions.

Oeufs "à la tripe" is a very old dish, a very old title. Sometimes it is also called *"à la béchamel"* or *"Soubisée."* The dish has nothing to do with tripe, but probably acquired its name because the onions are cooked as tripe are. They are hard boiled, cooked with onions and butter, highly seasoned with saffron and nutmeg, and coated with a béchamel sauce. The recipe requires 3½ cups of sliced onions, and should peeling all those onions alarm you, there is a most wonderful *truc* to know. Simply take a wooden kitchen match, light it, blow it out, and hold it between your teeth while slicing the onions. For some mysterious reason, this will keep you from crying.

If you would prefer an even richer dish, you could serve *les rognons à la Madras*, curried lamb kidneys. This dish is in fact so substantial that it could well serve as the main course for a light supper. It can also be made with veal kidneys, but these present certain problems. For one thing, they are much more expensive than lamb kidneys and, for another, one can never be sure that the calves have been truly "milk-fed" as they were in former times. In the old days in France, the butchers would pay the farmers who grew the calves 22 quarts of milk a day for one calf! But today, with the uncertainty and the expense, I think it is better to speak only about lamb.

The pear tart shows another application of the *truc,* mentioned earlier, for keeping a tart shell from swelling when it is baking, unfilled, in the oven; in this case the raw crust is painted with egg yolk beaten with a tablespoon of water, and sprinkled with sugar. The sugar will render the pastry still more impermeable after the cooking, and permit it to be covered with juicy fruits without its turning soggy. It is best to obtain for this tart as hard a type of pear as possible. I would use the *poires de Fizet,* which are quite firm when ripe, and which in Normandy one cooks only in cider, without adding either water or sugar, the pears cooking for at least 2 days until they are almost a marmalade. But other firm pears will do.

Conseils: The eggs can be prepared in advance and reheated as described in the recipe. The kidneys are easily reheated in a bain-marie. The tart shells can be made one or two days ahead of time and filled about an hour before being served.

—•—

Oeufs "à la tripe"

SLICED HARD-BOILED EGGS AND ONIONS IN CREAM
SAUCE, BROWNED WITH CHEESE

This dish can be prepared in advance and reheated and browned at the last minute. To reheat, set the baking dish into a shallow pan; pour a small amount of water into the pan, and bring it to the simmer; simmer for 10 or 15 minutes before browning and serving.

For 10 to 12:

14 medium-sized eggs, *hard boiled* p. 297)	8 tablespoons butter 2½ tablespoons oil

1 pound (about 6 medium-sized)
    yellow onions, to yield 3½
    cups *sliced*
Pinch of saffron
Salt

6 tablespoons flour
2½ cups milk
Black pepper, *freshly ground*
Nutmeg, *freshly grated*
¾ cup heavy cream

Shell the hard-boiled eggs and cut them into slices about ⅓ inch thick. Set aside.

Heat the butter and oil in a heavy-bottomed skillet (about 2½-quart capacity), and add the sliced onions, saffron, and ¼ teaspoon salt. Cover and cook gently, stirring from time to time, until the onions are tender and lightly colored but not browned (20 to 30 minutes).

Sprinkle on the flour and continue to cook, stirring, for 2 or 3 minutes. At the same time bring the milk to the boil.

Remove the onions from the heat, pour in the boiling milk, and stir until smooth; return to the heat and simmer for 2 or 3 minutes, still stirring, until smooth and thick. Season with salt, pepper, and nutmeg. Pour in the cream by spoonfuls and stir until smooth again.

Preheat the oven to 425°.

Spread half of the onions in an even layer in a buttered shallow baking dish. Cover with half of the sliced eggs in one layer, a layer of the remaining onions, and finally with the remaining eggs.

To complete and serve

⅓ cup imported Swiss cheese,
    grated
2 tablespoons butter

Sprinkle on the grated cheese, dot with butter, and set in the preheated oven for 2 or 3 minutes, until the top is brown. Serve immediately.

—————•◆•—————

Rognons à la Madras

CURRIED LAMB KIDNEYS

These can be made in advance and reheated over simmering water.

For 10 to 12:

10 to 12 lamb kidneys
Salt
Black pepper, *freshly ground*
10 tablespoons butter
2 tablespoons peanut oil
8 shallots or scallions, *minced*
2 tablespoons flour

2 tablespoons curry
1 cup dry white wine
Cayenne pepper
1 cup cream (*optional*)
About 1 tablespoon parsley,
   minced

Wipe the kidneys and remove the fat. Cut them into ¼-inch slices, and season with salt and pepper. Melt 3 tablespoons of the butter, and roll the kidneys in the butter to keep them from discoloring.

Heat the oil and 3 more tablespoons of the butter in an enameled saucepan; when the fat is beginning to smoke, add the kidneys and sauté them, turning constantly, for 3 or 4 minutes until they are grayish and stiff. Remove them with a slotted spoon and keep them warm. Pour the liquid into a bowl and clean the saucepan.

In the same pan sauté the minced shallots or scallions in 4 table-spoons of butter until they are tender and translucent. Sprinkle on the flour mixed with the curry, and stir for a minute or two, still over the heat. Pour in the wine and stir until the mixture is smooth. Add the re-served cooking liquid from the kidneys. *The kidneys may be served at this point, in the sauce, seasoned with salt, pepper, and cayenne pepper and sprinkled with parsley. But for a much richer and more unctuous dish, proceed as follows.*

Stir in the cream by tablespoonfuls. Season with salt, pepper, and cayenne pepper, and let simmer for 6 or 7 minutes. Finally, add the kidneys, to warm them in the sauce. (The kidneys should *never boil* in the sauce, or they will turn tough.)

Serve the kidneys in a warmed serving dish, decorated with parsley.

———— • • ————

Deux tartes aux fruits:
aux poires, aux prunes et bananes

PEAR TART AND PLUM TART WITH BANANAS

For 10 to 12:

Two 10-inch tart shells

2 recipes *pâte sablée* (*p. 314*)
1 egg yolk *beaten with* 1 tablespoon water

About ¾ cup apricot jam
2 tablespoons granulated sugar

Recommended equipment: Two 10-inch tart molds or rings.

Make the pastry and set it into the refrigerator to firm.

Preheat the oven to 375°.

Divide the pastry into two pieces. Roll them out to a thickness of ⅛ inch and line the two tart molds (*technique, p. 324*). Warm and strain the apricot jam and spread it on the bottom of one of the unbaked tart shells. Paint the second shell with the beaten egg and sprinkle it with the sugar.

Prick the bottom of each shell in several places with a fork and refrigerate to firm again before baking.

Bake the tart shells in the preheated oven for 15 to 18 minutes until they have drawn slightly away from the sides of the molds and are very lightly colored.

Pear tart

To cook the pears

1 orange
A bottle (about 3 cups) of red
wine
⅔ cup sugar

2 cloves
2½ to 3 pounds firm ripe pears
Juice of 1 lemon

Wash the orange and grate half of the rind into an enameled saucepan. Add the strained juice of the orange, the wine, the sugar, and the cloves. Bring slowly to a simmer, and simmer for about 5 minutes to melt the sugar.

Peel, quarter, and core the pears. Sprinkle them with the strained lemon juice, add them to the simmering liquid, and simmer them for about 5 minutes until they are tender. Remove them with a slotted spoon and set them aside to cool. Boil down the syrup over a brisk fire until reduced by about half and thick enough to glaze the tart. Let cool.

To assemble the pear tart

4 tablespoons apricot jam,
  warmed and strained

About 1 hour before serving, paint the egg-yolk glazed tart shell with apricot jam. Arrange the pears in attractive rows in the shell, and then coat them with the wine syrup.

Plum tart

To cook the plums

About 2 pounds ripe plums, fresh   About ½ cup sugar
  or canned   Juice of 1 lemon

If the plums are fresh, skin them and remove the pits. Put them into an enameled saucepan with the sugar and the strained lemon juice. Let them macerate for about 1 hour. Then set the pan over moderate heat, bring to a boil, and turn down to simmer, uncovered, for about 20 minutes (or less time if the plums are very tender). Remove from the pan. Strain the juice, return it to the pan, and boil it down until it is syrupy.

For canned plums, remove the pits, add lemon juice and sugar to taste to their syrup, and boil down the syrup until thick.

To assemble the plum tart

2 ripe bananas   4 tablespoons apricot jam,
Juice of 1 lemon   *warmed and strained*
2 tablespoons sugar

About an hour before serving, fill the apricot-glazed tart shell with a layer of sliced bananas. Sprinkle with lemon juice and then with sugar. Cover with the plums and their syrup, and glaze with apricot jam.

26. *Un pique-nique élégant*

AN ELEGANT PICNIC

Canapés basque aux sardines
Sardine butter on toast or
Couronne rose de l'océan
Rose-colored ring of fish mousse

Quichettes aux champignons
Small mushroom quiches

Terrine de porc en verdure
Terrine of pork, lamb, ham, tongue, and spinach

Salade verte vinaigrette
Green salad vinaigrette

Salade d'aubergines et jambon en friquette
Cold eggplant and ham salad

Fromages: Comté, Beaufort, ou Emmenthal

Tarte à l'orange à la Valenciana/Orange tart

Champagne blanc de blancs ou Champagne rosé

A picnic should always be an occasion for good food: you go to a beautiful place, and you want to spread out an attractive array of dishes. The picnics that follow are both typically French.

I remember many picnics in my life, and they changed a great deal as the years went by. Before World War I, when I was a tiny little girl, there were very, very elegant picnics, which I can just barely remember. After the war life seemed more informal, though still very elegant. I remember especially a picnic that my father arranged in 1922 for some English people whom he had met during the war. We picnicked on the grass above the Falaise at Varengeville. I don't remember everything that was served, but I remember a wonderful *poulet en gelée,* chicken in aspic, each piece wrapped in a large leaf of romaine so that you could eat it without a knife and fork. There were also some "bouquets," little pink shrimps, with buttered bread. And I remember the cheese, Pont l'Evêque, and some sweet pears and a chocolate cake. My father and mother had special low folding chairs, the chauffeur-butler was there to serve everyone, and we drank only champagne.

Then World War II came, and after that life changed again and became more informal still. Today my brother and I take picnics with his children, my nieces and nephews, in the woods down the little River Saane, which flows by our family house in Normandy, where he still lives. Another kind of picnic is the kind my husband and I pack when we go from Provence to Paris. We usually drive, and we never stop in a restaurant but instead in various places along the way that we call our "dining rooms out of doors." We have "dining rooms" in Bourgogne, some with a long view, some in the woods, very pretty places that no one else knows.

Canapés basques aux sardines

Sardine butter on toast. See page 238. The toast will remain crisp if prepared as described.

Couronne rose de l'océan

Rose-colored ring of fish mousse. This cold ring of fish mousse (see recipe, p. 121) can easily be transported in its mold, along with a separate container of green mayonnaise, and then unmolded on a serving plate after your arrival. It would be, perhaps, a lighter beginning to an elegant picnic.

Quichettes aux champignons

Little individual mushroom quiches, to be found on page 232.

Terrine de porc en verdure

TERRINE OF PORK, HAM, TONGUE, AND SPINACH WITH HERBS

For 10:

1 pound fresh pork breast, half fat and half lean

½ pound boiled ham, *in one piece*

½ pound salty country ham, prosciutto, or Westphalian ham, *cut in thick slices if possible*

½ pound pickled or smoked tongue

2 pounds fresh spinach, or 1 pound frozen, to make 1 cup when cooked

Salt

3 tablespoons peanut or vegetable oil

2 medium-sized yellow onions, to make 1 cup, *chopped*

3 large cloves garlic, *minced*

½ cup mixed parsley, chervil, tarragon, and savory, *chopped* (¼ cup if dried)

1 teaspoon bay leaf, *pulverized*

Black pepper, *freshly ground*

1 egg, *beaten*

¼ cup Cognac

Pinch of allspice

Dash of cayenne pepper

Recommended equipment: An oval 2½-quart terrine, with a lid.

Cut the pork breast into ½-inch dice and the boiled ham into slightly smaller dice. Cut the country ham or prosciutto and the tongue along their full length into strips about ⅓ inch thick. Set aside.

Thoroughly wash and trim the spinach if fresh. Bring a large quantity of water to the boil, add the fresh spinach, and when the water returns to the boil, toss in a handful of salt. Let the spinach boil uncovered for 5 minutes. (If the spinach is frozen, cook it according to the package directions.)

Immediately refresh the spinach in a colander under cold running water. Then by handfuls squeeze it in the corner of a towel, twisting to remove as much water as possible. Set aside in a mixing bowl.

Heat the oil in a frying pan, add the chopped onions, and cook, covered, stirring from time to time, until they are soft but not colored (10 to 12 minutes). Add the minced garlic and cook 2 or 3 minutes longer. Stir the onions and garlic into the spinach. Season highly, adding the herbs, the bay leaf, and salt and pepper to taste.

Combine the pork and the boiled ham with the beaten egg and the Cognac, and season with the allspice, a dash of cayenne pepper, and salt and pepper.

To assemble and bake   *Preheat the oven to 375°.*

A strip of lard to line the terrine   1 cup flour
  (or melted lard)

Line the bottom of the terrine with a strip of lard or coat it with melted lard. Cover with a third of the spinach and onion mixture in an even layer. Add a layer of the pork and ham mixture and then half of the strips of ham and tongue, facing along the length of the terrine. Press them lightly and cover with a second layer of spinach and then the remaining meat mixture. Place the remaining strips of tongue and salty ham on the meat, and cover all with the remaining spinach, making a dome.

Lightly rap the terrine against the table to settle the ingredients. Cover with a thin layer of lard or a piece of waxed paper greased on one side with melted lard and placed with the greased side down.

Put the lid on the terrine. Make a thick, fluid paste of 1 cup flour and ¼ cup water, using more water if necessary. Use the paste to seal completely the edges of the terrine, extending under the rim.

Set the terrine into a shallow pan, pour 1½ inches of boiling water into the pan, and set the pan with the terrine into the preheated oven to bake for 1 hour. Then turn the oven down to 350° and cook for another hour. Remove the paste and look at the terrine. It will be finished if, as you prick it, the juice runs clear like bouillon. If it is not, reseal it and return it to the oven until done.

Uncover the terrine and place a weight on top of the meat to pack it down tightly. Leave for 12 hours with the weight, and then refrigerate for another 24 hours.

Serve either unmolded or in the terrine, cut in slices.

Salade d'aubergines
et jambon en friquette

COLD SALAD OF MARINATED FRIED EGGPLANT AND HAM

For 6 to 8:

2½ pounds eggplants (tiny ones
    if available, 6 inches long by
    1½ inches, diameter)
Salt

½ cup flour
1½ to 2 cups olive oil
2 large cloves garlic, *unpeeled*
Black pepper, *freshly ground*

To fry the eggplant

Wash and dry the eggplants and remove the stems. Cut them, unpeeled, into rounds about ¼ inch thick. (If they are large eggplants—regular American eggplants—cut the rounds into quarters.) Spread the slices on absorbent paper, sprinkle them with salt, and leave them for about 15 minutes to exude their liquid, turning them once. Wash them in a colander under cold running water, and pat them dry.

Spread the flour on a board, and lightly flour the eggplant on each side, shaking each slice to remove excess flour. Warm half of the oil in a frying pan and add the unpeeled garlic. As soon as little bubbles form around the cloves of garlic, plunge a layer of eggplant slices into the oil and fry them for about 3 minutes on each side until they are golden brown. Put them to drain on absorbent paper and sprinkle them with salt and pepper. Repeat with the succeeding batch or batches.

To marinate the eggplant

¼ cup olive, vegetable, or peanut oil
½ cup wine vinegar
Juice of 1 lemon
1 teaspoon thyme, *minced*
3 bay leaves, *crushed*

2 tablespoons chervil, *minced* (If dried, use about 2 teaspoons)
Dash of mace or nutmeg
Dash of ginger (*optional*)

Pour the oil and the vinegar into a small saucepan. Add the strained lemon juice, thyme, crushed bay leaves, chervil, mace or nutmeg, and ginger (if you like it). Simmer for 5 or 6 minutes and strain. Put the fried eggplant into a bowl and moisten it with the warm marinade. Let cool slightly. Then refrigerate for at least an hour or put into the freezer if time is short.

To assemble and serve

1 head of Boston lettuce, *washed and separated into leaves*
½ pound thick boiled or baked ham, *diced*

2 eggs, *hard boiled*
1 or 2 tablespoons chervil, basil, or parsley, *chopped*

Spread the lettuce leaves in a salad bowl and cover them with diced ham and sliced hard-boiled eggs. Just before serving, add the eggplant, and sprinkle with the chopped herbs. Toss the salad at the table.

Tarte à l'orange à la Valenciana

Orange tart. See page 117 for the recipe.

27. *Un pique-nique en famille*

A FAMILY PICNIC

Le céleri-rave à la provençale/Salad
of celeriac, olives, and anchovies

Les oeufs en bohèmienne
Ratatouille with eggs

Pâté pantin de Fontainebleau/Onions,
mushrooms, and brown rice in pastry

Gâteau d'Hélène/White cake with
coconut cream and apricot

Fruits frais/Fresh fruit

Vin blanc: Maçon

Céleri-rave à la provençale

SALAD OF CELERIAC WITH OLIVES, ANCHOVIES,
CAPERS, AND EGGS

For 6:

6 anchovy fillets
½ cup tepid milk
1 medium-sized celeriac (celery
    root) (1½ to 2 pounds)
Juice of 1 large lemon
Salt
4 large or 6 medium eggs
½ cup olive oil
1 small onion, *chopped*
2 cloves garlic, *peeled and crushed*

1 cup *purée de tomate provençale*
    (*p. 299*), or canned to-
    matoes, *drained and puréed*
½ tablespoon sugar
3½ tablespoons wine vinegar
1½ tablespoons capers
3 ounces (⅝ cup) small black
    Mediterranean olives
Black pepper, *freshly ground*
¼ cup flour
1½ tablespoons parsley, *chopped*

Put the anchovies to soak for a good hour in the tepid milk to re-move the salt. When the taste of salt is no longer strong, drain the an-chovies, dry them on paper towels, and cut them into dice.

Peel the celeriac, cutting deeply to remove all the blackish parts. Wash, dry, and cut into even slices. Cut the slices into strips and the strips into ⅓-inch dice. Put into a bowl, sprinkle with the strained juice of the lemon, and let macerate for one-half hour.

Put the diced celeriac into 6 cups of boiling water, add 2 tablespoons of salt as soon as the water returns to the boil, and boil for 10 minutes. Remove with a slotted spoon, refresh under cold running water, dry on paper towels, and set aside.

In the same water hard-boil the eggs for 10 minutes. Remove them, let cool in cold water, and shell them.

Heat ¼ cup of the oil in a frying pan, add the chopped onion and the garlic, and cook until lightly colored, stirring with a wooden spoon. Pour in the tomato sauce and the sugar, and stir constantly until the sauce has thickened and is lightly browned. Remove the pan from the heat, and add the vinegar, capers, olives, and anchovies. Taste, and correct the seasoning, adding pepper.

Heat the remaining oil in the frying pan. Roll the pieces of celeriac in the flour, shaking off the excess flour, and fry them until they are lightly browned. Drain and dry on paper towels.

Spread the tomato mixture in the middle of a serving dish, and cover with the fried celeriac. Surround with quartered eggs, sprinkle with parsley, and serve cold (but do not refrigerate).

Oeufs en bohèmienne

RATATOUILLE WITH EGGS

For 6 to 8:

2½ pounds eggplant
Salt
About 1 cup olive oil
1½ pounds onions (preferably
    sweet Bermuda or Spanish),
    chopped
1½ pounds green peppers
3 pounds ripe tomatoes
2 or 3 large cloves garlic, *unpeeled*
½ bay leaf

1 stalk thyme
1 teaspoon sugar
Black pepper, *freshly ground*
Paprika to taste
4 tablespoons wine vinegar
Tabasco to taste
6 to 8 eggs, *hard boiled*
2 tablespoons parsley, *minced* (if
    dried, use less)

Recommended equipment: A shallow baking-serving dish.

Peel and dice the eggplant and sprinkle the pieces with salt. Set into a colander for 10 minutes to exude their liquid, then turn and let drain 10 minutes more. Rinse and pat dry with paper towels.

Heat 3 tablespoons of the olive oil in a skillet, add the chopped onions, and cook them slowly, stirring from time to time, until they are tender but not brown.

Parboil the peppers for 10 minutes in boiling salted water. Refresh under cold running water, and dry on absorbent paper. Remove the segments and the seeds, cut into strips, and add the strips to the onions. Finish cooking together for about 15 minutes, stirring occasionally.

Heat 4 tablespoons of oil in another skillet, add half of the diced eggplant, and sauté slowly for 15 to 20 minutes, until tender and lightly golden brown. Remove with a slotted spoon and drain on absorbent paper. Add more oil to the pan and fry the remaining eggplant in the same way. When all the eggplant pieces are fried, stir them into the onions and peppers.

Quarter the tomatoes, add more oil to the skillet, and cook them very slowly for about 20 minutes with the unpeeled garlic, bay leaf, thyme, sugar, and freshly ground pepper. Put through a food mill and then stir the purée into the onion and eggplant mixture. Correct the seasoning, adding paprika, vinegar, and Tabasco. If the mixture is too runny, reduce it over heat until thick. Refrigerate.

To serve warm: Preheat the oven to 375°. Put the ratatouille into the baking dish. Press the hard-boiled eggs, cut into quarters, into the mixture, and sprinkle with some drops of oil. Reheat and brown for 10 to 15 minutes in the preheated oven. Serve sprinkled with parsley.

To serve cold: Put the ratatouille into the serving dish and garnish with quartered eggs. Serve sprinkled with parsley.

Pâté pantin de Fontainebleau

ONIONS, MUSHROOMS, AND BROWN RICE IN PASTRY

For 6 to 8:

Pastry crust

2 recipes *pâte brisée "B"* (*p. 314*)

Make the pastry and put it into the refrigerator to firm.

Brown rice

1 cup uncooked brown rice

Soak the rice in cold water for 3 hours. Pour out the water and rinse the rice. Then boil it for 45 minutes in 3 cups of salted water. Again drain and rinse it, and set it aside.

Mushroom-onion filling

3 ounces (⅝ cup) almonds,
  blanched and slivered
¼ cup olive oil
2½ pounds onions (preferably
  sweet Bermuda or Spanish),
  to yield about 10 cups,
  chopped
1 cup chicken bouillon or homemade beef bouillon
Pinch of saffron (*optional*)
Salt
Black pepper, *freshly ground*
Nutmeg, *freshly grated*

1 pound mushrooms (if large
  mushrooms, *stemmed and
  quartered*), *cleaned*
1 cup cold milk
2 tablespoons cream
1 egg
1 tablespoon flour
2 slices (6 ounces) boiled or
  baked ham, *diced*
1½ tablespoons parsley, *chopped*
1½ tablespoons mixed parsley,
  chervil, and tarragon, minced
  (if herbs are dried, use less)
Mace

Put the slivered almonds on a baking pan and brown them very lightly in a 375° oven, shaking the pan from time to time to brown evenly. Chop them finely and set them aside.

Warm the oil in a large heavy skillet. Add the chopped onions and cook them very slowly, stirring from time to time, until they are soft but not brown. Add the bouillon and bring to the boil. Stir in the saffron if you wish, and season with salt, pepper, and nutmeg. Continue to cook slowly, uncovered, for 35 to 45 minutes, until the onions are very soft and tender. Gently simmer the mushrooms with the milk in a covered skillet, for about half an hour, until the mushrooms are tender and have absorbed the milk. Season with salt and pepper and set aside.

Drain the onions and put them through a food mill, or spin them briefly in a blender at low speed, to make a thick purée. Return the purée to the skillet. Beat the cream thoroughly with the egg and the flour and stir into the onion purée. Then set over low heat and continue to stir until the mixture is very thick.

Let cool slightly, and combine with the almonds, mushrooms, and diced ham. Add the herbs and mace, taste, and correct the seasoning.

To assemble,
bake, and serve   *Preheat the oven to 375°.*

1 egg yolk

Roll out the pastry to a thickness of ¼ inch and trim into a large rectangle 11 by 26 inches. Lay the rectangle of pastry on a baking sheet, and brush it with egg yolk.

Spread half of the rice on half of the pastry in a neat layer, making a square of rice and leaving a ¾-inch border of uncovered pastry. Cover the rice with the filling, and top with the remaining rice. Then carefully fold the uncovered half of the pastry over the rice, and seal the three sides.

Brush the pastry again with egg yolk, and make two slashes in the top to allow steam to escape. If you like, decorate the top with shapes made from any remaining pastry. Brush the pastry again with egg yolk, and refrigerate for about 15 minutes to firm again before baking.

Bake the pâté in the preheated oven for 25 to 30 minutes. Serve it tepid.*

Gâteau d'Hélène

White cake with coconut cream and apricot. See page 84.

---

* If you are making the pâté as an entrée dish, serve it lukewarm with *beurre mousseux* prepared with mushroom jumet, page 302.

28. Thé

HIGH TEA

LES PREPARATIONS SALÉS

Canapés basques aux sardines
Canapés of sardine butter or
Tartelettes à la dijonnaise/Tomato tartlets

Les croque-madame/Hot cheese canapés

Croustades savoyardes/Cheese tartlets

GÂTEAUX ET TARTES

Gâteau au chocolat: Le Doris
Chocolate cake with almonds and whiskey

Gâteau d'Hélène/White cake with
coconut cream and apricot

Tourte créole/Pineapple, pears, and bananas
in sweet brioche

Tartes aux fruits, ou tarte de Nancy
Pear tart, plum tart, or almond tart

UNE CRÉATION

*Le Formidable aux trois crèmes et aux trois
liqueurs*/Mocha, orange, and chocolate
butter creams in layers of sweet pastry

UNE SELECTION DE PETITS FOURS

PETITS FOURS
Les rosetta/Petites sablées de Mélanie

PETITS FOURS À LA CRÈME AU BEURRE
Petits moka/Tartelettes Zalita
Les dollars/Mes truffes au chocolat

LES BOISSONS

Thé glacé d'Elizabeth au citron
Iced tea with lemon juice

Vin de pêches d'Arlette/Red wine
flavored with peach leaves

La Sangría de Bramafam/Spiced
red wine with oranges

A "high tea" in France is served on such occasions as a women's meeting, a gathering of people for business purposes, or a celebration to do honor to a particular person. Several sorts of drinks are usually provided: in winter, hot tea (either Ceylon or China), hot chocolate, café au lait; in summer, iced tea, different fruit juices, beer, perhaps some Coca-Cola with lemon juice, and other refreshing soft drinks. Salted as well as sweet dishes are served. Here I offer suggestions from which selections can be made. No matter how small the tea, one wants some variety, and it is always nice to have at least one spectacular cake to make the tea party festive.

The recipes for the dishes suggested here will be found as follows: *Canapés basques* (*p. 238*), *tartelettes à la dijonnaise* (*p. 234*), *croque-madame* (*p. 27*), *croustades savoyardes* (*p. 230*), *le Doris* (*p. 107*), *gâteau d'Hélène* (*p. 84*), *tartes aux fruits* (*p. 194*), *tarte de Nancy* (*p. 99*). The *vin de pêches d'Arlette*, red wine flavored with peach leaves, which must be made at least a week ahead, can be found on page 241 and *La Sangría de Bramafam*, which should be prepared the day before, on page 242. The *tourte créole* and *le Formidable*, as well as recipes for all of the petits fours and iced tea, are on the pages that follow.

The *tourte créole* is another version of the Normand *tourte*, described in Menu 22. It is a flat covered pie—in this case made with a special sweet brioche pastry and filled with pears, bananas, pineapple, and raisins soaked in lemon juice. I have called it "Creole" for the tropical islands of Martinique, Guadaloupe, and Madagascar, where the bananas and pineapples grow. The *tourte*, which is served warm, can be made in advance and reheated.

Tourte créole, Sauce d'abricot

TOURTE OF SPECIAL SWEET BRIOCHE PASTRY
FILLED WITH PINEAPPLE, PEARS, AND BANANAS,
SERVED WITH APRICOT SAUCE

This can be baked a day in advance and reheated in a 350° oven for 15 minutes.

Sweet brioche crust

1 recipe *pâte à brioche a l'huile*
(p. 315)

Make the brioche pastry a day ahead of time, using ½ cup of sugar, and refrigerate it.

Macerated fruit filling

1 good-sized pear, ripe but not overripe	⅓ cup raisins
	1 orange
1 cup chunks of fresh ripe pine- apple or canned pineapple	½ lemon
	¼ cup sugar
2 ripe bananas, *sliced*	

Peel and core the pear and cut it into 8 pieces; then slice each piece in half crosswise. Put the pieces in a mixing bowl with the pineapple (drained if canned), the sliced bananas, and the raisins. Grate the peel of the orange and the half lemon into the bowl (*technique, p. 324*). Add the juice of the lemon and the sugar, stir to blend, and set aside to macerate for 20 minutes—no longer—mixing once or twice.

Drain the fruits well, reserving the maceration liquid, and set aside.

To assemble

Oil for the tart mold	¼ cup sugar
5 tablespoons butter	1 egg, *beaten with* 1 tablespoon water

Recommended equipment: An 11-inch tart mold.

Remove the brioche dough from the refrigerator, and put it on a board or pastry marble. Divide the dough in two, and roll out one piece about ⅛ inch thick, returning the other half to the refrigerator. Oil the tart mold, roll the pastry lightly around the rolling pin, and line the mold (*technique, p. 324*).

Cream the butter with the sugar. Spread half of it carefully onto the bottom layer of dough. Place the macerated fruits on top, in an even layer. Dot the fruits with the second half of the butter-cream mixture. Brush the rim of the pastry with the beaten egg. Roll out the second piece of pastry to the same thickness as the first. Roll it lightly around the rolling pin and unroll it onto the *tourte.* Press down lightly to seal together the two pieces of pastry on the rim, and remove the excess dough.

With the back of a knife, lightly draw a flower-like design in the center of the top layer of pastry, and make a small hole in the middle of the design (through which steam will escape). Brush the pastry with beaten egg, and set it into the refrigerator to firm for about 20 minutes, or into the freezer for about 5 minutes.

To bake   *Preheat the oven to 375°.*

Bake the *tourte* for 20 to 25 minutes until it is golden brown and has drawn slightly away from the sides of the mold.

Fruit sauce

1 cup apricot jam	The maceration liquid from the fruit

Warm and strain the apricot jam. Put it into a saucepan with the maceration liquid from the fruit and stir over heat until warm and well blended. Serve it separately in a sauceboat.

Le Formidable aux trois crèmes et aux trois liqueurs

A CREATION OF THREE LAYERS OF PASTRY, SPREAD WITH MOCHA, ORANGE, AND CHOCOLATE BUTTER CREAMS AND GLAZED WITH APRICOT JAM

Le Formidable is made of three layers of pastry, each spread with a different butter cream. The sides are frosted with a mixture of the creams, a fourth round of the pastry is crumbled and pressed into the top layer of chocolate cream, and the top is glazed with apricot jam and sprinkled with toasted almonds. The pastry is the *pâte sablée de Mélanie,* especially devised for the petits fours *les petits sablés de Mélanie* on page 217.

This is even better when prepared a day in advance.

Four pastry crusts

Recommended equipment: A 7½-inch cake pan. (If you have 4 such cake pans, the 4 layers of pastry can be made and rolled out at the same time. Otherwise, make and bake them in succession.)

4 egg yolks	5 ounces almonds, enough to make
⅔ cup sugar	1¼ cups, *pulverized* (*tech-*
¼ teaspoon salt	*nique, p. 317*)
2 lemons	2 cups flour, preferably cake flour
	¼ pound butter, *softened*

Beat the egg yolks with the sugar until they are a pale creamy yellow. Add the pinch of salt and grate in the rind of the lemons.

Add the pulverized almonds, the flour, and then the softened butter, to make a dough. Form it into a ball, flour it, and put into the refrigerator to firm.

Remove the dough from the refrigerator, divide it into 4 pieces and return 3 of them to the refrigerator. Roll out the first piece into a circle the size of the cake pan. Turn one cake pan upside down and lightly butter and flour the upended bottom. Lay the dough on the pan and flick off the excess pastry all around with the back of a knife. Prick the pastry in several places with a fork, and refrigerate to firm again before baking.

Preheat the oven to 400°.

Bake in the preheated oven for about 10 minutes until lightly golden. Remove from the cake pan or pans and set on a rack to cool.

To prepare the three butter creams

Mocha butter cream

2 egg yolks
⅔ cup confectioners' sugar
2 tablespoons powdered instant
   coffee

1½ tablespoons rum, preferably
   dark rum
¼ pound sweet butter

Put the egg yolks into a heatproof (nonaluminum) bowl. Gradually add the sugar, beating until the mixture is a pale creamy yellow. Set the bowl over simmering water, and continue to beat until the mixture has thickened and is sticky. Dissolve the instant coffee in the rum. Blend thoroughly into the egg mixture and remove from the heat. Then add the butter by bits, waiting until each piece of butter has been thoroughly incorporated before adding the next. Refrigerate to firm the butter cream, but not to harden it completely.

Orange butter cream

1 large thick-skinned orange
2 egg yolks
¼ cup confectioners' sugar

¼ pound sweet butter, *softened*
2 to 3 tablespoons orange liqueur
   or Benedictine

Grate the orange peel into a bowl (*technique, p. 324*). Add the egg yolks, and then the sugar by small quantities, beating until the mixture is a pale creamy yellow.

Blend in the butter. Finish the cream by adding some orange liqueur or Benedictine, which will give an incomparable aroma. Refrigerate to firm.

Chocolate butter cream

5 ounces German's sweet chocolate, *broken into small pieces*
3 tablespoons strong coffee

5 tablespoons sweet butter
2 tablespoons orange liqueur or
Benedictine

Put the chocolate and the coffee in the top of a double boiler, set over simmering water, and stir until smooth. Remove from the heat and stir in the butter, by bits, waiting until each piece of butter has been thoroughly incorporated before adding the next. Add the liqueur, and refrigerate to firm.

To build up the cake

¼ cup apricot jam, *warmed and
strained*

½ cup almonds, *blanched and
roughly chopped and lightly
toasted*

Place one of the baked rounds of pastry on a serving dish. Set aside 2 or 3 tablespoons of mocha cream for covering the sides. Spread the pastry layer with the remaining mocha cream, using a knife or spatula (warmed under hot running water and dried) to spread it evenly. Press the second crust neatly on top of the first and spread it with the orange butter cream. (The pastry is fragile and may crack; but have no concern, because the whole cake will be covered.) Top with the third crust, and spread on all but 2 or 3 tablespoons of the chocolate cream.

Roughly crumble the fourth crust, and press the crumbs neatly into the top layer of chocolate cream. Mix the remaining mocha and chocolate creams and spread this around the sides of the cake to fill in all the gaps between the layers. Refrigerate to firm the creams.

Spread the top with the strained apricot jam, and sprinkle the toasted almonds over the top and press them around the sides. Refrigerate until time to serve.

Les Petits Fours

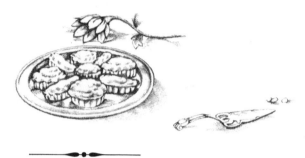

Les rosetta

ROSETTES

Les rosetta go perfectly with any frozen desserts, especially fruit sherbets. They are very easy to make, the mixing requiring only three or four minutes and the baking about five. They can be baked ahead of time if they are then stored in a closed metal box so they will not be softened by humidity.

For about 25 cookies:

4 tablespoons butter
⅓ cup sugar
¼ teaspoon vanilla or large pinch
    of lemon rind, *grated*
2 egg whites

Pinch of salt
½ cup flour
Oil and flour for the baking sheet
3 or 4 tablespoons almonds,
    slivered, or lemon rind,
    grated

Preheat the oven to 425°.

Rinse a mixing bowl in hot water and dry it. Cream the butter in the warm bowl and add the sugar, working until thoroughly mixed. Add the vanilla or grated lemon rind. Beat the egg whites with a pinch of salt until they are stiff but not dry and fold them into the mixture; then add the flour by tablespoons.

Oil and lightly flour a baking sheet, tapping it to remove excess flour. Make circles in the flour about 2¼ inches in diameter with a cookie cutter or a glass. Spread the cookie pastry very thinly within the circles. (This is most easily done with the back of a teaspoon.) Sprinkle the circles of pastry with the slivered almonds or grated lemon rind. Set into the preheated oven to bake for about 5 minutes. Watch carefully: as soon as the edges of the cookies are colored, remove them from the oven and set them on a rack to cool. They will keep for a few days in a closed container.

Petits sablés de Mélanie

LEMON ALMOND COOKIES

Les petits sablés de Mélaine are a little more substantial than *les rosettas* and have more flavor. The preparation time is slightly longer, because the dough must be chilled to firm it before baking. This is the dough used in making *le Formidable* on p. 213.

For 25 to 30 cookies (about 1¾ cups of pâte sablée de Mélanie):

2 egg yolks	6 tablespoons almonds, *pulverized*
⅓ cup sugar	(*technique, p. 317*)
Pinch of salt	1 cup flour, preferably cake flour
1 lemon	4 tablespoons butter, *softened*

To make the dough

Beat the egg yolks with the sugar until they are a pale creamy yellow. Add the salt and grate in the rind of the lemon (*technique, p. 324*).

Add the pulverized almonds, the flour, and then the softened butter, to make a dough. Form it into a ball, flour it, and put into the refrigerator to firm.

To bake the cookies   *Preheat the oven to 400°.*

1 tablespoon oil for the baking   10 almonds, *slivered*
   sheet

Recommended equipment: A round or oval fluted cookie cutter (or a glass) about 2 inches across.

Roll out the dough on a lightly floured board to a thickness of ¼ inch. Cut out the dough into 2-inch rounds or ovals and place them on a well-oiled baking sheet. Decorate with the slivered almonds and refrigerate to firm again before baking.

Bake the cookies in the preheated oven for 8 to 10 minutes until the sides are lightly golden and the centers lightly colored. Remove and set to firm on a cake rack. They will keep for a few days to a week in a tin box.

————◦•◦————

Petits moka

LAYERED PETITS FOURS WITH
MOCHA BUTTER CREAM

If you can buy the cookies called *petits beurres,* which I know are available in many shops in the United States, this is a very quick and easy way to make some delicious petits fours with mocha butter cream. But if you cannot find *petits beurres,* you can bake these yourself, using the *pâte sablée de Mélanie* in the preceding recipe.

For about 35 petits fours:

Cookie dough

A 6¼-ounce box *petits beurres*
    (bought in a fine food
    store), or 1 recipe *pâte sablée*
    de Mélanie (p. 217)

If making the cookies yourself, prepare the dough and put it into the refrigerator to firm.

Divide the dough into 3 pieces, roll out each one, and then trim to a 7-inch square. Refrigerate to firm again.

Bake in a 400° oven for 8 to 10 minutes.

Mocha butter cream

3 egg yolks
¾ cup plus 1 tablespoon confectioners' sugar

4 teaspoons powdered instant
   coffee
¼ pound plus 2 tablespoons cold
   sweet butter

Put the egg yolks into a heatproof (nonaluminum) mixing bowl. Set into simmering water and beat in the sugar gradually with an electric beater or a whisk, waiting each time for the sugar to dissolve before adding more sugar and beating constantly until the mixture is warm and absolutely smooth. Stir in the instant coffee and then the butter 2 tablespoons at a time, again beating constantly until all is thoroughly mixed. Refrigerate to firm.

To assemble

2 cups strong, sweet cold coffee

Preheat the oven to 400°.

⅔ cup almonds, *pulverized*
   (*technique, p. 317*)

Arrange the squares of pastry or *petits beurres* in a shallow pan and moisten with the coffee, being careful not to make the pastry soggy. Pour off any excess coffee. Spread with some of the chilled mocha cream. Repeat with a second and third layer of pastry and mocha cream. Spread mocha cream around the sides and on top to cover the *moka* and refrigerate to firm.

Toast the pulverized almonds in the oven for a few minutes at 400°. With a heated carving knife, cut the *moka* into small squares or rectangles.

Roll each piece on all sides in toasted pulverized almonds. Place in paper candy cups and refrigerate or freeze until time to serve.

———◆●●———

Tartelettes Zalita

TARTLETS OF CHOCOLATE-ALMOND CREAM, COVERED WITH CHOCOLATE MERINGUE

Les tartelettes Zalita are elegant little tartlets of chocolate-almond paste covered with a chocolate meringue. One could make this recipe in a large mold, but in that case the tart would be served as a dessert, not offered at a tea. These tartlets can be made partially a day in advance and completed on the day they are to be served.

For 20 tartlets:

Tartlet shells

1 recipe *pâte sablée (p. 314)*   ¾ cup apricot jam

Recommended equipment: 20 tartlet molds 1½ inches wide and ½ inch deep.

Make the pastry and put it in the refrigerator to firm.

Roll out the dough to a thickness of ⅛ inch. Warm and strain the apricot jam. Line the tartlet molds with the dough (*technique, p. 324*) and lightly brush the inside of each with a layer of apricot jam. Then prick in several places with a fork and refrigerate to firm again.

Chocolate-almond filling

2 egg yolks
1 egg white
½ cup granulated sugar
3 tablespoons powdered bitter
    cocoa

4 ounces (¾ cup) almonds,
    pulverized (technique,
    p. 317)

Preheat the oven to 400°.

Put the 2 egg yolks and the 1 egg white into a heatproof (non-aluminum) mixing bowl with the sugar. Set the bowl over simmering water and beat until the mixture is a pale creamy yellow. Stir in the cocoa and the pulverized almonds, blending well.

Spoon the mixture into the tartlet shells, smooth the tops with a wet knife or spatula, and bake in the preheated oven for 12 to 15 minutes until slightly set. *The recipe can be made a day in advance to this point.*

Chocolate meringue

2 egg whites
1 cup confectioners' sugar

1½ ounces German's sweet chocolate, *pulverized*

In a heatproof (nonaluminum) bowl beat the egg whites until they are frothy; then set over simmering water and gradually add the confectioners' sugar, still beating until the mixture is warm and creamy. Remove from the heat, stir in the pulverized chocolate, and beat until the chocolate has melted.

Spread a dome of meringue over each baked tartlet, smoothing it out with a wet knife or spatula.

Final baking and decoration

12 almonds, *blanched and chopped*

Preheat the oven to 350°.

Lightly toast the chopped almonds in the preheated oven, and sprinkle them over the meringue.

Return the tartlets to the oven to bake for 8 to 10 minutes until the meringue is dry and crisp.

Let cool before serving.

Les dollars aux raisins

FLAT OR ROLLED COOKIES

Les dollars can be served either as flat cookies (*petits fours secs*) or they can be formed into little cornets or "cigarettes" immediately after they are taken from the oven, and filled with one of the butter creams to be found in the recipe for *le Formidable* (p. 213). To serve them as plain cookies, set them immediately on a rack to cool. To make cornets or cigarettes, shape them one by one around a sharpening steel. This must be done rapidly, while they are hot. (Wear gloves if necessary.) If you wait, it will be too late to shape them, and the little cakes will break when they are folded.

For about 25 cookies, cornets (small cones), or "cigarettes":

1 egg
⅓ cup sugar
¼ teaspoon vanilla
⅓ cup flour
1 orange

3 tablespoons butter, *softened or creamed*
¼ cup raisins
Oil for the baking sheet

Preheat the oven to 400°.

Beat the egg with the sugar and the vanilla until the mixture is a pale creamy yellow. Blend in the flour, grate the orange rind (*technique, p. 324*), and stir in the softened butter.

Drop by teaspoonfuls onto an oiled baking sheet to make mounds about the size of a walnut. Carefully spread them out into circles about 2½ inches in diameter. (Smooth with the back of a wet teaspoon.) Put 2 or 3 raisins on each circle, and bake in the preheated oven for about 5 minutes until the edges of the cookies are golden brown.

To form into cornets or "cigarettes," see above.

I might have named *mes truffes au chocolat* to honor my grandfather, Alexandre le Grand, because they contain Benedictine, the liqueur that he, in a sense, created. Benedictine is generally believed to have been invented and perfected by the Benedictine monks in the fourteenth century, but the facts are not nearly as simple as that. So many people have asked me whether it is actually true that my grandfather invented Benedictine that I have decided to tell the story as I know it.

Some people, hearing of my grandfather's role in the story of Benedictine, believe that he must have been a monk. No, he was a happily married man with 21 children and 180 grandchildren, of whom I am one!

My grandfather was a *négociant*—a man who sells wines and spirits —and his travels in the mid-nineteenth century took him to many parts of France. He was a very clever man with a variety of interests who loved old furniture and old things in general. One day, in going through his attic, he found in a large wooden chest a manuscript written in Old French. It proved to contain formulas for making elixirs, balms, and ointments that had been used by the Benedictine monks over the centuries.

My grandfather looked at the formulas again and again over a long period of time; and finally he singled out the one that interested him the most and decided to try it. He gathered together everything that was needed, carefully blended his brew, and then tasted it—it was a kind of pick-me-up—much too strong! But the idea had been planted in his mind, and he—very Normand and very stubborn—determined to perfect it. He worked for many years, experimenting with different ingredients. It was his idea to add tea, which the early monks did not have, and he added more honey and many other special things. Finally there were more than 27 ingredients, such as hyssop, angelica, melissa, myrrh, thyme, as well as various spices, and he was finally satisfied with his liqueur. In 1860 Benedictine was born.

Now, more than 100 years later, it is an important flavoring for my chocolate truffles.

Mes truffes au chocolat, aux noisettes ou aux amandes

CHOCOLATE TRUFFLES WITH PULVERIZED NUTS AND LIQUEUR

For about 50 chocolate truffles:

10 ounces German's sweet chocolate

½ pound hazelnuts, filberts, or almonds (enough to make about 1 ½ cups, *pulverized*)

¼ pound sweet butter, *softened*

4 tablespoons Benedictine liqueur

⅔ cup powdered bitter cocoa

Preheat the broiler.

Grate the chocolate into a heatproof (nonaluminum) mixing bowl.

Spread the pulverized nuts on an oven tray, and set them under the preheated broiler for 5 or 6 minutes to brown them slightly, stirring every minute to make them color evenly, being very careful not to let them burn.

Set the bowl of chocolate over simmering water. Mix the toasted nuts into the grated chocolate and stir; the chocolate will melt completely. Let cool. Then add the butter, stir until thoroughly mixed, add the Benedictine liqueur, and refrigerate to firm.

When very hard, roll one large tablespoon at a time into the powdered bitter cocoa to make uneven balls about an inch or so in diameter.

These are attractive when served in fluted paper cups. Keep them in the freezer until time to serve.

Variation: Substitute for the butter ½ cup of thick heavy cream.

———— •❦• ————

Thé glacé d'Elizabeth au citron

ICED TEA WITH LEMON JUICE

For a 2½-quart pitcher (to serve about 5):

2 tablespoons good Ceylon tea	1 cup sugar
4 or 5 lemons, to make 1 cup	Ice cubes
lemon juice, *strained*	

Fill the pitcher with ice cubes.

Steep the tea in 2 cups of boiling water for 3 or 4 minutes. Strain, add the lemon juice and the sugar, pour into the pitcher, and serve.

Vin de pêches d'Arlette

Red wine flavored with peach leaves, which must be made at least a week ahead, can be found on page 241 and *la Sangría de Bramafam,* which should be prepared the day before, on page 242.

29. *Le Cocktail*

A COCKTAIL PARTY

AMUSE-GUEULE ET BOUCHÉES

Mélange de noix et raisins secs
Mixture of nuts and raisins

Les pruneaux farcis/Warm stuffed prunes

Croustades savoyardes/Cheese tartlets

Quichettes soubise/Tiny onion quiches

Quichettes aux champignons
Tiny mushroom quiches

Quichettes aux aubergines
Tiny eggplant quiches

Tartelettes à la dijonnaise
Tomato and cheese tartlets

Bouchées demi-lune aux crustacés
Small pastries of shrimp and crab

Les croque-madame/Small hot cheese canapés

Les croquemitaine/Hot ham and cheese bouchées

Canapés basques aux sardines
Sardine butter on toast

RAFRAÎCHISSEMENTS PERSONNELS

Vin d'orange de Bramafam/White wine
with essence of orange

Vin de pêches d'Arlette
Peach-flavored red wine

La Sangría de Bramafam
Spiced red wine with oranges

Le cognac moka/Coffee, milk, and cognac, iced

Un champagne cocktail/Champagne cocktail

*T*he French style of dining seems to be making itself more and more felt in some parts of America; the reverse is true for cocktail parties. New York and Chicago have come to Paris and the cocktail party is very common now. But, as with all adaptations, it is done with some special differences, a strong French accent. I often give cocktail parties in my apartment in Paris, and the selections in this chapter reflect the kind of food and drinks that I serve.

I always serve a great array of canapés, but since recipes for these are available in many other books, I will not give them here.

To begin with, in Paris I set up a beautiful buffet table and, in the center, an elegant arrangement of flowers. In my house in Provence in the summer I use instead a very large bowl filled with arrangements of colorful vegetables—raw or partially raw—surrounded by smaller bowls of cold sauces or "dips." I fill the bowl first with tender leaves of lettuce; then, several "flowers," taken from a large head of cauliflower, which have been first blanched for 2 minutes in boiling water. This blanching is done to eliminate the rather bitter taste of the raw cauliflower, but still leave it quite crisp; it also makes the cauliflower a little more pliable so that other vegetables can be inserted, here and there, like bundles of colored crayons, in the cauliflower "flowers." Vegetables that lend themselves especially well to this treatment are clusters of raw carrots, cut into quarters and then into matchsticks, and raw celery stalks (first snapped in half and the strings removed), also cut into sticks. Next, if available, some new and very tender raw turnips; little radish flowers; cherry tomatoes; raw green and sweet red peppers cut into strips; some tender new scallions; green beans, or asparagus tips, peeled and blanched for a few minutes; fennel, the very tender heart, cut into pieces.

Two "dips" that I served frequently this past winter are the *sauce rosy* and the *mayonnaise au pistou*. *Sauce rosy* is a fresh dip of cream cheese whipped with grated raw cucumbers, then a little tomato paste to give flavor and make it pink. The *mayonnaise au pistou* is a very strongly flavored Provençal sauce with garlic and basil. These recipes will be found on page 307 and page 308.

Next, always, some of the little morsels that can be eaten in a single bite, which we call in France *amuse-gueule*. *Gueule,* in French slang, means mouth, and sometimes face—often of an animal. If you say, *"Quelle gueule!"* you mean, "What a face!" A difficult word to translate, perhaps; in the context of *amuse-gueule* it simply means something to "amuse your mouth." Some typical *amuse-gueule,* for example, would be bowls of olives or salted nuts. I find salted nuts, served alone, too salty and prefer to mix them with raisins, in the following combination:

Mixture of nuts and raisins to serve with cocktails

⅓ cup cashew nuts, ⅓ cup blanched, toasted almonds, cut into thick slivers, ⅓ cup pignolias, or pine nuts, to 1 cup of raisins. I usually combine half dark raisins with half yellow raisins, but I advise that you use yellow raisins only if you are sure that they have not been sulfurized. Other salted nuts can well be used; the only thing to remember is that the mixture is best when the total quantity of nuts equals the total quantity of raisins.

Other *amuse-gueule* that I like to serve at cocktail parties are steamed sausages with Dijon mustard, or:

----•◦•----

Les pruneaux farcis

WARM STUFFED PRUNES

For 20 to 25 stuffed prunes:

20 to 25 prunes	4 or 5 chicken livers
A pot of tea	2½ tablespoons butter

1½ tablespoons oil
Thyme, *pulverized*
Salt

Black pepper, *freshly ground*
2 or 3 tablespoons Cognac
12 small slices bacon

First make a pot of tea and put the prunes to steep in the tea. When they have swelled, carefully remove the pits without splitting the prunes all the way open. Clean the chicken livers and cut them in half. Heat the butter and oil in a frying pan, and sauté the livers for 2 or 3 minutes on each side, adding thyme, salt, and pepper. As soon as they have been turned, add the Cognac. Scrape the bottom of the pan to deglaze it, then flame the pan juices, and shake until the flame goes out. Let the chicken livers cool in their juice, then drain them on absorbent paper and cut them into pieces approximately the same size as the prune pits. Put a piece of liver into each prune, close up the prunes, and roll them each in a piece of bacon, securing it with a toothpick if necessary. Arrange them on an oven-proof plate.

Ten minutes before serving, put the prunes in a 400° oven or under the broiler and grill the bacon, turning them once during the cooking. Serve them warm.

For a simpler version of this recipe, one can stuff the prunes with a little piece of well-cooked salt pork or bacon, rolled, or a little piece of cooked sausage. The prunes should be grilled before serving them.

Another type of *amuse-gueule* is the bouchée, or "little mouthful," often made with pastry. I offer first some recipes for *quichettes* and tartlets. The recipes follow for the *croustades savoyardes* (with cheese), *quichettes aux champignons* (with mushrooms), and *quichettes soubise* (with onions). *Quichettes aux aubergines* (with eggplant) is a variation of the recipe on page 82. The *tartelette à la dijonnaise,* made with tomatoes, herbs, and cheese, is also made in little molds, but is not a quiche because it has no eggs or cream.

Croustades savoyardes

CHEESE TARTLETS

These can be made a day in advance and reheated for 10 minutes in a 375° oven.

For 25 to 30 tartlets:

Tartlet shells

1 recipe *pâte brisée "A"* (*p. 313*)

Recommended equipment: 25 tartlet molds 2 inches in diameter and ½ inch deep.

Make the pastry and put it into the refrigerator to firm.

To make the tartlets

1 cup imported Swiss cheese, *finely diced*
2 eggs
1 cup heavy cream
Salt

Black pepper, *freshly ground*
Nutmeg, *freshly grated*
¾ cup imported Swiss cheese, *grated*

Preheat the oven to 400°.

Roll out the pastry to a thickness of ⅛ inch. Line the tartlet molds (*technique, p. 324*) and prick in several places with a fork. In each tartlet shell, make a layer of the tiny squares of cheese, not too close together, pressing them slightly into the pastry. Refrigerate while preparing the filling.

Beat the eggs with the cream and season lightly with salt and liberally with pepper and nutmeg. Fill the tartlet shells and sprinkle with the grated cheese. Bake in the preheated oven for 12 to 15 minutes until the tartlets have swelled and the color is golden.

Unmold and serve tepid.

Note: The tartlets will deflate when cold.

————— •◦• —————

Quichettes soubise

TINY ONION QUICHES

These may be baked the day before and reheated for about 8 to 10 minutes in a 375° oven just before serving.

For 2 dozen quichettes:

Tartlet shells

1 recipe *pâte brisée "A" (p. 313)*

Recommended equipment: Two dozen 2-inch tartlet molds.

Make the pastry and put it in the refrigerator to firm. Roll it out to a thickness of ⅛ inch and fill the tartlet molds (*technique, p. 324*). Refrigerate to firm again before baking.

Onion filling

1½ tablespoons butter	2½ tablespoons flour
1 tablespoon peanut oil	¾ cup milk
About 7 medium-sized yellow onions, to make 3½ cups, *roughly chopped*	1 egg
	½ cup cream
Salt	Black pepper, *freshly ground*
¼ teaspoon saffron	Nutmeg, *freshly grated*

Heat the butter and oil in a large heavy skillet, add the chopped onions and ¼ teaspoon of salt, and stir over moderate heat for a few minutes to coat the onions with the butter and oil. Add the saffron, stir, cover the skillet, and let the onions cook very gently for 30 to 40 minutes, stirring from time to time, until they are golden and very tender.

Sprinkle the onions with the flour and stir over heat for 2 minutes longer. Remove from the heat, pour in the milk, and stir constantly until smooth. Return to the heat and continue to stir until thick. Remove from the heat. Beat the egg and cream together and add to the pan. Season with salt, pepper, and nutmeg.

To bake and serve   *Preheat the oven to 375°.*

Fill the uncooked pastry shells three-quarters full with the filling and bake in the preheated oven for about 12 to 15 minutes. Unmold and let them cool slightly before serving.

———— •◦• ————

Quichettes aux champignons

SIMCA'S SPECIAL MUSHROOM QUICHETTES

For 24 tartlets:

Pastry shells

1 recipe *pâte brisée "A"* (*p. 313*)   ½ cup imported Swiss or creamy Dutch cheese, *slivered*

Preheat the oven to 400°.

Recommended equipment: Two dozen tartlet molds 2 inches in diameter and ½ inch deep.

Make the pastry and put it into the refrigerator to firm.

Roll out the pastry to a thickness of ⅛ inch. Line the molds with the pastry (*technique, p. 324*), spread the cheese evenly on the bottom in one layer, pressing it into the dough, prick the bottom in several places with a fork, and refrigerate to firm again before baking. Bake in the preheated oven for about 10 to 12 minutes until crisp and *very* lightly colored. Set aside to cool.

Creamy mushroom filling

2 pounds white mushrooms   3 shallots or scallions, *minced*
Lemon juice   2½ tablespoons butter

1½ tablespoons oil   1 cup light cream, unsweetened
                                         evaporated milk, or milk

Thoroughly clean the mushrooms. If they are very small, leave them whole; otherwise, stem them and cut them into quarters. Sprinkle them with a little lemon juice to keep them white. Cook the shallots or scallions gently in the butter and oil for about 2 minutes until they are tender but not colored. Add the mushrooms in one layer, and cook, stirring, for about 3 minutes to heat them through. Cover them with the cream or milk and simmer very slowly for 15 to 20 minutes until the liquid has almost evaporated and the mushrooms are very lightly colored. *The mushrooms can wait a few hours before being baked.*

To assemble, bake, and serve

2 medium-sized eggs   Nutmeg, *freshly grated*
About ¾ cup heavy cream   2 tablespoons imported Swiss
Salt   cheese, *grated*
Black pepper, *freshly ground*

Preheat the oven to 375°.

Lightly beat the eggs with half of the heavy cream and season with salt, pepper, and nutmeg. Put a little of the mixture into each of the partially baked shells and add the mushrooms and more cream if necessary.

Top with the grated cheese, and place in the preheated oven to bake for about 15 to 20 minutes, until the top is golden brown.

Serve hot.

The *quichettes* may be reheated 8 to 10 minutes in a 375° oven.

Quichettes aux aubergines

Tiny eggplant quiches. Follow the recipe for the *quiche aux aubergines,* page 82, filling two dozen tartlet molds. The eggplant must be cut into smaller dice but otherwise the directions for filling and baking the *quichettes* are the same.

Tartelettes à la dijonnaise

TARTLETS OF TOMATOES AND CHEESE
WITH GARLIC AND HERBS

For 24 two-inch tartlets:

Tartlet shells

1 recipe *pâte brisée "A"* (*p. 313*)
2 tablespoons Dijon mustard

½ cup imported Swiss or
creamy Dutch cheese,
slivered

Recommended equipment: 24 tartlet molds or muffin tins 2 inches in diameter and ½ inch deep.

Make the pastry and set it into the refrigerator to firm.

Roll out the pastry to a thickness of about ⅛ inch and line the molds (*technique, page 324*). Brush the shells evenly with mustard, and sprinkle with the slivered cheese. Prick the bottom crusts in several places and refrigerate to firm before baking.

Preheat the oven to 375°.

Partially bake the shells for 10 to 12 minutes in the preheated oven. *The recipe can be made in advance to this point and the tart shells refrigerated or frozen.*

Tomato filling

3 pounds fresh ripe tomatoes, or 2 cups *purée de tomate provençale,* or 2 two-pound cans whole Italian plum tomatoes, *drained, refreshed with herbs* (*p. 301*)
3 tablespoons olive oil

1 small onion, to make ¼ cup, *chopped*
2 large cloves garlic, *minced*
½ teaspoon *each* dried thyme, oregano, marjoram, savory
Salt
Black pepper, *freshly ground*

If the tomatoes are fresh, skin, seed, and juice them (*technique, p. 325*). Chop them roughly.

Heat the olive oil in a skillet, add the chopped onions, and cook them, stirring from time to time, until they are soft but not colored. Add the tomatoes, the minced garlic, half of the herbs, and salt and pepper. If the tomatoes are fresh, simmer them for 5 to 10 minutes to cook them, but do not allow them to become a pulp; the pieces should retain their shape.

To bake and serve   *Preheat the oven to 375°.*

About 1 tablespoon olive oil   ½ cup cheese, same type as above,
                                                                    grated

Fill the partially baked tart shells with the tomato mixture. Sprinkle with drops of olive oil and the remaining herbs, and spread with the grated cheese. Finish baking the tartlets in the oven for about 15 minutes —just long enough to heat the pastry and the tomatoes and melt the cheese, which should form a glazed crust hiding the tomatoes.

Unmold, and serve.

———◆●◆———

Bouchées demi-lune aux crustacés

SMALL PASTRIES FILLED WITH SHRIMP AND CRABMEAT

In addition to the above, I often serve little pastries that I like to call *demi-lunes,* because they are rounds of pastry, covered with a filling, and folded over into the shape of a half-moon. The *demi-lunes aux crustacés* offered here are filled with shrimp and crabmeat, but once you have made these bouchées, you can vary the fillings endlessly. They are very easily and quickly made for drinks before dinner if you have some pastry in your freezer.

These can be made and baked in the morning, and reheated just before serving for 10 minutes in a 350° oven.

For 45 to 60 bouchées:

2 recipes *pâte brisée "A"* (*p. 313*)

Make the pastry and put it in the refrigerator to firm.

Shrimp and crabmeat filling

1 large or 2 medium apples, to make 1 cup, *peeled and diced*
Juice of ½ lemon
¼ pound tiny canned shrimps
½ pound canned crabmeat
3 tablespoons butter
1½ tablespoons peanut or vegetable oil

1 large or 2 medium-sized yellow onions, to make 1 cup, *chopped*
2 tablespoons flour
1 teaspoon curry powder
½ cup heavy cream
Salt
Black pepper, *freshly ground*
Tabasco

Peel, core, and dice the apples and sprinkle them with strained lemon juice to keep them white.

Strain the shrimps and crabmeat and combine their juices. There should be 1 cup of juice; if not, add some bottled clam juice or some water. Go over the crabmeat carefully to remove all the little pieces of cartilage.

Heat the butter in a skillet, add the shrimps, and sauté them for 2 minutes. Remove them with a slotted spoon and set them aside. Add the oil to the pan, heat it briefly with the butter, add the chopped onions, and cook them gently until they are soft and very lightly colored. Add the diced apples and cook until tender. Sprinkle with the flour and stir for about a minute to cook the flour; then moisten with 1 cup of the juice from the shrimps and crab, and continue to stir until smooth. Add the shrimps, the crabmeat, and the curry, and stir in the cream. Season with salt, pepper, and a little Tabasco to taste. Set aside to cool.

To assemble and bake

1 egg *beaten with* 1 tablespoon water

Preheat the oven to 400°.

Roll out the dough to a thickness of ⅛ inch. Using a round cutter about 4 inches in diameter (a saucer can be used if you do not have a cutter), cut out 60 rounds of dough. Place on a baking sheet or sheets, separating any layers with waxed paper. Refrigerate to firm again.

Put about 1 teaspoon of the shellfish mixture in the middle of each round of pastry, moisten the edges with cold water, and fold over to make "half-moons." Press the edges all around with a fork to seal the pastry tightly and make a decorative border, and glaze them with the beaten egg. Refrigerate for a few minutes to firm again before baking. Then bake in the preheated oven for 12 to 15 minutes until nicely browned. Serve hot.

The *croque-madame* and the *croquemitaine* are hot canapés made with ham and cheese. The *croque-madame,* for which the recipe will be found on page 27, is made with bread, the *croquemitaine* without it. It is best to serve little paper napkins with the *croquemitaine.*

——◆•◆——

Les croquemitaine

TINY HOT "SANDWICHES" OF HAM AND CHEESE

For 32 cocktail bouchées:

16 large, neat slices of boiled ham, about ¼ inch thick

8 slices imported Swiss cheese the same size as the ham, *at room temperature*

Spread 8 pieces of the ham on a board. Cover each with a slice of cheese and then with a second piece of ham, and press together thoroughly. Cut each into four squares to make the bouchées, or "little mouthfuls."

To prepare for baking

1 teaspoon peanut oil	A dash of cayenne pepper
1 egg	5 tablespoons flour
Salt	1 cup stale bread crumbs, *home-*
Black pepper, *freshly ground*	*made from good bread*

Lightly beat the egg with the oil and season it with salt, black pepper, and cayenne pepper. Spread the flour on a plate and the bread crumbs on another plate. Roll each bouchée in flour, dip into beaten egg, and roll in bread crumbs, using a knife or spatula to spread the bread crumbs and pat them down very neatly and evenly.

To bake and serve

Butter for the baking sheet	4 tablespoons butter, *melted*

Preheat the oven to 400°.

Put the bouchées onto a buttered baking sheet, sprinkle them with melted butter, and bake them in the preheated oven for about 5 minutes until they are nicely golden brown. Serve them piping hot, in little paper napkins or paper cases.

Canapés basques aux sardines

COLD CANAPÉS OF SARDINE BUTTER ON TOAST

The *canapés basques aux sardines* are cold canapés of sardine butter on toast. A *truc* for making the toast for cold canapés is to use stale bread, toast and butter it, and let it cool before spreading it with the covering mixture. This will ensure good, crisp toast when it comes time to serve the canapés.

A day or two ahead of time, slice the bread into halves (for a first course or luncheon) or into quarters (for a cocktail party), and set it aside to get stale.

To make 4 servings for lunch, or 32 cocktail bouchées:

8 slices *pain de mie* or other good sandwich bread
6 tablespoons butter
6 fine, fat French or Portuguese sardines (canned)
1 tablespoon wine vinegar

1½ tablespoons tarragon mustard or Dijon mustard mixed with tarragon
3 tablespoons mixed fresh tarragon and parsley, *chopped* (if dried, use less)
Black pepper, *freshly ground*

Lightly toast the stale bread, melt 2 tablespoons of the butter, and brush a little on each piece of bread. Set aside.

Crush the sardines with a fork. Blend in the remaining butter, the vinegar, and the mustard, working the mixture thoroughly. Add 1½ tablespoons of the chopped herbs, season with pepper, and refrigerate to firm. *The recipe may be prepared in advance to this point.*

Just before serving, spread the toast with the sardine butter, using a wet spatula to make it spread neatly, and garnish with the remaining chopped herbs.

At cocktail parties in France, we usually offer one or two plates of petits fours, particularly when serving champagne. Recipes will be found in the Tea section.

In addition to champagne and alcoholic drinks—iced whiskey, gin, or vodka—we always serve some nonalcoholic drinks such as fruit juice. For a refreshing orange drink, I use the juice of 4 large oranges, with 1 lemon, to 3 cups of water (this yields about 1 quart). Then I add sugar, and serve over ice.

I also serve some brews of my own invention.

———— ◆•◆ ————

Vin d'orange de Bramafam

WHITE WINE WITH ESSENCE OF ORANGE

The dry bitter oranges of Provence are what I ordinarily use in this *vin d'orange,* white wine flavored with orange rind, Cognac, and sugar. But it can be made with the oranges ordinarily found in the United States if only the peels are used.

This wine requires from 8 days to about a month of preparation, depending on whether or not you have dried orange peel on hand.

For about 1 quart:

8 large oranges, to yield about 4 ounces of dried peel
2 cloves
Small piece of cinnamon bark

1 quart dry white wine, of good quality
¼ to ⅓ cup sugar to taste
3 or 4 tablespoons *marc de Provence* or good Cognac

Remove the peel from the orange, and set it out to dry for at least two weeks (see page 324).

Put the dried orange peel into a jug or pitcher. Add the cloves and the cinnamon bark. Pour in the wine, plug or cover, and set in a cool place, sheltered from the light, to macerate for 8 to 10 days until the wine is imbued with the taste of orange. (If you must use the refrigerator, use the least cold part.)

Strain the wine. Pour 1 cup into an enameled saucepan, add sugar to taste, and stir over gentle heat, without letting the mixture boil, until the sugar has melted. Pour back into the wine in the jug, add the marc or Cognac, and stir.

You can serve the orange wine at once, or you can keep it for months in corked wine bottles. Serve it very cold, with a sliver of fresh orange peel in each glass.

———— ◆•◆ ————

Vin de pêches d'Arlette

RED WINE FLAVORED WITH PEACH LEAVES

The *vin de pêches d'Arlette* is the creation of my good friend Arlette Glaënzer. It is a light red wine with an elusive taste of almonds imparted by the leaves of peaches.

This wine is to be made about a week in advance.

For 2½ quarts:

120 peach leaves collected in springtime or 80 collected in the autumn
2 quarts good red wine
2 cups sugar

½ cup good *marc de Provence,* if you have the luck to have some; otherwise, good Cognac

Recommended equipment: 3 or 4 wine bottles, old or new; new corks.

If there is any chance that the peach leaves have been sprayed, wash them and dry them thoroughly between paper towels. Put them into a jug and pour in the wine. (If you do not have a jug large enough to hold all the wine, keep the remaining wine to add later.) Cork or cover the jug and put it in the coolest part of the house.

Taste the wine after 6 days; if it has the almond taste that will be imparted by the leaves, it is ready. If not, leave it for a few days longer, tasting it every day. (It is unlikely to need longer than 8 days.)

Strain the wine and discard the leaves. Put 3 cups of the wine and the 2 cups of sugar into an enameled saucepan, set over heat, and stir until the sugar has melted, without letting the mixture come to the boil. Pour back into the wine and add any reserved wine and the marc or Cognac. Fill and cork the wine bottles.

This *vin de pêches* can be kept a few weeks in a cool place away from the light. It may keep even longer, but I have never had the opportunity to find out, since my guests love it so much!

Serve the wine well chilled.

———◦•◦———

La Sangría de Bramafam

SANGRÍA

I often make this version of Sangría—a traditional drink from Spain—at our home in Provence.

This should be made in the morning for the evening, or a day in advance.

For about 3 quarts:

3 oranges
1 lemon
3 cloves

¾ cup confectioners' sugar
About 3 quarts good red wine
Branch of fresh mint

Wash the oranges and the lemon and cut them into thin slices. Put them into a large glass pitcher, add the cloves and sugar, and cover with the wine. Place in the coolest part of the kitchen until time to serve. Two hours before serving, stir, and add the branch of fresh mint.

Stir again, and serve with ice.

———◦•◦———

Le Cognac moka

EQUAL PARTS OF COFFEE, MILK,
AND COGNAC, ICED

This explosive mixture, *le Cognac moka,* will create atmosphere; the guests will see *la vie en rose.*

1 cup very good strong coffee
Sugar to taste

1 cup evaporated milk
1 cup Cognac

Pour the above into a cocktail shaker and shake vigorously. Pour into a jug of ice cubes, stir well, and serve.

Finally, a champagne cocktail:

———◆●◆———

Un champagne cocktail

This should be made 5 or 6 hours in advance.

For about 15:

1 orange
2 lumps sugar
Angostura bitters

¼ cup Cognac
3 bottles dry champagne

Wash and peel the orange, carefully removing only the orange skin, not the pith.

Put the orange peel into a cocktail shaker with the sugar (moistened with 3 dashes of Angostura bitters), the Cognac, and the champagne, and mix.

Serve chilled.

*A*long with the American concept of the cocktail party itself, we in France have also adopted the idea of the cocktail/buffet. The word *buffet* is French, meaning a side table on which refreshments are served, for example at a ball.

But the cocktail/buffet dinner, like the cocktail party itself, has come only fairly recently to France. However, it is done a little differently from the way it is customarily done in the United States. Dinner is formally announced and though the guests help themselves from the buffet table, they seat themselves at formal dining tables. Following are two typical French cocktail/buffet dinners, one for winter and one for summer.

Most of the recipes for these two buffets are to be found elsewhere in this book. The amounts to be served will vary. Even if you wish to serve a cocktail/buffet dinner for twice the number of people served by the recipe, you will not necessarily precisely double the ingredients. Because there are so many more dishes than at a normal dinner, guests will usually take less of each.

30. *Un buffet en hiver*

A WINTER BUFFET

Soufflé roulé farci aux crabes
Rolled crab soufflé

Vin blanc sec: Chablis

Quasi de veau en gelée, à l'anchois/Jellied
roast of veal, with anchovies

Vin rouge de Bordeaux: St.-Émilion

Gratin de céleri-rave à la dauphinoise
Gratin| of celeriac and potatoes

Salade de haricots verts provençale
Green bean salad Provençal

*Plateau de fromages: Bleu de Bresse ou
d'Auvergne, Pont l'Évêque ou Liverot,
Poivre d'Âne, St. Marcellin*
Assorted cheeses

Le "Mont Blanc" en surprise/Snow mousse
with center of walnut brittle or rum and raisins

Gâteau au chocolat: Le Doris
Chocolate cake with almonds

Les rosetta/Rosette cookies

Mes truffes aux chocolat/Chocolate truffles

Champagne demi-sec or:
Tout au Champagne brut
(or champagne, brut, throughout)

The winter buffet can be made almost completely in advance. The recipe for the crab soufflé will be found on page 75. It can stay warm, wrapped in foil in the turned-off oven, for about 20 minutes. But since it will stay on the buffet table for a certain period of time, it is best made as close to the last minute as possible. It is a dish that will look very attractive on the table, especially if formed into the shape of a fish, as described in the recipe. The tomato sauce (page 301) can be made in advance and reheated at serving time. The veal, designed to be served cold, can be prepared as long as 48 hours in advance. The recipe will be found on page 139. Should you wish to serve a hot vegetable, you might choose the *gratin de céleri-rave à la dauphinoise* on page 284. The rest of the dinner will be cold: the green bean salad on page 106, the *Mont Blanc* on page 185, the cake on page 107, the chocolate truffles on page 223, and the petits fours on page 216. The *Mont Blanc,* a frozen dessert, should not be set out until dessert time.

31. *Un buffet en été*

A SUMMER BUFFET

Barquettes de concombre aux crustacés
Cucumbers filled with crab and hard-boiled egg

Sardines en gelée Sainte Marine en timbales
Cold timbales of puréed sardines in aspic

Champagne rosé

Porc braisé au whiskey, froid
Pork braised with bourbon, cold

Vin rouge: Mâconnais ou Côtes de Beaune

Asperges vertes en vinaigrette "mimosa"
Asparagus in vinaigrette "mimosa"

Salade verte en vinaigrette
Green salad vinaigrette

Plateau de fromages variés:
Petit Suisse, Demi-Sel, Cantal, Brie
Assorted cheeses

Coupe de fruits glacés/Chilled fruits
with orange syrup and liqueur

Petits fours: Les dollars

Crème au chocolat meringuée
Frozen chocolate mousse

Petits fours: Les petits moka

Or *Tout au Champagne*
(or champagne throughout)

The summer buffet will begin with either the *barquettes de con-combre aux crustacés* or the *sardines en gelée Sainte Marine en timbales* —or both, for a large buffet. The first is cucumbers cut into little bar-quettes, or "boats," and piled with a filling of crabmeat and hard-boiled eggs bound with *sauce tartare.* The latter is timbales of puréed sardines in aspic. Both will be attractive on the buffet table. For the cucumbers I al-most always use canned crabmeat, the Russian Chatka variety, and I find the results perfectly satisfactory. These can easily be made a day in ad-vance, but in that case it is best not to cover them with the final garnish of cream and cream cheese until shortly before serving them. They should be served very cold and should therefore be quite highly sea-soned because chilling always tends to mute flavors. The sardines can also be prepared a day ahead of time and refrigerated before being deco-rated with chopped aspic and minced parsley.

The pork braised with bourbon will be found on page 6. Served cold, it is best cut into thin slices and surrounded with watercress. The recipe for asparagus mimosa is on page 90, *salade verte* on page 304, the petits fours on page 216, and the chocolate mousse on page 125. The other recipes follow.

— • • —

Barquettes de concombre aux crustacés

CUCUMBERS STUFFED WITH CRAB AND HARD-BOILED EGGS

For 10 to 12:

Salt
8 to 10 firm cucumbers (depending on size)
About ¾ pound crabmeat, fresh
or canned

About 6 ounces fresh shrimps
cooked and peeled, or small
canned shrimps
Black pepper, *freshly ground*
2½ cups boiled rice, *drained,*
dried, and cooled

Cut the cucumbers (unpeeled) into half lengthwise. Then cut in
half crosswise to make 40 pieces. Put the cucumbers into a large quantity
of boiling water; bring again to the boil, add a tablespoon of salt, and let
simmer, uncovered, for 15 to 18 minutes, until the cucumbers are tender
but not overcooked.

Drain in a colander and dry the pieces on paper towels. Then scrape
out the seeds with a teaspoon, leaving the shell, or barquette. Sprinkle
the barquettes with salt and pepper.

Drain the crabmeat and shrimps if canned and dry them on paper
towels (save the liquid for use in another recipe, such as a fish fumet).
Go over the crab to remove all tiny pieces of cartilage, and chop the
shrimps if they are large.

Sauce tartare

8 eggs, hard boiled plus 3 raw
egg yolks
2 tablespoons wine vinegar
2 tablespoons Dijon mustard
2 cups vegetable oil
Tabasco

2½ tablespoons mixed parsley,
chervil, and dill, *minced* (if
dried, use less)
½ cup heavy cream
4 ounces Philadelphia cream
cheese
Salt
Black pepper, *freshly ground*

Pound all of the hard-boiled egg yolks in a mixing bowl (reserving the white part to be used later), and work to a paste, adding the three raw egg yolks, the vinegar, and the mustard, pounding thoroughly until smooth. Add the oil by drops to begin with, then half a cup at a time until the sauce is thick and smooth. Season highly, adding a little Tabasco to taste. Put the egg whites through a food mill, ricer, or sieve, and add them to the sauce.

Mix the rice, crabmeat, and shrimps in the sauce; add 2 tablespoons of the minced herbs. Whip the cream and the cream cheese together and fold three-fourths of it into the mixture. Taste, and correct the seasoning.

Fill the barquettes, making a dome over each, coat with the remaining cream, and sprinkle with the remaining herbs. Refrigerate until time to serve.

Sardines en gelée Sainte Marine en timbales

COLD TIMBALES OF PURÉED SARDINES IN ASPIC

These can be made a few days in advance and refrigerated.

For 8 to 12:

20 medium-sized canned boneless Portuguese sardines
2 tablespoons butter
6 eggs, *hard boiled, 3 sieved, the rest sliced*
About ¼ cup lemon juice
Black pepper, *freshly ground*

2 packages gelatin
3 cups cold chicken stock or beef bouillon
1 cup sherry, white port, or dry white wine
Tabasco (*optional*)

Recommended equipment: 18 third-cup or 8 half-cup timbale molds.

Remove the skin from the sardines (leaving the bones) and mash them with a fork, adding the butter, to make a smooth purée. Add the 3 sieved hard-boiled eggs, and the strained lemon juice to taste, and season with pepper.

Dissolve the gelatin in ¾ cup of the cold stock. Bring the rest of the stock and the wine to a boil. Remove from the heat and stir in the dissolved gelatin. This jelly should be very highly seasoned: add pepper, or a dash of Tabasco.

Pour ¼ inch of jelly into each mold and set the molds into the refrigerator for a few minutes until the jelly is partially set. Press a slice of hard-boiled egg into the jelly, then fill the molds three-fourths full of the sardine mixture and fill to the top with jelly. Put the remaining jelly into a square dish. Set all in the refrigerator to chill.

To serve

Tender leaves of Boston lettuce · 1 tablespoon parsley, *chopped*

Chop the reserved jelly.

Line a serving dish with tender leaves of lettuce. Unmold the aspics onto the bed of lettuce by running a warm, wet pointed knife between the mold and the aspic. Surround the timbales with the remaining sliced eggs and chopped aspic, sprinkle with parsley, and serve.

Coupe de fruits glacés

MIXED CHILLED FRUITS
WITH ORANGE SYRUP AND LIQUEUR

This is best when made a day or a few hours ahead of time, and chilled.

For 6:

1 lemon
5 oranges
⅔ cup sugar
1 beautiful apple, *cut into ½-inch dice*

1 juicy ripe pear, *cut into ½-inch dice*
2 fine ripe bananas, *sliced*
2 or 3 branches of fresh mint (if possible)

½ pound red fruits: frozen raspberries or strawberries, *de-*
 frosted and drained; or
 canned dark cherries, *drained*

⅓ cup walnuts, *roughly chopped*
3 or 4 tablespoons kirsch, rum,
 Benedictine, or orange
 liqueur, to taste

Squeeze the juice from the lemon and 2 of the oranges into an enameled saucepan. Add the sugar and 1 cup of water to the juice, set over heat, and stir until the sugar has melted and the syrup is beginning to reach the thread stage (230° on a candy thermometer, or until a teaspoon dropped into a bowl of cold water is sticky to the touch). Let cool.

Peel the 3 remaining oranges and cut them into thin slices, removing the seeds; put them into a crystal serving bowl. Add the diced apple and pear, and the sliced bananas, and toss all with the syrup and one stalk of fresh mint, being careful not to bruise the fruit. Refrigerate for 2 or 3 hours.

About half an hour before serving, add the drained raspberries, strawberries, or cherries, the walnuts, and the liqueur. Mix gently and remove the mint.

Serve very cold, with a branch or two of fresh mint broken into pieces and inserted here and there in the bowl of fruit in "bouquets."

Note: If you cannot find fresh mint to make a nice decoration, you can add some glacéed fruits (like green angelica cut into dice or pieces of candied orange rind, or any other glacéed fruit cut into small dice). This can also be served accompanied by a sabayon (p. 290).

LES AUTRES
PLATS DE CHOIX

Other Favorite Dishes

*T*he following collection of recipes consists of dishes, some of them my very favorites, which for one reason or another did not lend themselves to inclusion in a menu. They comprise a few hot and cold entrées, some main courses, vegetables, *salades composées,* and desserts. Some of them, like the *crème au chocolat de Zulma,* which was often made by our family cook Zulma in Normandy, or the *oeufs farcis à la Chimay,* which was originated by the great Antonin Carême, are very old dishes. Others, like the *poulet Île de France en ramequins* or *canards en cocotte aux deux purées,* are special creations or adaptations of my own, which require a little more time and trouble than other recipes in this book, but which I hope will please more advanced cooks. Others, like the *filets de poisson à la normande,* are dishes that I have created especially for American students who have requested recipes that can be quickly made. The recipes in this section, however, have one thing in common— I could not bear to leave out any one of them!

Soupe normande

PURÉED SOUP OF BEANS WITH
BUTTER AND CREAM

For 6:

1 pound flageolet beans, dried pea
    beans, or dried baby lima
    beans
1 cup celery, *sliced*
5 tablespoons butter
2 medium onions, to make 1 cup,
    sliced
4 medium carrots, *sliced*

½ cup leeks, *sliced*
2 tablespoons flour
3 to 5 tablespoons heavy cream or
    evaporated milk
Bunch of chervil, *finely chopped*
    (2 to 2½ teaspoons if dried)
Salt
Black pepper, *freshly ground*

Put the beans into a heavy-bottomed 3-quart saucepan and cover them liberally with cold water. Bring slowly to the boil, add 2 tablespoons of salt, and simmer until the beans are tender and slightly in purée (about 1 to 1½ hours).

Remove the beans with a slotted spoon and set them aside. Add the sliced celery to the cooking liquid, and simmer until it has reduced to 7 cups. Strain the cooking liquid into a bowl, set the celery aside with the beans, and clean the pan.

Heat 3 tablespoons of butter in the pan, add the sliced onions and carrots, and sauté them slowly for about 10 minutes, stirring occasionally to cook them evenly. Then add the sliced leeks and cook for about 5 minutes longer. Sprinkle on the flour, and stir for 2 to 3 minutes to coat the vegetables with the flour. Remove from the heat.

Pour in the cooking juice from the beans, return to the heat, stirring until smooth, add a little pepper, bring to the boil, cover, and simmer for 20 to 30 minutes until all the vegetables are tender.

Add the celery and the beans, reserving 18 beans for decoration, and reheat the soup. Then put it through a food mill or spin briefly in the blender at low speed. Pour the purée back into the pan, set over medium heat, and stir in the cream or milk by spoonfuls. Remove from the heat, season with salt and pepper, and add half of the chervil.

Serve in warm soup cups or a tureen, decorated with the remaining chervil and the reserved beans.

Velouté de tomate

TOMATO SOUP

For 6:

8 fine well-ripened tomatoes	3½ tablespoons flour
1 cup onions, *sliced*	6 cups chicken bouillon
3 to 4 tablespoons olive oil	1 stalk celery
1 clove garlic, *crushed*	Bouquet of parsley
1 tender leek or scallions, to make	Salt
¼ cup, *minced*	Black pepper, *freshly ground*
1 large carrot, *cut in small rounds*	

Skin, seed, and quarter the tomatoes (*technique, p. 325*).

Sauté the sliced onions in the olive oil until golden, stirring from time to time. Add a little more oil, if necessary, 8 of the tomato quarters, and the crushed garlic, and cook until the tomatoes are brown and the juice has evaporated. Add the minced leek or scallions and the carrot slices and continue cooking until the edges of the vegetables are lightly brown and the moisture has evaporated.

Sprinkle on the flour, and stir for 2 or 3 minutes to coat the vegetables with the flour. When the mixture is thick and smooth, pour in 2 cups of the bouillon, stirring over heat until smooth, add the remaining tomatoes, the stalk of celery, and the bouquet of parsley, and continue to cook over a moderate heat for about 20 minutes, stirring occasionally, until the tomatoes have rendered their juice and a sort of purée has formed. Pour in the remaining bouillon, mix thoroughly until smooth, and let simmer for 20 minutes longer.

Pass the soup through a vegetable mill. Correct the seasoning, and return the velouté to the saucepan. *The soup may be made 24 hours in advance to this point.*

To serve

1½ tablespoons parsley, *minced*   Small croutons (*p. 320*)

Pour the soup into a warmed soup tureen or into individual soup cups, and sprinkle with minced parsley and croutons.

———————•◦•———————

Oeufs farcis à la Chimay

EGGS STUFFED WITH MUSHROOMS AND
SHALLOTS, IN MORNAY SAUCE

This dish can be prepared ahead of time and reheated before serving.

For 4 to 5:

½ pound white mushrooms, *cleaned and stemmed*
Lemon juice
2 tablespoons butter
4 shallots or scallions, *minced*
6 eggs, *hard boiled*

2 tablespoons mixed parsley and chervil, *finely chopped* (if dried, use half the amount)
1 to 3 tablespoons heavy cream
Salt
Black pepper, *freshly ground*

Mince the mushrooms and sprinkle them with a few drops of lemon juice to keep them white. Heat the butter in a skillet, add the minced shallots or scallions, and cook until they are tender but not colored, stirring from time to time with a wooden spoon. Add the chopped mushrooms and sauté, stirring, until all the juice has evaporated; the mushrooms must be dry.

Cut the hard-boiled eggs very evenly in half lengthwise and pound the yolks in a bowl with the mushrooms, chopped parsley, and chervil, working the mixture to make a paste.

Stir the cream in by spoonfuls, being careful not to let the mixture become runny, and season highly with salt and pepper. Fill the egg whites with the mixture, making a dome; then set aside while preparing the sauce.

Mornay sauce

2 tablespoons butter	¼ cup heavy cream
3 tablespoons flour	Salt
2 cups milk	Black pepper, *freshly ground*
¼ cup imported Swiss cheese, *grated*	Nutmeg, *freshly grated*

In a heavy-bottomed enameled saucepan set over heat, melt the butter. Stir in the flour and cook, stirring, for a few seconds. Remove from the heat and pour in all the milk. Return to the heat and stir vigorously until the sauce is smooth; then bring to the boil and simmer for 2 minutes. Stir the cream into the sauce, add half of the cheese, and season highly with salt, pepper, and nutmeg.

To assemble, cook, and serve	*Preheat the broiler.*
2 tablespoons bread crumbs, *made from stale homemade brown bread*	1½ tablespoons chilled butter

Spread a film of the sauce into a shallow baking-serving dish. Place the eggs in the dish in a nice arrangement and coat them with the remaining sauce. Cover with the remaining cheese combined with the bread crumbs, and dot with tiny pieces of butter.

A few minutes before serving put under the preheated broiler for about 5 minutes, until brown. *If the dish has been prepared ahead of time, it should be reheated in a 375° oven for about 15 minutes before being browned under the broiler.*

Serve in the baking dish.

Ramequins forestières

MUSHROOMS IN CREAM WITH HAM,
SHALLOTS, AND HERBS, MOLDED

These ramekins are named for hunters who come home with nothing to show for their day's hunting but a few handfuls of woodland mushrooms. They can either be presented in their molds, or unmolded and served in a tarragon cream sauce. They can be prepared in advance and reheated in the oven in a bain-marie.

For 6 to 8:

Butter and bread crumbs to coat
    the ramekins
2 pounds white mushrooms,
    cleaned and trimmed
Juice of 2 lemons
2 tablespoons shallots or scallions,
    minced
5 tablespoons butter
2 cups plus 4 tablespoons heavy
    cream
6 eggs

About 1 cup bread crumbs, *home-
    made from good toasted stale
    bread*
½ pound boiled or baked ham,
    diced
2½ tablespoons tarragon or half
    tarragon and half parsley,
    chopped (if dried, use less)
Salt
Black pepper, *freshly ground*
Nutmeg, *freshly grated*

Preheat the oven to 375°.

Recommended equipment: 12 half-cup ramekins, or 18 third-cup ramekins (individual baking dishes), or a 2-quart charlotte mold, soufflé dish, or casserole.

Butter the ramekins or mold and sprinkle the bottom and sides with bread crumbs. Shake off excess bread crumbs.

Cut the mushrooms into thin slices (vertically) and sprinkle them with the lemon juice, to keep them white.

Cook the minced shallots or scallions in the butter for a few minutes until they are soft. Add the sliced mushrooms and sauté them, stirring, for about 5 minutes. Then pour in 1 cup of the cream and cook the mushrooms gently for 15 to 20 minutes, continuing to stir from time to time, until they are tender and have absorbed almost all the cream. Remove from the heat.

Beat the eggs lightly with a fork, and add them to the mushrooms, with the bread crumbs, the diced ham, and the remaining cream, stirring thoroughly. (The mixture will be thick.) Add the herbs, and season with salt, pepper, and nutmeg to taste.

Fill the ramekins or the mold three-fourths full, and put into a shallow pan with water to come a third of the way up the sides of the ramekins or 1½ inches up the sides of the mold. Bring the water to the simmer on top of the stove. Then set the pan into the oven to cook 10 to 12 minutes for the small ramekins, 13 to 15 minutes for the half-cup size, or 20 to 25 minutes for a large mold.

Serve in the ramekins or mold.

Variation: Serve unmolded, coated with 2 cups tarragon cream sauce, page 303.

Courgettes panachées

COLD DISH OF ZUCCHINI AND TOMATOES
WITH OLIVE OIL, GARLIC, AND LEMON

This refreshing cold hors d'oeuvre is suitable for a luncheon or picnic. Very simply made, it can be prepared in advance and kept several days in the refrigerator. It can be accompanied by slices of salami or radishes and butter.

For 6:

2 pounds small zucchini
1 pound small ripe tomatoes

2 large cloves garlic, *peeled and minced*

3 tablespoons olive oil
2 tablespoons lemon juice
1 tablespoon chervil, *finely chopped*

1 tablespoon tarragon, *finely chopped* (if dried, use half the amount)
Salt
Black pepper, *freshly ground*
1 large lemon

Peel the zucchini and cut into ¾-inch slices. Peel and seed the tomatoes (*technique, p. 325*) and chop roughly.

In an enameled skillet, put the zucchini, the tomatoes, the minced garlic, the olive oil, 2 tablespoons of strained lemon juice, and half of the chopped herbs. Season with salt and pepper. Stir, bring to the boil, and let simmer uncovered until the zucchini are tender (25 to 30 minutes).

Peel the lemon, remove the seeds, and roughly chop the pulp. Remove the vegetables from the heat and stir in the lemon. Let cool. When cold, put into a serving dish, sprinkle with the remaining herbs, and refrigerate to be served nicely chilled.

Timbale de poisson, Selma

FILLETS OF FISH MOLDED IN TOMATO PURÉE

This recipe can be prepared a day in advance.

For 6 to 8 (8 as a first course):

1½ pounds red snapper or flounder fillets
2½ pounds ripe tomatoes, or canned Italian plum tomatoes, *drained and refreshed with herbs*
2 or 3 large cloves garlic, *peeled*
Pinches of thyme, oregano, and savory
2 tablespoons olive oil

½ pound onions (about 3 medium onions), *finely chopped*
Pinch of saffron
Salt
Black pepper, *freshly ground*
4 eggs, *beaten with a fork*
2 tablespoons butter
½ recipe *sauce rosy (p. 307)*
Parsley, *chopped*

Recommended equipment: A 2-quart charlotte mold, soufflé mold, or other deep baking dish.

Wash the fish fillets and pat them dry.

Peel and seed the tomatoes if fresh (*technique, p. 325*), or drain and refresh if canned. Cut the tomatoes into quarters, press them lightly to remove their juice, and simmer them in a large heavy skillet or omelet pan with the peeled garlic and the herbs.

Warm the olive oil in a smaller skillet, add the chopped onions, and cook them slowly until they are a light golden brown. Stir them into the tomatoes and continue to cook gently until the mixture has almost the texture of a purée. Then put through a food mill, season with salt, pepper, and saffron, and return to the pan.

Cut the fish fillets into pieces 2 inches long and 1 inch wide, and sprinkle them with salt and pepper. Add to the tomato purée as many fillets as will fit in one layer and poach them over gentle heat for 5 minutes. Remove them with a slotted spoon and replace with another layer. Continue until all the fillets have been poached. Return them all to the pan and gently stir in the beaten eggs and 2 tablespoons of melted butter; do not let the mixture boil. Taste, and correct the seasoning.

To assemble and bake   *Preheat the oven to 375°.*

Butter for the mold

Cut a round of waxed paper to fit the bottom of the mold. Butter the paper and press it into the mold, buttered side up. Butter the sides of the mold. Put the fish mixture into the mold, and the mold into a shallow pan. Pour about an inch of water into the pan, and bring the water slowly to a simmer on top of the stove. Then cover the mold and bake for 35 to 40 minutes until the timbale is set.

Let the timbale cool and put it into the refrigerator to chill.

Prepare the *sauce rosy* (*p. 307*).

To serve

Unmold the timbale, coat it with a little of the sauce, and sprinkle it with chopped parsley. Serve the remaining sauce in a sauceboat.

———— ◆•◆ ————

Couronne de poisson en gelée à la portuguaise

RING OF FISH MOUSSE IN ASPIC

This fish purée can be made up to two days in advance.

Fish fumet

For 6 to 8:

1 medium carrot, *thinly sliced*
1 medium onion, *thinly sliced*
Approximately 2 cups fish trim-
    mings—head, skin, and
    bones
4 sprigs parsley
½ bay leaf
¼ teaspoon thyme

Pinch of saffron, fennel, or dill
Pinch of chili powder
Black pepper, *freshly ground*
¼ teaspoon salt
2 cups dry white wine
1 pound lean skinned fish fillets
    (lemon sole, flounder, whit-
    ing, silver hake)

Put the sliced carrot and onion into a saucepan (preferably enamel) with the fish trimmings, the herbs, and the seasonings. Add the wine, bring to a boil, and simmer for 30 minutes.

Strain the fish fumet, return it to the pan, and let it cool. Add the fish fillets, bring slowly to the simmer, and cook them at just below the simmer for about 8 minutes, until a fork will easily pierce the fish but the fish is not dry and flaky. Drain the fish, return the fumet to the pan, and boil it down until it has reduced to 1 cup. Set aside.

Mousse mixture

2 tablespoons tomato paste
2 tablespoons mixed fresh green
    herbs (dill, parsley, chives
    or scallion tops, basil),
    minced

About ⅛ teaspoon garlic, *peeled
    and mashed*
1¼ cups tiny fresh or canned
    shrimps, *cooked*
2 tablespoons gelatin
¾ cup chilled heavy cream

Recommended equipment: A 4- or 5-cup ring mold, fish mold, or other mold.

Put the cooked fish fillets through the finest blade of the food mill. Mix the fish purée with the tomato paste, the herbs, the mashed garlic, and all but a dozen of the shrimps.

Soften the gelatin in ½ cup of the fish fumet, and then heat gently to dissolve completely. Add it to the fish and beat vigorously until the mixture is smooth. Correct the seasoning.

Whip the cream over ice cubes until soft peaks are formed. Delicately fold the cream into the fish mixture. Set aside.

To prepare the mold

1 tablespoon gelatin	1 teaspoon tomato paste

Soften the gelatin in the remaining ½ cup of fish fumet; when softened, stir over gentle heat to dissolve. Beat in the tomato paste, season to taste, and stir over cracked ice until the gelatin is cold and almost syrupy. Pour about ⅓ inch into the bottom of the mold, swirl it around, and place the mold into a bowl of ice cubes long enough to coat the bottom. After about 3 minutes, when the jelly is beginning to set, press the remaining shrimps against the jelly lining in a decorative pattern. Chill until set. Mix the remaining shrimps into the fish mixture, then pack all into the prepared mold and chill until set.

To serve

½ recipe *sauce rosy* (*p. 307*)

Serve, unmolded, with *sauce rosy.*

———•••———

Filets de soles, d'Eve

ROLLED FILLETS OF SOLE ON BAKED APPLES,
MASKED WITH A VELOUTÉ SAUCE

For 8:

Fish fumet

16 fillets of sole, ¼ pound each
Bones and trimmings from the
    sole
1 carrot, *sliced*
1 onion, *sliced*

Bouquet garni of thyme, ½ bay
    leaf, parsley, celery stalk
1¾ cups dry white wine
Salt
Black pepper, *freshly ground*

Wash the bones and trimmings from the fish and chop them roughly. Combine them in a saucepan with the sliced vegetables and the bouquet garni. Add the wine, and bring to a boil. Add 4 cups of cold water and salt and pepper, and let barely simmer for 25 minutes.

Strain the fish fumet, return it to the pan, and simmer it, uncovered, until it has reduced to 2 cups. Taste, correct the seasoning, and set aside.

Herb butter

4 or 5 tablespoons tarragon, pars-
    ley, chervil, or dill, or com-
    bination, *minced* (if dried,
    use half the amount)

1½ sticks butter, *softened*
Salt
Black pepper, *freshly ground*

Blend the herbs into the butter with a fork. Season with salt and pepper and refrigerate until firm.

Apple garniture

16 medium-sized Golden De-
    licious apples

1 lemon
Butter for the baking dish

Preheat the oven to 350°.

Carefully peel and core the apples, removing as little of the flesh as possible. Rub them with lemon, and arrange them in a buttered shallow baking dish. Bake them in the preheated oven for 25 to 30 minutes until they are tender but still hold their shape well. Arrange them on an oval serving platter, and keep them warm.

Duxelles filling

1 pound very fresh white mush- rooms	3 shallots or scallions, *minced*
	Salt
Juice of 1 lemon	Black pepper, *freshly ground*
2½ tablespoons butter	Nutmeg, *freshly grated*
½ tablespoon oil	

Thoroughly clean and dry the mushrooms and remove the stems (which can be saved for another purpose). Chop them very finely and sprinkle them with strained lemon juice. Put a handful of the chopped mushrooms in the corner of a towel, wrap tightly, and squeeze out all the liquid; the mushrooms must be as dry as possible.

Heat the butter and the oil in a skillet, add the minced shallots or scallions, and cook until soft but not colored. Stir in the mushrooms, and sauté them, stirring from time to time, for about 7 or 8 minutes. They will begin to separate, forming little dry particles. Season highly. The mushroom *duxelles* is now ready to be spread over each fillet.

To prepare the fillets and the stock

Butter for casserole	2 cups fish fumet (*above*)

Preheat the oven to 375°.

Make slashes with a knife on the skin side (back) of the fillets, and spread a spoonful of the herb butter and the *duxelles* on each fillet. Then roll the fillets into *paupiettes* and arrange them carefully in a buttered casserole, preferably an enameled one. Cover them to three-fourths of their height with the fish fumet, then with a buttered piece of waxed paper (buttered side down). Bring to a simmer on the top of the stove; then bake in the preheated oven for 7 to 10 minutes, depending on the thickness of the fish. Drain the fish, pouring off the liquid and straining it (there should be 2¼ to 2½ cups). Reduce over high heat to 2 cups. Meanwhile, place a fillet on each apple, and keep warm.

Velouté sauce

2½ tablespoons butter
3 tablespoons flour
2 cups reduced fish cooking liquid
    (*above*)
Salt

Black pepper, *freshly ground*
Juice of ½ lemon
1 cup heavy cream
4 to 5 egg yolks, depending on size

In a saucepan, preferably enamel or glass, melt the butter, add the flour, and cook, stirring, for a few seconds. Remove from heat and add the reduced fish cooking liquid. Blend thoroughly until smooth, correct the seasoning, and if desired add lemon juice to taste. Beat the cream with the egg yolks. Reheat the sauce, incorporate a little of the hot sauce with the cream and eggs, and finally combine the two over heat until smooth.

To assemble

1 lemon, *fluted and cut into slices*

Spread the sauce over the sole and apples and decorate the serving platter with slices of lemon. Serve immediately.

——•◦•——

Filets de poisson à la normande

FISH FILLETS AND MUSHROOMS
BAKED IN A VELOUTÉ SAUCE

For 6:

6 fillets of sole, whiting, cod, or
    comparable fish
About 1 tablespoon butter,
    melted
2½ tablespoons tarragon, *minced*
    (if dried, 2 to 3 teaspoons)

Salt
Black pepper, *freshly ground*
½ pound small white mushrooms
    (or larger mushrooms,
    stemmed)
⅓ cup milk or evaporated milk

Recommended equipment: A baking-serving dish, about 12 inches long, 8 inches wide, and 2½ inches deep.

Split the fish fillets in half; wash and dry them.

Brush the baking dish with melted butter and sprinkle in half of the tarragon. Make some slashes with a sharp knife on the skin side of the fillets. Season with salt and pepper and fold them each in half, skin side inside. Arrange them in the dish and set aside.

Slice the mushrooms. Put them into a frying pan in one layer, cover them with the milk, and set over low heat. When they have absorbed all or almost all of the milk, they will be done (10 to 15 minutes).

Velouté sauce

2½ tablespoons butter
3½ tablespoons flour

1½ cups fish fumet (*p. 298*)
or canned clam juice

In an enameled saucepan set over heat, melt the butter. Stir in the flour, and cook, stirring, for a few seconds. Remove from heat and pour in the fish stock or clam juice, stirring. Return to the heat and continue to stir until the sauce is smooth.

To bake and serve

Juice of 1 lemon
½ to ⅔ cup heavy cream

Nutmeg, *freshly grated*

Preheat the oven to 375°.

Turn the cooked mushrooms and any milk remaining in the pan into the velouté sauce, and season with salt, pepper, and a dash of nutmeg. Sprinkle with strained lemon juice to taste, add the cream, and mix thoroughly over the heat. Pour the sauce over the fish fillets, and set into the preheated oven for about 12 to 15 minutes, depending on the thickness of the fillets. The top should be nicely browned.

Serve in the baking dish, sprinkled with the remaining tarragon.

————— ◆◆ —————

Poisson braisé au cidre
ou au vin blanc

FISH BRAISED WITH
CIDER OR WHITE WINE

For 6 to 8:

A 4- to 5-pound bass   Black pepper, *freshly ground*
Salt

Thoroughly clean and rinse the fish. Season it inside with salt and pepper.

Filling

5 shallots or scallions, *minced*   2 hard-boiled egg yolks, *pounded*
2½ tablespoons butter   Salt
4 tablespoons stale bread crumbs,   Black pepper, *freshly ground*
   homemade from good bread   Nutmeg, *freshly grated*

Cook the shallots or scallions in the butter for 2 or 3 minutes, until they are soft but not brown. Add the bread crumbs, stir, and then add the pounded egg yolks. Mix thoroughly, and season with salt, pepper, and nutmeg.

To bake

Oil for baking dish   3 tablespoons butter, *melted*
1 lemon, *cut into 6 very thin*   3 cups hard dry cider (*bought in a*
   wedges   *liquor store*) or good dry
2 to 3 tablespoons stale bread   white wine
   crumbs, *homemade from*   2 to 3 tablespoons heavy cream
   good bread   ½ teaspoon cornstarch

Preheat the oven to 375°.

Fill the fish with the stuffing, close it with toothpicks, and place in an oiled baking dish. Make 2 or 3 slits on the back of the fish to help the cooking, and insert the wedges of lemon, like a fan. Sprinkle the fish with bread crumbs and then melted butter. Pour in the cider or wine, and set into the oven to bake for 25 to 30 minutes, depending on the thickness of the fish, basting two or three times, until the skin has burst a little near the fins and the flesh is milky white. Do not overcook. When the fish is almost done, remove from the oven. Pour the cooking juices through a strainer into an enameled saucepan, add the cream mixed with cornstarch, set over heat, and let it blend with the cooking juices to thicken them slightly, stirring over heat with a fork or whip to make it all smooth. Return the sauce to the pan and the fish to the oven to finish cooking. Taste the sauce, and correct the seasoning.

To serve

Remove the fish to a platter, coat it with some of the sauce, and serve the rest of the sauce in a sauceboat.

Variation: Fillets of red snapper or flounder can be used instead. Fold or roll the fillets to enclose the filling, and reduce the cooking time to 10 to 12 minutes, depending on the thickness of the fillets.

———— •◦• ————

Chapon d'Honfleur

CAPON OR CHICKEN WITH CIDER OR
WHITE WINE, COOKED WITH CREAM AND APPLES,
SERVED WITH RICE

For 6:

4 pounds tart cooking apples
Lemon juice
About ½ pound butter
2 tablespoons peanut oil

Cinnamon or ginger
A 4- to 5-pound capon or fat
  chicken
4 or 5 shallots or scallions, *minced*

Pinch of thyme

2 cloves

2 teaspoons sugar

2 cups hard dry cider (bought in a
   liquor store) or dry white
   wine

1½ cups uncooked rice

1 teaspoon arrowroot or cornstarch

1½ cups heavy cream

Salt

Black pepper, *freshly ground*

Chervil or parsley, *finely minced*

Preheat the oven to 400°.

Peel, core, and quarter the apples and sprinkle them with lemon juice to keep them white.

In a large heavy skillet, heat ⅓ cup of butter and the oil. Add half of the quartered apples and sauté them in one layer over moderate heat, turning them once, until they are lightly colored and half cooked—5 or 6 minutes. Remove and season the sautéed apples lightly with cinnamon or ginger. Sprinkle the inside of the capon or chicken with salt and pepper and fill it with the sautéed apples, reserving their cooking juices. Sew the openings with thread or secure with skewers, and rub the capon liberally with butter. Put it into a heavy pot, and set, uncovered, into the preheated oven for about 20 minutes to brown well on all sides, turning it as each side browns.

Remove the pot from the oven, set it over moderate heat, and add 2 tablespoons of butter.

When the butter is melted, stir in the minced shallots or scallions, the remaining apples, additional cinnamon or ginger, the thyme, cloves, and sugar, and cook for 6 to 7 minutes very gently; then add the reserved cooking juices from the sautéed apples.

Turn up the heat to high and pour in the cider or wine, ½ cup at a time, waiting each time for the liquid to return to the boil before adding the next ½ cup. Cover the capon with waxed paper. Then put the lid on the pot and return to the oven to cook for 45 to 55 minutes longer until the capon is tender. Halfway through the cooking time turn the capon and add more salt.

Rice

Cook the rice in boiling salted water for 10 minutes. Rinse it under cold water, put it in a buttered baking dish, dot with butter, and let it finish cooking in the oven with the capon for the last 15 to 20 minutes.

To serve

Remove the capon to a warm serving dish and keep it warm while completing the sauce.

Strain the cooking juices and remove the fat (*technique, p. 320*). Return the juices to the pot; if too thin, reduce them over high heat. Dissolve the arrowroot or cornstarch in 2 tablespoons of the cream, then blend with the rest of the cream and pour into the pot. Stir the sauce as it thickens. Taste and correct the seasoning.

Carve the capon and arrange it on the serving platter, placing the apple stuffing in the middle and the rest of the apples around the outside. Spread a little of the sauce on the capon, and sprinkle it with the minced chervil or parsley. Serve the remaining sauce in a sauceboat.

Serve the warm buttered rice separately in a warm vegetable dish.

Poulet gratiné savoyard

CHICKEN AND SMALL ONIONS
IN CHEESE AND CREAM

For about 4:

16 small white onions, about ½ inch in diameter
¼ pound butter
1½ tablespoons oil
1 cup dry white wine
1 medium yellow onion, to make ½ cup *chopped*

1 frying chicken, about 3 to 4 pounds, *cut into 8 pieces*
Black pepper, *freshly ground*
Salt
½ cup chicken stock
Sprig of thyme
½ bay leaf

Preheat the oven to 375°.

Recommended equipment: A large, shallow, buttered baking dish.

Peel the small onions, being careful not to cut into the skin.

Heat half of the butter with the oil in a medium-sized skillet, add the small onions, and cook them for about 5 minutes, shaking the pan from time to time to brown them evenly. Pour in the white wine and parboil for about 5 minutes longer.

Heat the remaining butter in a heavy-bottomed saucepan or skillet with a lid. Add the chopped onions, and sauté them gently for 2 or 3 minutes. Dry the pieces of chicken on paper towels. Add the neck, drumsticks, and all the dark meat to the pan. Remove them when they are slightly colored and add the white meat. When these pieces are lightly browned, return all the chicken to the pan and add the small onions and wine. Season with pepper and a small amount of salt. (The cheese that will cover the top is salty.) Pour in the chicken stock, add the thyme and bay leaf, cover, and finish cooking in the oven for 25 to 30 minutes, checking after 20 minutes to be sure that the chicken does not overcook.

Remove the chicken and onions to a serving platter (reserving the cooking liquid) and keep warm while making the sauce.

Sauce

2 tablespoons butter
2½ tablespoons flour
¾ cup cooking liquid from the
   chicken
2 egg yolks

¾ cup light cream, or 1 cup milk,
   or ¾ cup evaporated milk
Salt
Black pepper, *freshly ground*

Strain the cooking liquid from the chicken over a small bowl and remove the fat (*technique, p. 320*). Melt the butter. Stir in the flour, and cook, stirring, for a few seconds. Remove from the heat and stir in ¾ cup of the cooking liquid, return to medium heat, and beat with a whisk until smooth.

Beat the egg yolks with the cream or milk, and stir into the sauce over low heat, continuing to stir constantly until the mixture is smooth and coats the spoon. Taste and season with salt and pepper. *The recipe can be made a couple of hours in advance to this point. Then it can be reheated, covered with foil, in a preheated 375° oven for 15 minutes.*

To gratiné and serve   *Preheat the broiler.*

1 cup imported Swiss cheese, or
   half Swiss and half Parmesan, *grated*

Spread half of the grated cheese on the bottom of a large shallow buttered baking dish. Arrange the warm chicken and onions on the cheese, coat all with the reheated cream sauce, and spread with the grated cheese. Five minutes before serving, run under the broiler to lightly color the top.

Serve in the baking dish, accompanied by the same dry white wine.

Poulet Île de France, en ramequins

PURÉE OF CHICKEN IN RAMEKINS
WITH VELOUTÉ SAUCE

For 6 as a luncheon dish; 12 as a first course:

A 3-pound chicken with its giblets
1 carrot, *sliced*
2 small onions, *peeled and stuck*
    with 2 cloves
1 leek, *sliced (optional)*
Bouquet garni: thyme, ½ bay leaf,
    and parsley
1 medium onion, to make ½ cup,
    chopped
3 tablespoons butter

¼ cup Cognac
2 eggs, *separated*
1 cup heavy cream
½ cup almonds, *pulverized*
    (technique, p. 317)
2 tablespoons parsley, *minced*
Salt
Black pepper, *freshly ground*
Nutmeg, *freshly grated*

Recommended equipment: 12 half-cup ramekins. (This can be made in one large casserole, but the result will not be quite as satisfactory.)

Chicken bouillon and chicken purée

Clip off the ends of the chicken wings just above the joint. If you have the feet, blanch them in boiling water and remove the skin. Put the wings and feet into a kettle with the gizzard and neck of the chicken, add the sliced carrot, the 2 onions with cloves, the leek if you wish, and the bouquet garni. Cover with about a quart of cold water, bring to the boil, and simmer slowly for about 2 hours. Remove the scum that arises to the surface at the beginning of the simmering to keep the bouillon clear. After half an hour add salt and pepper.

Using a very sharp knife, cut the meat from the chicken, scraping each little bone to remove it all. Add the bones to the simmering bouillon.

Put the chicken meat through a meat grinder and then through a food mill to make a fine purée.

Preheat the oven to 400°.

Sauté the chopped onions in the butter until they are soft but not colored. Stir in 2 tablespoons of the Cognac. Then put through a food mill to make a fine purée.

Beat the 2 egg yolks with the cream. Spread the almonds evenly over an oiled oven tray and put them into the oven for a few seconds to toast them slightly.

Turn the oven down to 375°.

Combine the chicken, toasted almonds, onions, cream and egg yolks, and the minced parsley, and season highly with salt, pepper, and nutmeg; the mixture will be thick.

Beat the egg whites with a pinch of salt until they are stiff but not dry. Fold 2 tablespoons of the beaten egg whites into the chicken mixture to lighten it. Then fold lightly and evenly into the remaining egg whites (*folding technique, p. 321*).

Fill the ramekins two-thirds full of the mixture. Put them into a shallow pan, pour an inch of water into the pan, set over the heat, and bring the water to a simmer. Then set the pan with the ramekins into the preheated oven and bake for about 20 minutes until set.

Sauce velouté

Chicken bouillon (*above*)
3 tablespoons butter
3 tablespoons flour
Salt

Black pepper, *freshly ground*
¼ cup dry white port or sherry
1½ cups heavy cream

Strain the chicken bouillon into a bowl. Let it cool briefly while the fat rises to the surface, and remove the fat (*technique, p. 320*).

In an enameled saucepan set over heat, melt the butter. Stir in the flour, and cook, stirring, for a few seconds. Remove from the heat and pour in ¾ cup of the chicken bouillon, stirring vigorously until the sauce is smooth. Return to the heat, let the sauce come to a simmer, and season it highly with salt and pepper. Let the sauce boil for 4 minutes, stirring constantly. Then pour in the port or sherry, and let the sauce simmer 3 or 4 minutes longer, adding cream by tablespoonfuls to taste.

To serve

Unmold the ramekins onto a warmed serving dish, and coat them with some of the sauce, serving the remaining sauce in a sauceboat.

Canards en cocotte aux deux purées

TWO BRAISED DUCKS WITH ONION
PURÉE AND BROCCOLI PURÉE, SERVED WITH
CARAMEL VINEGAR SAUCE AND CROUTONS

In France I make this dish with wild ducks that my husband, when he is lucky, brings home from hunting. But if you cannot get wild ducks (the best being mallards), the recipe can be made perfectly with American domestic ducks.

For the stuffing, I use a little ginger with the onions. Ginger is not a traditional French seasoning, but I remember that about thirteen years ago Julia Child and I made a special mixture called rougail—a very highly spiced condiment served with various Créole dishes. I thought the ginger gave a wonderful taste, and it gave me the idea for using the spice in this recipe.

A *truc* to be used in duck recipes, which will keep the ducks from being too rich and greasy, is first to brown the birds, then prick the skins all over with a fork so that the fat runs out, and rinse the fat away with hot water. This is especially useful for American domestic ducks, which are much fatter than the French ones.

For 8:

2 ducks, *cleaned,* with their gizzards

Recommended equipment: A heavy cooking pot with a lid, large enough to hold the ducks.

Stock

2 tablespoons goose fat or lard, or
   3½ tablespoons cooking oil
½ cup onions, *sliced*
½ cup carrots, *sliced*
½ cup celery, *sliced*
3 ounces boiled ham, *diced*

3 tablespoons flour
1 cup dry white wine
Bouquet garni of parsley, thyme,
   and ½ bay leaf
Black pepper, *freshly ground*
Salt

Roughly chop the necks and the gizzards of the ducks. Heat the fat or oil in the heavy pot, add the necks and gizzards, and sauté for 5 or 6 minutes over medium heat until very lightly browned. Add the sliced onions, carrots, and celery, and stir until the edges of the vegetables are beginning to color lightly. Add the diced ham, and cook, stirring occasionally, for 4 or 5 minutes longer. Sprinkle on the flour, and stir for 2 or 3 minutes until the flour is browned. Pour in the white wine, bring to a boil, and stir constantly until the flour is thoroughly amalgamated. Stir in 2½ cups of hot water. Bring to a boil, then turn down the heat and let the stock simmer very slowly, uncovered, for half an hour. Add the bouquet garni, season with pepper and a little salt, and simmer for another half-hour, until stock has reduced to about 2 cups.

Remove the pot from the heat, strain the liquid, and let it cool before removing the fat (*technique, p. 320*). Taste, correct the seasoning, and set the stock aside. Clean the pan.

To cook the ducks

Preheat the oven to 375°.

2 lemons
Salt
Black pepper, *freshly ground*
1 large onion, to make 1 cup,
    chopped

½ teaspoon powdered ginger
2½ tablespoons butter
2 tablespoons cooking oil

Cut the zest of the 2 lemons into matchlike strips. Blanch these strips in boiling water to cover for approximately 10 minutes; then dry on paper towels. Season the inside of the ducks with salt and pepper. Sprinkle the chopped onions with the ginger, add half the lemon peel, and put the mixture into the ducks. Cut off the fat around the tail opening and discard it. Then sew up the opening.

Dry the ducks thoroughly. Heat the butter and oil in the heavy pot, and lay the ducks on their sides in the pot. Cook over medium heat for 10 to 12 minutes, turning the ducks to color them evenly on all sides to a golden brown.

With a fork prick the skin of the ducks all over to release the fat. Then pour on a cup of boiling water. Remove the ducks from the pot, drain them, pour off the fat and water, and rinse and dry the pot.

Replace the ducks in the pot, and pour in 1 cup of the stock (*above*). Cover and cook in the preheated oven for 40 minutes, turning the ducks after 20 minutes.

Two purées

Meanwhile, prepare the broccoli purée and the soubise purée that follow this recipe.

Caramel vinegar sauce and croûtons

6 tablespoons granulated sugar
4 tablespoons red wine vinegar
The remaining cup of stock
Juice of 1 lemon
The remaining lemon peel strips
  (*above*)
Salt

Black pepper, *freshly ground*
3 tablespoons butter
8 slices stale *pain de mie* or other
  good sandwich bread, *cut
  into half on the diagonal* (*if
  fresh, dry in a slow oven*)

In a small enameled saucepan, simmer the sugar with the vinegar until it makes a light syrup. Immediately pour in the remaining cup of stock (*above*), and simmer very slowly, stirring, to dissolve the caramel. Pour in the strained juice of the lemon and add the remaining lemon peel. Do not let the sauce reduce. Season it, if necessary, with salt and pepper, and keep it warm over a very low flame.

Melt the butter in a large frying pan, add the bread one layer at a time, and fry for a few seconds on each side until golden brown. Drain on paper towels.

To serve

Lemon juice
Salt

Black pepper, *freshly ground*
3 tablespoons butter

Remove the ducks from the pot and keep them warm.

Strain the cooking liquid from the ducks and remove the fat (*technique, p. 320*).

Return the liquid to the pan and stir in the caramel vinegar sauce. Correct the seasoning with lemon juice, salt, and pepper to taste, and keep warm while carving the ducks. Remove some of the strips of lemon peel to garnish the platter.

First cut the breasts into strips, 3 or 4 on each side. Remove the wings and the drumsticks. Put the carcasses on a very large warm serving platter and reconstruct the ducks, placing the pieces of breast on the middle of each carcass and the wings and drumsticks on each side. Coat the pieces with some of the sauce, garnish with lemon strips, and surround with the croutons.

Stir the butter by pieces into the remaining sauce and pour into a sauceboat. Put some of the broccoli purée on one side of the ducks, some soubise purée on the other side, and the remaining purée into one or two warmed vegetable dishes.

———— •◆• ————

Brocoli en purée

PURÉED BROCCOLI

For 8:

3 pounds fresh broccoli
Salt
6½ tablespoons butter

Black pepper, *freshly ground*
1 egg, *hard boiled and sieved*

Separate the broccoli into stems and flowerets, and cut the stems into large pieces. Peel each very carefully. In a salad basket or colander wash the broccoli under cold running water, being gentle with the flowerets. Plunge the stems into a large quantity of boiling water, adding salt as soon as the water returns to the boil. Boil the stems uncovered for 5 minutes, then add the flowerets and boil 5 minutes longer, until a sharp knife easily pierces the stalks. Refresh the broccoli in a colander under cold running water and let it drain. *The broccoli can be made a few hours in advance to this point.*

Melt the butter in a large pan and add the broccoli. Shake the pan to coat the broccoli with the butter. Season with salt and pepper, and sauté, tossing every few minutes, until the broccoli is heated through.

Purée the sautéed broccoli by putting it through a food mill, then return the purée to the pan and heat it gently, adding more butter if desired. Correct the seasoning if necessary. Serve sprinkled with sieved hard-boiled egg.

Soubise purée

ONION PURÉE

2 pounds yellow onions, to make 7 cups, *roughly chopped*	1½ tablespoons cooking oil
5 tablespoons butter	1⅔ cups light beef bouillon or stock

Recommended equipment: A heavy-bottomed 2-quart casserole, with lid.

Preheat the oven to 375°.

Blanch the chopped onions for 5 minutes in boiling water. Drain and dry. In the heavy-bottomed casserole, warm the butter and oil, add the blanched onions, and stir for 5 minutes until the moisture has evaporated. Pour in the bouillon or stock, cover the casserole, and bake for 35 to 40 minutes, stirring from time to time, until the mixture is dry.

Velouté sauce

2 tablespoons butter	Salt
3 tablespoons flour	Black pepper, *freshly ground*
1 cup beef stock or bouillon	Nutmeg, *freshly grated*

While the onions are cooking, prepare the velouté: Melt the butter, add the flour, and stir while the mixture boils; remove from the heat and pour in the cup of stock; return to the heat and reduce a little (the velouté should be very thick). Season with salt, pepper, and nutmeg.

To finish the purée

½ cup heavy cream

Mix the cooked onion into the velouté and put through a food mill to make a smooth purée. If the purée is too thin, return to the heat and reduce to a thicker consistency. Taste, correct the seasoning, and return to the heat. Then stir in the cream by spoonfuls until all the cream has been added and the purée is warmed through.

Sauté d'agneau aux lingots

SAUTÉED LAMB SHOULDER WITH WHITE BEANS

For 6:

5 cups dry white beans, or 7 cups fresh small white beans

3 tablespoons rendered pork fat or cooking oil

4 pounds lamb shoulder, *cut into 2½-inch squares, 1 inch thick, all fat and gristle removed*

Bones from the lamb

3 or 4 large cloves of garlic, *peeled*

3 medium onions, *stuck with 3 cloves*

Bouquet garni of thyme, ½ bay leaf, oregano

1 medium tomato, *coarsely chopped*

½ pound fresh unsalted lean bacon or boiled ham shoulder, *cut into pieces ½ inch square*

Salt

Black pepper, *freshly ground*

1½ tablespoons parsley, *chopped and worked into* 2 tablespoons softened butter

½ tablespoon parsley, *chopped,* for garnish

If the beans are dry, bring them to a boil in 2 quarts of cold water and boil for 2 minutes. Turn off the heat and let them soak for 1 hour. Then bring them to a boil again and cook for 45 minutes. Drain, reserving 1 cup of the cooking liquid.

If the beans are fresh, cook them for only 15 minutes and drain.

Preheat the oven to 350°.

Coat a large, heavy-bottomed casserole with 1½ tablespoons of the rendered fat or the oil. Add the beans, the lamb bones, the garlic, the onions stuck with cloves, the bouquet garni and the chopped tomato. Pour in cold water just to cover and bring to a boil. Remove any scum that rises to the surface. Cover and put in the preheated oven while you prepare the lamb.

Heat the remaining pork fat or oil in a heavy skillet or pot and sauté the pieces of bacon or ham. Remove them and add them to the bean pot.

Then, in the same skillet, brown the lamb thoroughly on all sides, one layer at a time; as each batch is done, add it to the beans. When all the lamb is browned, deglaze the pot with the reserved cup of bean liquid (or if you are using fresh beans, with a cup of water), scraping up all the bits in the bottom of the pot. Add this liquid to the beans, taste, and season if necessary. Then remove the bouquet garni and bring to a boil on top of the stove, again removing any scum.

Cover, and return to the oven to finish cooking for 30 to 40 minutes.

When the meat is done, if you find it necessary to thicken the cooking juice, pour it off and reduce it over high heat. Then return it to the casserole and reheat the dish before serving. Remove from the heat, stir in the parsley butter, and serve sprinkled with the chopped parsley.

Carottes au Malaga

CARROTS WITH ONIONS AND SWEET WINE

For 4 or 5:

1½ pounds tender new carrots, *cut into ¼-inch slices* (or older carrots, *quartered and then sliced*)

¼ cup olive oil

1 medium onion, *cut into ¼-inch slices*

2 large cloves garlic, *mashed*

Salt

Black pepper, *freshly ground*

Paprika to taste

¼ cup brown stock or beef bouillon

¾ cup Malaga, Madeira, or sweet red port wine

1 tablespoon parsley, *chopped*

Prepare the carrots. If they are older carrots, remove and discard the woody centers.

Heat the olive oil in a heavy-bottomed enameled saucepan, add the sliced onions, and cook gently for 3 or 4 minutes, stirring, until soft. Add the carrots and cook very slowly, covered, for about 10 minutes (longer for mature carrots), tossing from time to time. Add the garlic, season with salt, pepper, and paprika, and simmer for 10 minutes longer.

Bring the stock or bouillon and the wine to the boil. Pour over the carrots, and when the liquid returns to the boil, reduce the heat and finish cooking the carrots very, very slowly, uncovered, for about 15 minutes longer until tender.

Correct the seasoning, and serve sprinkled with parsley.

———•••———

Gratin de céleri-rave à la dauphinoise

GRATIN OF CELERIAC AND POTATOES
WITH CREAM AND CHEESE

For 6 to 8:

1 pound celeriac (celery root)
Juice of 1 lemon
2 pounds boiling potatoes
Salt
2 cups cold milk
Black pepper, *freshly ground*
Nutmeg, *freshly grated*

Butter for the baking dish
1 cup heavy cream
¾ cup imported Swiss cheese, or half Swiss and half Parmesan, *grated*
2 cloves garlic, *grated* (*optional*)

Recommended equipment: An oval baking dish about 12 inches long, 6 inches wide, and 2½ inches deep.

Peel the celeriac and cut it into rounds ½ inch thick. Put into a saucepan with the strained juice of the lemon and cover with cold water. Bring the water to a boil, then add 1½ tablespoons of salt, lower the heat, and simmer very slowly, uncovered, for 10 minutes. Drain the celeriac. When it is cool, slice into rounds ¼ inch thick.

Peel the potatoes and cut them into slices ¼ inch thick. Put them into a saucepan, and cover with cold milk. Bring to a boil, season with salt, pepper, and nutmeg, lower the heat, and simmer for 10 minutes. Then remove the potatoes with a slotted spoon and set the milk aside.

Butter the baking dish and spread it with alternating layers of potatoes and celery root, spreading 3 tablespoons of cream and 2 tablespoons of grated cheese between each layer (but not over the top layer), and seasoning each with salt, pepper, nutmeg, and, if you wish, a little grated garlic. *The dish may be prepared one or two hours in advance to this point.*

To bake and serve   *Preheat the oven to 375°.*

Bring the reserved milk to a boil and pour it over the vegetables. Bake them in the preheated oven for 30 minutes; then remove them and turn up the oven to 425°. Coat the vegetables with the remaining cream, sprinkle on the rest of the cheese, and return the dish to the 425° oven for 5 to 8 minutes to brown the top slightly.

Serve in the baking dish.

(This can be reheated, but it is always best when the potatoes have just been cooked.)

Salade du Broc

PROVENÇALE SALAD OF COLD VEGETABLES
IN VINAIGRETTE

For 6:

1 package frozen artichokes
1 large head chicory
3 small firm ripe tomatoes
1 red bell pepper or 1 whole
    canned pimiento

1 egg, *hard boiled*
½ cup small black Mediterranean
    olives
1 teaspoon fresh tarragon or
    ½ teaspoon dry tarragon

Thaw the artichokes and cut them into quarters.

Wash the leaves of chicory, dry them well, and cut the larger leaves in two. Peel the tomatoes (*technique, p. 253*), stem and quarter them, and press to remove the seeds and excess water. Cut the pepper or pimiento into very thin strips. Roughly chop the egg.

Special vinaigrette

½ tablespoon mustard
4 tablespoons olive oil
1 tablespoon wine vinegar

2 tablespoons mixed basil or tar-
    ragon and parsley, *minced*
Salt
Black pepper, *freshly ground*

Prepare the vinaigrette and season highly, adding the minced basil or tarragon and parsley.

To assemble and serve

Place the chicory leaves in a salad bowl and cover them with an attractive arrangement of quartered artichokes, tomatoes, strips of pepper or pimiento, and olives. Just before serving pour on the vinaigrette, and sprinkle with the chopped hard-boiled egg and the tarragon. Bring to the table and toss several times before serving, using a large wooden fork and spoon, and pressing the leaves a little to saturate them with the dressing.

Salade Phano

SALAD OF APPLES AND BEETS
WITH CELERY AND WALNUTS

A very charming individual came one day, unexpectedly, to our farm in Provence. He was sympathetic and affectionate, and he has stayed ever since. He has long legs, rough brown fur, and a happy bark. Except that I am very fond of Phano, I have no recollection whatever of why I named this salad for him.

For 6 to 8:

1 large or 2 small very tender
    celery hearts
2 medium beets, *cooked*
1 large green apple

7 leaves of chicory, or half chicory
    and half endive
¾ cup walnuts, *shelled and
    halved*
1 tablespoon chives, *minced*

Cut the celery, the beets, and the apple into ⅓-inch dice. Wash and thoroughly drain the salad leaves. Place all the ingredients in a salad bowl.

Vinaigrette à la moutarde

3 tablespoons Dijon mustard	½ tablespoon parsley, *minced*
3 tablespoons wine vinegar	Salt
8½ tablespoons olive, peanut, or vegetable oil	Black pepper, *freshly ground*

Beat the mustard thoroughly with the vinegar; then add the oil by spoonfuls, continuing to beat with the parsley and seasoning to taste.

To serve

2 eggs, *hard boiled*	Parsley, *minced*

A few minutes before serving, pour the vinaigrette over the salad, and mix it for a good minute; the red color of the beets will tint the salad and the apple. Then put the eggs through a food mill, combine with parsley, and sprinkle onto the salad. Serve at once.

———◆●◆———

Salade de Fontenay

COLD SALAD OF MARINATED VEGETABLES
WITH MAYONNAISE

This should be prepared one day in advance.

For 6 to 8:

½ pound beets	½ pound tart apples, *diced*
1½ pounds boiling potatoes	Salt
¼ cup dry white wine	1 fennel bulb, *thinly sliced*
2 tablespoons wine vinegar	¾ cup mayonnaise (*p. 306*)
2 tablespoons shallots or scallions, *minced*	2 tablespoons parsley, *minced*
	1 tablespoon chives, *minced*

Black pepper, *freshly ground*

½ pound Belgian endive, *sliced lengthwise*

1 egg, *hard boiled (optional)*

2 tablespoons dill, *minced*

Boil or bake the beets, then cut them into dice. Next boil the potatoes until tender and, when they are cool enough to handle, skin them and cut them into even slices. Place them, still warm, in a bowl, pour on ¼ cup of hot water, and toss until the potatoes have absorbed the water. Then pour in the wine, toss again thoroughly, and add the vinegar, shallots or scallions, diced apples, and beets, and a little salt.

Marinate overnight in the coolest part of the kitchen, tossing once or twice.

When time to serve, toss the marinated vegetables and sliced fennel with the mayonnaise, add the parsley and chives, and correct the seasoning, adding more salt and pepper. Place the endive by bouquets into the salad mixture, put the hard-boiled egg through a food mill onto the salad to make a "mimosa," and serve sprinkled with dill.

Salade andalouse

COLD SALAD OF RICE, RAISINS, LITTLE PEAS, HAM, AND ARTICHOKE HEARTS

For 6 to 8:

2½ cups boiled rice (*p. 309*)

⅓ cup raisins

⅔ cup tiny sweet green peas, fresh or frozen, *cooked*

6 ounces boiled ham, *diced*

5 ounces tiny canned Italian artichoke hearts

1 tablespoon chives, *minced*

½ cup *vinaigrette classique* (*p. 304*)

1 cup *mayonnaise au pistou* (*p. 308*)

A bunch of watercress, Bibb lettuce, or field salad

About 2 tablespoons parsley, *finely chopped*

When the rice is cold and dry, put it in a salad bowl with the raisins, green peas, diced ham, artichoke hearts, and chives, and toss with the vinaigrette. Refrigerate 1 or 2 hours to marinate the ingredients and keep them cold and fresh, tossing the salad from time to time.

Just before serving, prepare the *mayonnaise au pistou.*

Remove the salad from the refrigerator, toss it again, and pour three-quarters of the mayonnaise over it. Toss, then place bunches of green leaves here and there in the salad, like bouquets. Decorate with dollops of the remaining mayonnaise, sprinkle with the minced parsley, and serve.

Variation: Instead of artichoke hearts, you could use raw mushrooms—sliced and marinated for 5 minutes in olive oil and lemon juice with salt and pepper.

——•◆•——

Soufflé au chocolat sans beurre

SPECIAL CHOCOLATE SOUFFLÉ

For 6:

Recommended equipment: A buttered 2-quart soufflé dish with a 2-inch foil collar.

7 ounces German's sweet choco-	½ teaspoon vanilla
late, *broken into small pieces*	4 eggs, *separated*
3 teaspoons powdered instant	2 extra egg whites
coffee	Pinch of salt
⅓ cup flour	½ cup sugar
2 cups cold milk	Confectioners' sugar

Combine the chocolate, the instant coffee, and 5 tablespoons of water in the top of a double boiler, and stir until the mixture is completely smooth. Set aside over hot water to keep warm.

Put the flour in an enameled saucepan and slowly add the cold milk, stirring vigorously with a whisk until smooth. Add the vanilla, set over moderate heat, and stir constantly until the mixture is thick and free of lumps. Continue to stir for a minute or so. Then blend in the melted chocolate and remove from the heat.

Stir the 4 egg yolks, one at a time, into the chocolate mixture. Beat the 6 egg whites with the salt until they are white and frothy; then slowly beat in the sugar to make a meringue-like mixture. Warm the chocolate mixture. Stir in 2 large spoonfuls of meringue to lighten; then lightly fold in the remaining meringue.

To assemble and bake   *Preheat the oven to 375°.*

Pour the soufflé mixture into the buttered dish and bake in the center of the preheated oven for 25 to 30 minutes.

Sprinkle the finished soufflé with confectioners' sugar, and serve immediately, removing the collar only after the first helping.

Sabayon au vin, rhum, ou Cointreau

SABAYON WITH SAUTERNES, COINTREAU, OR RUM

A sabayon is best made on a relaxed occasion because it must be done at the last moment. I like to serve the sabayon with chilled mixed fruit, such as the *coupe de fruits glacés* on page 251. The warm, creamy sabayon, with its strong taste of wine or rum, makes an exciting combination with the cold fresh taste of the fruit.

1 orange
2 large or 3 small lumps of sugar
6 to 8 egg yolks
½ cup sugar (or 1 cup of sugar
    if not using sweet wine)

1½ to 2 cups Sauternes or other sweet white wine or 1¼ cups white wine plus ¼ cup dark rum or 2 to 3 tablespoons Cointreau

Wash and dry the orange, then rub it with the sugar lumps to impregnate them well with the essence of orange contained in the rind. Put the sugar and the wine in an enameled saucepan over gentle heat to melt, without allowing the wine to boil. At the same time beat the egg yolks and the granulated sugar in a heatproof (nonaluminum) mixing bowl until the mixture is a pale creamy yellow. Set the bowl over simmering water, add the white wine, and stir constantly, *not allowing the sabayon to boil,* until it has the consistency of a light foamy cream. If using rum or Cointreau, add it at this point, continuing to whip the mixture.

The sabayon cannot wait and should be served immediately—either in tall glasses or, spooned over fruit, in a shallow serving dish. If fruits are used, they should be well drained.

———— ◆•◆ ————

Crème au chocolat de Zulma (au lait)

INFORMAL DESSERT OF CHOCOLATE
WITH COFFEE AND MERINGUE

For 6:

½ pound German's sweet choco-
    late, *broken into small pieces*
3 tablespoons strong coffee
3 eggs, *separated*
1 cup milk

½ teaspoon vanilla extract
Salt
½ cup sugar
Small pieces of candied orange
    (*optional*)

Chocolate and coffee mixture

Put the chocolate and the coffee into an enameled saucepan, set over heat, and stir until completely smooth. Remove from the heat and stir in the egg yolks and the milk. Return to the heat, and cook, stirring constantly, until the mixture begins to thicken. Add the vanilla, continuing to stir until the simmer is almost reached. Set aside.

Meringue

Beat the egg whites with a pinch of salt until they are beginning to turn white and frothy; then beat in the sugar a spoonful at a time to make a shiny, firm meringue. Fold a quarter of the meringue into the chocolate cream, then fold all back into the remaining meringue (*folding technique, p. 321*).

Pour into a serving dish. When cool, refrigerate.

Decorate, if you like, with candied orange. Serve chilled.

Variation: Before making the meringue, partially melt an additional ¼ pound of chocolate, broken in pieces, with 2 tablespoons coffee. Before the chocolate is completely melted, stir it into the chocolate cream. Then proceed with the recipe. There will be tiny bits of hard chocolate distributed throughout the cream.

———— ◆◆ ————

Pommes en crème, meringuées

BAKED CRUSHED APPLES WITH BLUEBERRIES, RAISINS, ALMONDS, AND MERINGUE

For about 6:

Butter for the baking dish
2 pounds green apples
6 tablespoons butter
¾ cup sugar
About 1 teaspoon cinnamon
¾ cup raisins
2 cups blueberries, or 1 extra cup
    raisins

1 tablespoon cornstarch, *dissolved*
    in 2 tablespoons kirsch or
    Cognac
3 large egg yolks
3 ounces (⅝ cup) almonds,
    blanched and pulverized
    (technique, p. 317)

Recommended equipment: A shallow baking-serving dish, about 7-cup capacity.

Butter the baking dish.

Peel and core the apples and cut them into large dice. Melt the butter with 3 tablespoons of water in a heavy saucepan. Add the diced apples and the sugar and simmer over medium heat for about 10 minutes, stirring occasionally, until the apples are tender. Remove from the heat and sprinkle the apples with cinnamon. Then crush them roughly with a fork and set them aside to cool.

Combine the apples with the raisins and blueberries and stir in the cornstarch dissolved in the kirsch or Cognac. Add the egg yolks and the almonds, blend the mixture thoroughly, and pour it into the buttered dish. *The recipe may be made 6 to 8 hours in advance up to this point.*

To bake   *Preheat the oven to 375°.*

About 1 hour before serving time, put the dish of apples in the preheated oven to bake for 18 to 20 minutes until set. While the apples are baking, make the meringue.

Meringue

3 egg whites   ¾ cup confectioners' sugar

Beat the egg whites until they are just beginning to become white and frothy; slowly fold in the confectioners' sugar, and continue to beat until thick and shiny.

Final baking and serving

Remove the apples from the oven, and turn the oven down to 250°. Coat the apples evenly with the meringue and return the dish to the oven for 20 to 25 minutes, to dry the meringue slowly.

Serve in the baking dish, warm or cold.

POT
POURRI

———◆———

Some Basic Recipes, Notes,
and an Aide-mémoire

Basic Recipes and Notes

How to Boil an Egg

How to boil an egg? Surely everyone must know from birth how, and how many minutes, a fresh egg must be boiled to be at its very peak of "hard-boiled" perfection—that is to say, with a beautiful yellow yolk, cooked just to the right point, but not *too cooked*. And if I volunteer some advice it is because, common sense to the contrary, one often finds a hard-boiled egg that has been *too cooked,* with the result that a green line appears around the yolk, marking the beginning of its transformation into sulfur. In the belief that few people could actually desire the strong, and moreover indigestible, presence of sulfur in their hard-boiled eggs, I offer some suggestions that will help you to arrive at a perfect hard-boiled egg.

The egg begins with the eggshell—and sadly today, in France as elsewhere, eggshells do not always have quite the quality that they did in days gone past. A most interesting *truc* for preventing eggshells from breaking while cooking is to rub a cut lemon over the surface of the egg. While I am not quite certain as to why this works, I can assure you that it does work—at least for me. Perhaps the acidity of the lemon juice solders together the more feeble parts of the shell, should such exist?

Next, the vessel in which the eggs are cooked. Ideally it should be of a size and shape to hold one layer of eggs comfortably. Put the eggs into the chosen pan, pour on some hot but not boiling water, set the pan over a brisk fire, and await the boil. Then count *exactly 10 minutes* for an egg of 2 to 2¼ ounces (a small egg); for medium and large eggs, 2½ to 3 ounces, add 2 minutes to the timing. Immediately plunge the eggs into a bowl of cold water and run more cold water over them. After a few minutes, tap each egg very lightly against the bowl to break the shell and allow the water to go between the shell and the egg. In about half an hour, when the eggs are absolutely cold, you will be able to remove the shells easily.

Two Bases

Le fumet de poisson ou court-bouillon

FISH STOCK

Ingredients for 2½ cups, sufficient to poach a 4-pound fish:

1 pound fish bones and trimmings	A bouquet garni of thyme, ½ bay
1 medium carrot, *sliced*	leaf, parsley, celery stalk
1 medium onion, *sliced*	2 cups dry white wine
2 tablespoons butter	Salt
	Black pepper, *freshly ground*

Clean and roughly chop the fish trimmings.

In a heavy pot, sauté the sliced carrot and onion in the butter for 5 minutes. Add the fish trimmings, the bouquet garni, the wine, and 4 cups of water, and boil for 25 minutes.

Strain, return to the saucepan, and reduce to 2½ cups, or less if you need a stronger flavor. Taste, and season with salt and pepper. *This can be kept for a few days in the refrigerator or frozen.*

To refresh bottled clam juice as a substitute for fumet de poisson

Bring the clam juice to the boil with a bouquet garni of parsley, thyme, celery, ½ bay leaf and fennel. Some white wine can be added if appropriate for the recipe.

Purée de tomate provençale, à la Jeanne

TOMATO ESSENCE

Made with the finest tomatoes, at the height of the tomato season, this purée can be frozen in small plastic bags and used in almost all preparations requiring tomatoes.

For about 2½ cups:

5 pounds very fine ripe tomatoes
2½ tablespoons olive oil
About 4 medium onions, to make 1 cup, *minced*
3 or 4 large cloves garlic
A large bouquet garni of thyme, savory, basil, and oregano

A 1-inch piece of dried orange peel (*p. 324*)
Salt
Black pepper, *freshly ground*
1 to 2 tablespoons sugar, to taste
1 large clove garlic, *pressed* (*optional*)
Tabasco (*optional*)

Wash and quarter the tomatoes. Warm half of the olive oil in a large heavy skillet. Add the quartered tomatoes and cook them uncovered over moderate heat, stirring from time to time, until they have rendered all their juice. Put them through a food mill and set them aside.

Heat the remaining oil in the same skillet. Add the minced onions and cook them slowly, stirring occasionally, until they are tender but not brown (about 15 minutes). Add the tomatoes, bring to a simmer, and add the garlic, the bouquet garni, a little salt, and the dried orange peel. Simmer uncovered for 15 to 20 minutes.

Remove the bouquet garni, and purée the tomatoes again through the food mill. Season with salt, pepper, and sugar to taste and return to the heat. If the mixture is too liquid, reduce it over heat to 2½ cups, watching carefully, and stirring to keep it from burning.

Let cool. When cold correct the seasoning, adding some fresh garlic and Tabasco if you wish and salt and pepper to taste.

Hot Sauces

Sauce hollandaise à la Simca

SPECIAL HOLLANDAISE SAUCE SIMCA

I devised this special hollandaise sauce made with fish fumet for James Beard's cooking classes during my last visit to New York. It is very easily made and always works.

For about 1 cup:

3 egg yolks
3 to 4 tablespoons fish fumet
    or bottled clam juice
    (p. 298)
10 tablespoons butter
3 tablespoons heavy cream

1½ to 2 tablespoons mixed
    parsley, tarragon, and
    chervil, *minced*
Salt
Black pepper, *freshly ground*

Put the 3 egg yolks into an enameled saucepan with the fish fumet. Set over very low heat or barely simmering water, and stir constantly until the egg yolks thicken and you can see the bottom of the pan between strokes. Remove from the heat and add the butter, 1 or 2 tablespoons at a time. When the butter is no longer easily absorbed, return the saucepan to the heat or hot water for a few seconds; then remove and add more butter and the cream until all is added and the sauce is thick and smooth. Season to taste with chopped herbs, salt, and pepper.

Sauce tomate pour le poulet
ou le poisson

TOMATO SAUCE FOR CHICKEN OR FISH

For about 2½ cups:

Velouté

2 tablespoons butter
2 tablespoons flour
About ½ cup chicken bouillon
   or fish fumet * (*p. 298*)

1½ cups *purée de tomate proven-*
   çale (*p. 299*)
Salt
Black pepper, *freshly ground*

In a heavy-bottomed enameled saucepan, melt the butter. Stir in the flour, and cook, stirring, for a few seconds. Remove from the heat and pour in all the bouillon or fish fumet, stirring constantly. Then cook slowly, stirring constantly, until thick. Pour in the *purée de tomate provençale* and continue to stir until the sauce is smooth. If the sauce is too thick, add a few more tablespoons of bouillon. Taste, and season with salt and pepper. *This sauce can be kept and reheated. It can also be frozen.*

Improvised tomato sauce
from canned tomatoes and tomato paste

Stir about 2 tablespoons of tomato paste into 2 cups chopped canned tomatoes. Add a bouquet garni of parsley, thyme, celery, and ½ bay leaf and one or two cloves of unpeeled garlic. Cook over gentle heat for 30 to 40 minutes. Then purée through a food mill. Season if necessary with salt and freshly ground black pepper.

* Depending on whether sauce is to be used for chicken or fish.

The *beurre mousseux* is a variation of the classic sauce of whipped butter. In both versions of the recipe that follows (which was developed by Mme. Françoise Régnier), the special quality of the sauce is achieved by the substitution for water of a special liquid, depending upon what dish the sauce will accompany. For fish dishes, such as the salmon in brioche in Menu 19, a *fumet de poisson* is used. For a dish including mushrooms, such as the *pâté de Fontainebleau,* mushroom fumet is substituted for the water. A recipe for mushroom fumet appears after the following recipe.

————————————◆◆◆————————————

Le beurre mousseux de Françoise

WHIPPED BUTTER SAUCE

For about 1 cup:

½ pound sweet butter
⅓ cup fish fumet, clam juice,
    mushroom fumet (*see be-
    low*)
⅓ cup lemon juice

Salt
Black pepper, *freshly ground*
1 tablespoon mixed parsley and
    tarragon, *chopped* (if dried,
    use half the amount)

Work the butter with a fork, spatula, or electric beater (at the lowest speed) until it is malleable. Very gradually, beat in the fish or mushroom fumet (or clam juice), then the lemon juice. Next whip with a balloon whip or electric beater until the butter has the consistency of whipped cream (7 to 10 minutes). Taste, and season with salt and pepper. This is best served immediately, but it will keep for up to an hour in a cool place (not the refrigerator). Just before serving, stir in the minced herbs. Serve tepid.

Le beurre mousseux de Françoise avec crème

Whipped butter sauce with cream. After the fumet has been incorporated into the butter, add ⅓ cup heavy cream.

———•◦•———

Fumet de champignons

MUSHROOM FUMET

¼ pound white mushrooms,   Lemon juice
    cleaned   Salt
1½ tablespoons butter

Put the mushrooms in a saucepan and barely cover them with water. Add the butter, drops of lemon juice, and some salt, bring to the boil, and boil for 10 minutes. Strain, return to the saucepan and reduce over heat to enhance the flavor. Let cool.

———•◦•———

Sauce crème a l'estragon

TARRAGON CREAM SAUCE

1½ cups heavy cream   Salt
2 tablespoons fresh tarragon (or   Black pepper, *freshly ground*
    2 teaspoons dried)

Bring the cream to the boil with the tarragon, salt, and pepper. Let simmer 7 or 8 minutes until you can feel that the sauce has the taste of the tarragon. Serve immediately.

Salads, Salad Dressing, and Cold Sauces

In France we eat green salads every day, and sometimes twice a day, both at lunch and at supper. The salad is served after the main course or vegetable course, and at family dinners often on the same plate. The most commonly used greens are endive, watercress, escarole, chicory, and what we call *laitues*—the soft lettuces such as Boston or butter lettuce or garden lettuce. The most common dressing for these is the classic *sauce vinaigrette*, the simple combination of wine vinegar and oil with salt and pepper. The classic proportions are 1 tablespoon of wine vinegar to 4 tablespoons of peanut oil or 3 tablespoons of olive oil, the proportions differing because olive oil is so much heavier and richer than peanut oil. I almost always use olive oil, which we make from our own olives in Provence. I suggest if you have nuts in the salad, that you make the vinaigrette with walnut oil.

Vinaigrette classique

CLASSIC VINAIGRETTE

For a green salad serving 4:

Salt
1 tablespoon wine vinegar
Black pepper, *freshly ground*
3 tablespoons olive oil, or 4 tablespoons peanut oil

2 tablespoons mixed parsley, chervil, and tarragon, *minced* (if dried, use only ½ teaspoon each of the aromatic herbs)
1 egg, *hard boiled* (*optional*)

Mix first the salt and vinegar and pepper, then add the oil. Blend thoroughly with a whisk and pour over the salad greens just before serving, tossing and turning the leaves to coat them evenly. Sprinkle on the minced herbs. Make a "mimosa," if you wish, by putting the hard-boiled egg through the food mill and sprinkling over the top.

Other ingredients are sometimes added to the classic vinaigrette. One variation, typically French, is used in salads served with roasted meat or poultry. One or two tablespoons of the cooking juice from the roast—reduced and degreased—is added to the vinaigrette, giving a very special flavor.

Another addition is mustard, the strong mustard of Dijon. The *vinaigrette à la moutarde* is especially appropriate for the stronger greens such as endive, watercress, escarole, chicory, and Romaine. This dressing is my particular favorite.

Vinaigrette à base de moutarde

Mustard vinaigrette. To the preceding recipe, add 1 tablespoon Dijon mustard, blending it with the vinegar and salt and pepper before slowly adding the oil. The optional mimosa may also be added to the salad.

Often, with stronger greens, other ingredients are added to the salad itself—such as diced ham or Gruyère cheese, sliced apples, chopped walnuts, sliced cooked beets, thinly sliced cucumbers. To salads based on Romaine lettuce, I sometimes add a sprinkling of grated Roquefort cheese. One combination I like especially is Romaine, watercress, and Roquefort.

A lovely dressing, very *normande,* to be used only with very tender new lettuces, is the *assaissonnement à la normande,* made only with lemon juice and cream.

A salad of soft lettuce leaves should be mixed at the table for about 10 seconds; mixing it earlier will cause the vinegar to "cook" the leaves. Salads of stronger greens can be tossed in advance.

For *salades composées*—salads based on rice, potatoes, or cooked vegetables—a different type of dressing is used—frequently a *sauce may-*

onnaise or its variation *mayonnaise verte*—green mayonnaise made with herbs. The following is a very sure and easy recipe for mayonnaise. It is facilitated by the *truc* of making it in a warm bowl, over steam. Among the advantages of this method is that you can make it with chilled eggs taken directly from the refrigerator.

Mayonnaise classique à ma façon

CLASSIC MAYONNAISE

2 egg yolks
1 tablespoon Dijon mustard
¾ to 1½ cups oil
1 to 2 tablespoons wine vinegar, lemon juice, or water

Salt
Black pepper, *freshly ground*
1½ tablespoons fresh chives, chervil, and parsley, *minced* (if dried use less) (*optional*)

Put the egg yolks and mustard in a warm bowl and mix with a whisk. Then put the bowl over boiling water and continue to beat for 8 or 9 seconds to lightly poach the egg yolks with the mustard; you will feel a slight difference in the composition—it will be smooth and a little sticky.

Remove from the steam, and beat in the oil, first a teaspoonful at a time. When the mixture becomes creamy, add more oil, a little at a time, until you have used about ¾ cup oil and you can see that the mayonnaise is saturated. It is then necessary to give it the capacity to absorb more oil: add 1½ to 2 tablespoons of *boiling* vinegar, lemon juice, or water. When you see the mayonnaise become clearer and creamier, add the remaining oil, beating constantly. Then season well with salt, pepper, and, if you wish, the herbs.

Mayonnaise verte

Green Mayonnaise. To the *mayonnaise classique,* add at least 3 tablespoons of fresh minced chives, chervil, and parsley.

Mayonnaise aux anchois

Mayonnaise with Anchovies. This mayonnaise can serve either as a cold sauce or as a spread. As a cold sauce, it is suitable for dishes such as the ring of fish mousse on page 121 or the *timbale de poisson, Selma* on page 262. As a spread, it is good for canapés based on shrimps, tomatoes, or cucumber. It is also good with deviled eggs, cold artichoke hearts, or eggplant.

Prepare the *mayonnaise classique* (p. 306). Rinse 8 anchovy fillets. Chop and mash them into a purée. Add 1 tablespoon chopped capers, 4 small chopped gherkins, 2 tablespoons minced parsley, and some chervil or tarragon, or a combination of the two. Fold all into the mayonnaise. Season with salt, pepper, and a little Tabasco.

The following are two preparations that I serve frequently at cocktail parties as dips for raw vegetables. Both are made with whipped cream cheese. *Sauce rosy,* very light and fresh, includes grated raw cucumbers, as well as a little tomato paste to add flavor and color. The special *mayonnaise au pistou* combines with the cream cheese the pungent Provençal preparation of garlic, basil, and oil known as "pistou," which gives the sauce a very strong Mediterranean flavor.

Both of these dips also function as sauces for cold meat, eggs, fish, and *salades composées.*

Sauce rosy, aux concombres et au fromage blanc

SAUCE AND DIP WITH GRATED CUCUMBERS
AND CREAM CHEESE

For 2 to 3 cups:

1 pound ripe cucumbers
2 eggs, *hard boiled*

⅔ cup Philadelphia cream cheese
⅓ cup light cream

2½ tablespoons tomato paste
¼ cup capers, *chopped*
1 large clove garlic
1 tablespoon chives, *minced*
1 tablespoon shallots or scallions, *minced*

2 tablespoons parsley and basil or dill, *minced*
2 or 3 tablespoons Cognac (*optional*)
Salt
Black pepper, *freshly ground*
Tabasco to taste

Peel, seed, and grate the cucumbers. Sprinkle them with salt, and let them stand in a colander for about 15 minutes, stirring them from time to time, while they exude their liquid. Rinse them under cold running water, squeeze out the water, and dry them thoroughly on paper towels.

Put the hard-boiled eggs through a food mill to make a "mimosa." Work the cream cheese with an electric beater in a bowl set over ice cubes, add the cream by spoonfuls, and beat until smooth. Add the eggs, the cucumbers, the tomato paste, and the chopped capers. Season heavily with salt, pepper, and Tabasco, the garlic pressed through a garlic press, and the minced chives, shallots or scallions, and herbs. Add the Cognac if you desire, and beat again.

Set aside in the coolest part of the kitchen until time to be served.

----◆·◆----

Mayonnaise au pistou

COLD SAUCE WITH CREAM CHEESE AND GARLIC

3 cloves garlic, *peeled*
¼ cup fresh basil, *chopped*
¼ cup good olive oil
1 tablespoon tomato paste

½ to ¾ cup Philadelphia cream cheese, *softened with a little cream*
Salt
Black pepper, *freshly ground*

Recommended equipment: A mortar and pestle or a heavy bowl and a wooden spoon.

Crush the peeled garlic, put it into the mortar or bowl with the chopped basil, and pound to blend them thoroughly. Then stir in the oil, drop by drop, as for a mayonnaise, mixing constantly with a fork. When all the oil has been used, add the tomato paste and season lightly with salt and pepper. Blend in the cream cheese, preferably with an electric beater. Taste and correct the seasoning.

Rice

Riz "au blanc"

BUTTERED RICE

For 8:

Salt
2½ cups long-grain rice
4 tablespoons butter, *softened*

2 tablespoons fresh tarragon
or basil, *minced* (*optional*)
Black pepper, *freshly ground*

Bring 6 cups of water to the boil with one tablespoon of salt. Sprinkle the rice into the boiling water, reduce the heat, and simmer, uncovered, for 15 minutes or until just tender. Immediately pour it into a colander and rinse under the hot tap. Drain thoroughly, dry on paper towels, and while the rice is still warm, return it to the saucepan, stir in the butter and herbs, and season with salt and pepper.

Riz au safran
Saffron Rice

Pinch of saffron

After the rice has been added to the water in the preceding recipe, as soon as the water returns to the boil, add the saffron and finish cooking as described.

Riz avec petits pois
Rice with Peas

⅔ cup cooked tiny green peas,
    warmed

Add the peas when you add the herbs.

Risotto

For 6 to 8:

¼ cup olive oil
2 cups long-grain rice
Pinch of saffron (*optional*)
Salt

2 tablespoons butter
2 tablespoons basil, *chopped* (*optional*)

Preheat the oven to 350°.

Heat the oil in an ovenproof saucepan. Stir in the rice, and continue to stir over medium heat until milky. Pour in 5 cups of water, add the saffron and a little salt, and bring to a boil. Cover the saucepan tightly, and set in the oven to cook for 18 to 20 minutes, until all the water has been absorbed and the rice is fluffy and dry.

Mix the butter into the rice, using two forks, and sprinkle with chopped basil if desired.

Green Vegetables

Green vegetables are always boiled in a very large pot of water to establish their green color. The large quantity of water is less likely to cool as the vegetables are added, and the water can return quickly to the boil. A teaspoon of salt should always be added per quart of water as soon as the water has regained the boil. This will help in fixing the color of the vegetables. Unless the vegetables are to be used at once, they should be immediately drained and "refreshed" under cold running water. Otherwise, the steam from the water in which they were cooked will cause them to lose their crispness and color.

Following is the timing for boiling green vegetables mentioned in this book:

Spinach	5 minutes
Swiss chard	12 minutes
Green beans	
(depending on their	
freshness)	10 to 15 minutes
Fresh peas (mature)	20 to 30 minutes
Very tender young fresh	
green peas	5 to 8 minutes
Green asparagus	12 to 15 minutes

Pastry

One of the greatest fears of my cooking students, especially those from the United States, is of making pastry. This is not really a terrifying operation: it requires only a little knowledge and a little practice. Having worked for many years to help my students with their problems, I think that the following observations may be useful.

To begin with, I have noticed that a definite hindrance to making good pastry is hands that are not as cool or as dry as they should be. Some people naturally tend to have warmer hands or perspire more easily than others. Furthermore, perhaps the fear aroused by what seems an awesome undertaking causes the hands of some novices to perspire unduly. The first thing to remember, then, is that it is not necessary or even useful to use your hands during the first mixing of the pastry; I never do myself.

This first mixing should be done very roughly. Even if you have a few little pieces of butter—⅓ to ½ inch—that have not been incorporated into the flour, your pastry will be much better and lighter than if you work it too much trying to smooth them out. For the first mixing, of the flour and shortening, use a large fork or two knives (I do not like a pastry blender myself. I use a large aluminum fork, made in Italy.)

After the butter and flour have been blended, liquid must be added. Make a well in the center of the flour and put in either some water or an egg beaten with water—or in the case of *pâte brisée "B"* (below), white wine. You should scrape the flour into the liquid very slowly with a fork, then pat the liquid back into the flour and keep scraping with the fork toward the center. You now have the beginning of a dough.

It is at this point, when the mixing is half done, that you must use your hands. I suggest that if your hands are hot or damp you put on rubber gloves!

Put the fork aside, nicely flour the heel of your hand—gloved or un-gloved—and press to moisten the remaining pastry. If, for some reason, part of the pastry is still dry, remove the moistened dough and set it aside; sprinkle a few drops of the liquid over the dry pieces and continue to work lightly until all has been blended. Then combine the pieces of pastry and form them into a ball.

My own system in making pastry is to work in a bowl. Not everyone uses this method, and I have nothing against a pastry board or marble (marble being best, because it is so cold and smooth). But the problem with a flat surface is that you can make the mistake of adding too much liquid. In a bowl, you can see exactly how the pastry is developing.

After only a few times, I am sure that you will be able to say, as have countless numbers of my students who were so afraid at first, "I see! I understand! It is all so easy!"

The two recipes for *pâte brisée* are to be used for all the *preparations salées*—salted dishes using pastry—in this book. Both doughs, well wrapped, will keep for weeks in the freezer, and I always have some on hand to make quiches out of leftover fish, ham, or chicken, or to make bouchées to have with drinks if guests come unexpectedly.

Pâte brisée "A" is the classic recipe and makes a flaky crust without a strong individual taste, preferable for dishes in which the filling is highly flavored.

Pâte brisée "A"

FOR QUICHES

For ¾ pound of short pastry (enough for 20 to 24 tartlet molds, 2 inches in diameter and ½ inch deep or one 10-inch tart mold)

¼ pound (1 stick) chilled butter   1 egg yolk
1⅔ cups all-purpose flour   1 tablespoon oil
Pinch of salt

Cut the chilled butter into tiny bits and put it into a mixing bowl with the flour and the salt. Using a fork, a pastry blender, or two knives, work the butter and the flour until the mixture has the texture of oatmeal.

Beat the egg yolk with 4 tablespoons of cold water and the oil. Make a well in the center of the flour-butter mixture and pour in the egg. Mix with a fork, then use your hands to press the dough into a ball. Wrap the pastry in waxed paper and refrigerate until firm—at least 20 minutes. It will keep wrapped in foil or waxed paper for 3 or 4 days, refrigerated. It can also be frozen.

—•◆•—

Pâte brisée "B"

FOR PÂTÉS AND OTHER PREPARATIONS

In *pâte brisée "B,"* I have substituted white wine for the water, creating a *saveur* that I find quite interesting.

For about 1¾ pounds of pastry (enough for 40 to 48 individual bouchées 4 inches wide or three 8-inch tart molds):

½ pound (2 sticks) butter,   1 egg
   chilled   ½ cup dry white wine
3½ cups flour   ¼ cup oil
½ teaspoon salt

Follow the same process as that for the preceding *pâte brisée "A,"* but use a whole egg beaten with the white wine and the oil.

—•◆•—

Pâte sablée (sucrée)

FOR DESSERT TARTS

Pâte sablée, with sugar, is used for sweet tarts and tartlets. It will also keep for weeks in the freezer, and it is a versatile pastry to have on hand for making tartlets on the spur of the moment. It can also be used to make cookies decorated with almonds or candied fruits.

To make fruit tartlets, quickly roll out the pastry into a circle about ⅛ inch thick and 3 inches in diameter. Line the tartlet molds and sprinkle sugar over the pastry. Pour in a drop of sweetened heavy cream and add some pieces of pineapple, banana, drained canned cherries, pitted plums, cooked pears or apples—or some combination of these. Bake in a 350° oven for 5 to 10 minutes.

For about ¾ pound sweet pastry, enough for one 8- to 9-inch pastry shell:

¼ pound (1 stick) plus 1 tablespoon butter
1⅔ cup flour (pastry flour if possible; if not, all-purpose
flour)

Pinch of salt
2 tablespoons sugar
1 egg yolk, *beaten with* 3 to 4
tablespoons cold water

Follow the initial mixing process for *pâte brisée "A"* (*p. 313*). When all is molded in a ball, flour the heel of your hand, take portions of the pastry one by one, and push them down and away on the pastry board to complete the blending of the flour and the butter. No tiny lumps should remain. Wrap the pastry in foil or waxed paper and refrigerate it for at least 20 minutes. It will keep for 3 or 4 days refrigerated. It may be kept a few weeks in the freezer.

Pâte à brioche, à l'huile

LIGHT BRIOCHE PASTRY WITH OIL

This is a brioche that developed from an experiment Julia Child and I tried when making croissants. Since American flour is drier than French flour, we decided to try adding some oil. We found that the resulting pastry was much smoother, and I later applied the idea to brioche dough. This dough is very quickly made and gives extremely satisfactory results.

For 1½ pounds:

1 package dry active yeast
3½ cups pastry (preferred) or
    all-purpose flour
2 large eggs, *beaten*
¾ teaspoon salt

½ cup sugar (*for sweet pastry*)
    or 2 tablespoons sugar
    (*for a salted dish*)
½ cup peanut oil

Dissolve the yeast in ⅓ cup tepid water. Make a well in the flour and add the 2 beaten eggs, the salt, the sugar, and all the oil by tablespoons. Mix roughly with a fork or an electric beater for about 1 minute. (Do not try to mix thoroughly.) Add the yeast and work the dough for about 2 minutes longer to blend in the yeast.

Remove the dough to a board or pastry marble, scraping the bowl clean. Knead for 5 or 6 minutes, until it has enough elasticity to return to its shape when pulled out.

Flour a mixing bowl, slide the dough into it, and sprinkle the dough with flour. Cut a cross in the top of the dough, then cover with a damp towel and set in a warm place for 2 to 2½ hours, until the dough has doubled in bulk.

Flour your hand and deflate the dough with your palm, turning the bowl to push the dough down all around.

You can use the dough immediately, or you can wrap it tightly in strong paper and then in a cloth, tie it with strings to prevent it from rising again, and refrigerate it to use it the following day. You can also freeze it and let it defrost in the refrigerator for 5 to 6 hours before using it.

Aide-mémoire

I am setting down here certain notes and suggestions, which I hope will be helpful. For many readers, particularly those familiar with the two volumes of *Mastering the Art of French Cooking,* many of the basic processes used regularly in the French cuisine will be familiar, and these notes will serve simply as a reminder. But I have also included a few special *trucs* of my own.

Almonds

To blanch: Drop the almonds in boiling water for a few seconds. Then, while the almonds are still warm, press them between your thumb and index finger to slip off the skins.

To pulverize: After the almonds have been blanched and skinned, dry them out thoroughly in a low oven for at least five minutes. Then spin them, about half a cup at a time, in an electric blender at full speed for half a minute.

Bacon

French lard, often used in cooking, can be replaced by American bacon. But because American bacon is heavily smoked and salted, it should almost always be blanched to keep its taste from dominating the dish it is part of. Cover the bacon with a generous amount of cold water (at least a quart for ½ pound); bring the water to a boil and boil for 5 to 10 minutes. Then drain the bacon, refresh it under cold running water, and dry it on absorbent paper.

Bain-marie

The bain-marie, a gentle, smooth way to cook or heat—known to generations of French cooks—is simply a shallow pan of warm or simmering water into which another dish is set. A shallow roasting pan, a gratin dish, or any similar pan that can go both directly over heat and into the oven is suitable. The bain-marie often serves the same function as a double boiler, but it is used in other ways as well:

For cooking: The bain-marie is used in cooking delicate mixtures—such as timbales or dishes containing eggs—that need gentle, steady heat. Place the dish you are cooking in the shallow pan and then pour in enough water to come ½ to ⅔ of the way up the sides of the dish. Bring the water to a simmer on top of the stove, and then put the bain-marie and the dish in the oven. It is important that the water be simmering before it goes into the oven to insure that the proper temperature has been attained for the dish to cook properly in the time specified in the recipe. After reaching the simmer, the water must never be allowed to boil—either on top of the stove or in the oven. The point of a bain-marie is to maintain low, even heat.

For keeping dishes warm: In this case the water in the bain-marie should be hot but not simmering, and you will want to use as much water as possible so that it will retain its heat as long as possible.

For reheating: One of the advantages of the bain-marie for reheating is that the food being reheated can remain in whatever vessel it has been cooked or stored. Place the container in the bain-marie, bring the water to a simmer as directed above, and finish reheating either in the oven or on top of the stove.

Bread and bread crumbs

To stale bread quickly: Cut the bread into slices and dry them in a slow oven until they are hard.

To make bread crumbs: Bread crumbs are best made from stale or oven-dried bread—but it must be bread of a good quality and firm texture. Put the stale bread through the fine blade of a food mill, force it through the holes in a colander, or spin it, a little at a time, in an electric blender.

Burns

To soothe a minor kitchen burn, rub it gently with the cut surface of a raw potato—a *truc!*

Butter

To clarify: Melt the butter slowly in a heavy-bottomed saucepan, preferably enamel. Then carefully skim off as much as you can of the white froth, the *casein,* which is the part of the butter that burns easily. Finally, pour the clarified butter through a fine, clean strainer, making sure not to disturb the remaining residue clinging to the sides and bottom of the pan.

To incorporate into a hot sauce: Butter should be added to a hot sauce in small pieces, and each piece must be thoroughly incorporated before the next piece is added. Otherwise the butter will not blend easily with the other ingredients.

When making a sweet butter cream or a cake, a nice *truc* for softening butter, if you have forgotten to take it out of the refrigerator, is to work it with a fork in a bowl that has been warmed under hot running water and then dried.

Chicken

Because chickens in France as well as in the United States are much less carefully raised than they used to be, and less care is taken with their diet, the fat at the end of their tail may have an unpleasant taste. Unless I have a chicken I know to have been properly raised, I always remove this fat.

In France, before roasting a chicken, we always cut the wings off at the first joint. The wing tips are removed because they tend to burn in the oven; they are useful when added to the neck, gizzard, and feet—if you have them—to make a chicken stock.

To truss a chicken: Chickens are trussed slightly differently in France than they generally are in the United States. I find our system less complicated and think it gives a very nice presentation.

Thread a large trussing needle, insert it in one thigh of the chicken, and push it through the body and out the other thigh. Then run the needle into one wing of the chicken, through the body, and out the other wing. Tie the ends of the string together.

Coffee

The flavor of even the finest coffee will be enhanced if, at the moment of pouring boiling water over the coffee, one adds a tiny pinch of salt. The same is true for hot chocolate.

Cream

Crème fraîche: Crème fraîche, found widely in France, is cream that has matured and fermented to the point where it has thickened slightly and has a faintly acid taste, very pleasant with many dishes, especially cold preparations, when it is used uncooked. To make a good approximation of *crème fraîche,* shake 1½ teaspoons of buttermilk or ⅓ cup commercial sour cream in a jar with 1 cup of heavy cream. Keep in a warm place until the cream has thickened. (This will take about 5 to 8 hours on a hot day, 24 hours on a cool day.) Shake the jar again and refrigerate. The cream will keep, refrigerated, for as long as 10 days.

Whipping cream: It is always best to whip cream with a very clean whisk or beater in a chilled bowl (preferably metal, which gets and stays colder) set over ice cubes. Chilling helps keep the cream from turning into butter and makes it easier to whip it to the desired consistency.

Croutons

Croutons—small squares or large slices of sautéed bread—can be sautéed in either oil or butter, depending on the flavor you prefer and the dish the croutons will garnish. If butter alone is used, it should be clarified. Always make croutons with stale rather than fresh bread so that they do not absorb too much fat. Remove the crusts and cut the croutons into whatever shape you desire, then let them dry out in a low oven (less than 200°) for 15 to 20 minutes before sautéing them. For 8 slices of bread, use 6 tablespoons of butter and/or oil, and sauté the pieces briefly until they are browned on both sides.

Degreasing

Degreasing—removing the fat from a soup, a stew, or a sauce—may help to contribute to the more relaxed attitude toward calories that we have in France. We go to great pains to eliminate such unnecessary calories from a dish and leave only the essence.

The easiest way to remove grease, if you have the time, is to chill the dish and then take the congealed fat off the surface. But in many instances one wants to remove fat when the liquid is still warm. I suggest two different methods.

1. Let the liquid cool slightly and skim off as much fat as you can with a spoon. For some dishes this will be sufficient—a little fat gives body to hearty sauces. But you really want to remove every bit of fat from

a very delicate sauce. To do so, after you have skimmed off the fat, draw some absorbent paper across the surface of the liquid. This will soak up any fat still remaining.

Although I prefer the above technique, there is a second way of degreasing that is sometimes useful.

2. Let the sauce cool, then pour it through a sieve lined with several thicknesses of cheesecloth and filled with ice cubes. The fat will stiffen and congeal on the ice cubes. Although this method is faster, my objection to it is that the ice cubes will inevitably melt a little and add extra water to the sauce.

Eggs

Beating egg yolks: Many of the recipes in this book call for egg yolks beaten "to a pale, creamy yellow." This means they should also have a consistency thick enough to form a "slowly dissolving ribbon" on their surface when dropped from a lifted whisk or beater. They should not be beaten beyond this point; if they are, they will become granular when they are heated.

Folding technique for beaten egg whites: I have found this folding method—which is the opposite of that conventionally used—extremely successful for reasons I have discussed in the introduction to Menu 6. Stir a spoonful or two of the beaten egg whites into the warm base to lighten it. Pour the base back into the bowl of egg whites. With a spatula, cut down through the center and draw the more solid base up and out toward the edge of the bowl. Then, pressing the spatula lightly across the surface as you go, return to the center. Rotate the bowl with each fold.

Enameled saucepan

When I have specified an enameled saucepan it is because enamel is a nonstaining material that will not impart a taste or color to anything being cooked in it. The enamel covers cast-iron, which gives a slow, even heat, and under ordinary circumstances the pan will not scorch. Acceptable substitutes are heavy-bottomed stainless steel, heatproof glass, fireproof porcelain, or lined copper.

Fat

A *truc* when rendering fat is always to add a little cold water, which will help the fat melt.

To remove fat from a dish, see *Degreasing.*

Food mill

A food mill is an inexpensive utensil for puréeing various substances such as soups, thick sauces, mousses, vegetable mixtures, or fruits, by forcing them through holes with a rotary blade. Alternative equipment varies according to what you want to accomplish. A sieve and wooden spoon, a garlic press, a meat grinder, or an electric blender—each is useful on occasion.

I have an electric blender, and sometimes I find it valuable—for instance, in making butter creams—but I still prefer this wonderful little device, the food mill. A fixture in French kitchens, it is now readily available in the United States. A food mill has several advantages over a blender: It is less expensive, and also easier to control. I find that a blender sometimes purées a mixture too thoroughly and homogenizes it. In addition, a blender is annoying to use because the contents sometimes stick to the jar, and you have to stop to scrape them down. Thick mixtures are apt to get clogged. Finally, I never use a blender when the purée would have to be strained as well (to remove seeds or skins, for example) because this makes an extra step.

But if you do not have a food mill or an acceptable substitute and must use a blender, there are two important points to remember: (1) Run the blender very briefly and (2) add a small amount of liquid—appropriate to the recipe—so that the blades can work properly.

If you buy a food mill, the best kind is one with at least three different disks: one with tiny holes for a smooth purée, one with medium, and one with larger holes for rough mixtures.

Garlic

To give the aroma of *fresh* garlic to a sauce or to a dish that has been cooked with garlic, 10 minutes before the final cooking add more garlic. That way the garlic will release its pungent flavor, without being raw.

Herbs

Because fresh herbs are so superior to dried, I suggest that you might want to grow your own. Even if you live in the city, you might want to try growing them in a sunny window box. Chives, parsley, basil, and rosemary can easily be cultivated this way. Tarragon and chervil are a little more uncertain.

Lemons

When adding a small amount of lemon juice to a dish, cut the lemon in half, wrap it in the corner of a towel, and squeeze the juice through the towel. The fibers and seeds will be left behind.

Lemon peel: see under *Oranges*

Meat

Tenderizing: To tenderize a cut of meat that is insufficiently aged (such as freshly killed game), or of inferior quality, marinate the meat for 24 hours in good olive oil with some aromatic herbs—marjoram, thyme, laurel, oregano and freshly ground black pepper. If the meat is "white" meat (veal or pork, for example), add some lemon juice to the oil—a few drops to ½ cup of oil. For red meats like beef, substitute for the lemon juice a few drops of vinegar.

Salting: Meats, or dishes in which meat is the principal ingredient, should never be salted at the beginning of the cooking. *For a meat cooked in sauce,* salt halfway through the cooking and correct the seasoning when the dish is done, because the reduction of the cooking juices will increase the degree of saltiness. *For broiled or sautéed meats,* the meat should be salted at the end of the cooking only; otherwise the salt will draw out the blood and the meat will be dry instead of juicy. *For roasted meat,* salt halfway through the cooking, because some liquid is necessary to make the sauce.

Carving: Roast or braised meat should never be carved immediately upon being taken from the oven or cooking vessel, but should instead be set to "rest" for 15 to 20 minutes, covered with foil. In cooling slightly, the meat will lose some of its elasticity, the flesh will contract and become firmer, and it will be easier to carve the meat into even, attractive slices. In sum: never carve any meat as soon as it is done, but let it rest.

Mold/unmold

To unmold a frozen or chilled dish: Soak a towel with hot water, wring it out, and wrap it around the mold for 15 seconds. Then, using both hands, unmold with a fast downward snap of the wrists.

Oranges

To dry orange peel: Dried orange peel is used extensively in Provençale cooking and I always have some on hand. The zest of the orange— that is, the colored part of the rind, without the white (which is bitter) is peeled off and spread out (or sometimes tied in a bunch) to dry. Left in an open area it will dry in a few days to a week, depending on the humidity. But if you have several months in which to dry the peel, you can use the entire skin, including the white part, for its bitterness will diminish with the passage of time.

To peel orange and lemon rind: When only the zest is wanted, the best way to remove it is to use a potato or vegetable peeler.

Pastry

To line a pastry mold: Because a French tart or quiche is not served in the mold in which it is baked, but is free-standing, the sides of the crust must be thicker than the bottom so that they will not collapse. Roll out the dough into a rough circle a good inch and a half larger than the mold in which it will be baked, and lay it in the mold with about 1 inch hanging over on all sides. Gently press the pastry against the sides and the bottom. Then take the overlapping pastry and gently tamp it down along the insides of the mold to form the thick walls of pastry. Refrigerate for 15 minutes to 1 hour or more before baking.

How to form a tourte crust: Using only three quarters of the dough, follow the above directions for lining a mold with pastry. Then, with your fingers on the outside and your thumbs on the inside of the mold, gently pinch up a quarter-inch rim from the thick sides of pastry. Carefully push this rim toward the center all the way around, forming a lip upon which the top of the *tourte* will rest. When you fill the crust, fill it only to the level of the lip.

Roll out the remaining dough to make a cover for the *tourte.* Paint the lip with an egg beaten with water and then lay the cover on it carefully, pressing gently to make the two pieces of pastry adhere. Trim off any excess dough. Glaze the top with beaten egg.

Pepper

Pepper should always be freshly ground from peppercorns. The strength of pepper diminishes in cooking; for the full strength of pepper in a dish, it should always be added at the end.

To preserve pâtés that have been cooked in a terrine and then unmolded, cover the exterior with coarse pepper, freshly ground.

Reheating and keeping warm

To reheat: The best method of reheating something depends on the type of dish. Anything with a considerable amount of liquid, such as a soup or a stew, can be reheated over direct heat. In reheating a stew, it is almost always best to add 2 or 3 tablespoons of water or bouillon. Water is preferable if the dish has already been completely seasoned.

Dishes with very little liquid are better reheated in the gentler bain-marie (see p. 318).

When reheating a dish whose liquid has been considerably reduced, always add some water—a few tablespoons to half a cup, depending on the state of reduction. Otherwise the flavor will be too strong and the dish may be oversalted.

To keep warm: If a fully cooked dish must wait before being served, it can be kept warm in the following ways:

1. Place the dish in a bain-marie with hot but not simmering water, and keep renewing the water to keep it hot.

2. Put the food on a warm platter, cover it with foil, and leave it in a warm oven.

3. Small amounts of food can be put between two plates and set either over simmering water or in a warm oven.

Tomatoes

To peel, seed, and juice: The easiest way to peel tomatoes is to drop them, one or two at a time, into boiling water for 10 seconds. Immediately plunge them into cold water to stop the cooking. After that the skin will peel off easily. To seed and juice tomatoes, cut them in half and squeeze them gently.

To neutralize the acidity of sauces made with out-of-season tomatoes: For 2 cups of sauce: stir ½ teaspoon instant coffee into ½ cup of the sauce. Combine with the sauce. Repeat if necessary.

Zest

The zest of an orange or lemon is the orange or yellow part of the rind. For further details, see under *Oranges.*

A Memorable Ending

Knowing that this book was in preparation, a great connoisseur of Cognac recently suggested the following to me:

"A good Cognac is the inevitable conclusion to a fine dinner with fine wine. The choice of the Cognac will give the final impression; it is that which one's guests will remember. Having the same origins, Cognac and wine are natural companions. Furthermore, Cognac facilitates the digestion of the meal. How else to conclude a good meal if not with a Cognac served at the moment of serving the coffee? And what is more agreeable than warming a beautiful glass in which the master of the house has just served you a fine old Cognac?"

In these thoughts I concur.

Index

Biographical Note

Simone Beck received her nickname "Simca" from her husband, Jean Fischbacher. (She infinitely prefers it to Simone.) Her full name is Simone Suzanne Renée Madeleine Beck Fischbacher, and she was born in 1904 at Tocqueville en Caux, Normandy, into a family that had been *normand* for generations. At a time when "well-bred" French children did not go into the kitchen, she felt, very early, its lure. At six or seven one of her favorite pastimes was making toffee with her English governess and soon she was making cakes and desserts. On an old slate tablet on which her mother wrote the menus of the day, she remembers the frequent entry: "Mademoiselle Simone will make the dessert."

By her teens, Simca had begun to assemble in a number of black memorandum books the recipes that interested her. After the end of her first marriage, in 1933, she began to study at the Cordon Bleu, then the world's supreme school of cuisine. Her teacher was Henri-Paul Pellaprat, its *maître* and the author of *Modern French Culinary Art,* who, in the grand tradition of French chefs, had studied every aspect of professional cooking from the age of twelve. With the encouragement of her second husband, Jean Fischbacher, she focused her full talent and energy on the study and practice of cooking, entertained prodigiously, and joined a number of culinary societies.

In 1948 she was approached by a friend, Louisette Bertholle (now Comtesse de Nalèche), to collaborate on a French cookbook for Americans. In 1951, at the suggestion of her husband, they began to search for an American to help them, and a friend introduced Simca to Julia Child, then studying cooking in Paris. Soon afterward, the three women formed a cooking school, L'École des Trois Gourmandes, and began the collaboration that produced the first volume of *Mastering the Art of French Cooking,* published in 1961. Julia and Simca continued to work together writing the second volume of *Mastering the Art of French Cooking,* which was published in 1970. L'École des Trois Gourmandes still carries on in its unique way: Julia, of course, gives lessons on television to millions of Americans and Simca still gives private lessons at her apartment in Neuilly, where she and her husband live when they are not in Provence.

Simone Beck has made three extended visits to the United States, each time giving cooking demonstrations in various parts of the country and classes at James Beard's cooking school in New York. She insists that this book will be her last. Meanwhile, her experiments continue . . .

Patricia Simon

A Note on the Type

This book was set on the Linotype in Garamond, an adaptation of a famous series of old-style types preserved in the Imprimerie Nationale, Paris. Long attributed to Claude Garamond (1510–61), they are now known to have been cut about 1615 by Jean Jannon (fl. 1609–58). Jannon's types fell out of use and lay forgotten until early in the nineteenth century, when they were catalogued. Their origin now lost, they were attributed to Garamond, the most important French type founder of the sixteenth century, and were titled *caractères de l'Université*. Their revival in 1898 by the Imprimerie Nationale brought them to general attention, and in the present century their design has been widely adapted by commercial type founders. Finally, in 1926 M. Paul Beaujon discovered a unique copy of Jannon's specimen book and unraveled the history of their origin—though too late to correct their common identification with the name of Jannon's famous predecessor.

The book was composed, printed, and bound by Kingsport Press, Inc., Kingsport, Tennessee. The text and binding designs are by Anthea Lingeman.